Studies in the Book of Galatians

also called
Studies in Galatians—The Two Covenants

By
A.T. Jones

TEACH Services, Inc.
P U B L I S H I N G
www.TEACHServices.com

World rights reserved. This book or any portion thereof may not be copied or reproduced in any form or manner whatever, except as provided by law, without the written permission of the publisher, except by a reviewer who may quote brief passages in a review.

This book was written to provide truthful information in regard to the subject matter covered. The author assumes full responsibility for the accuracy of all facts and quotations as cited in this book. The opinions expressed in this book are the author's personal views and interpretation of the Bible, Spirit of Prophecy, and/or contemporary authors and do not necessarily reflect those of TEACH Services, Inc.

This book is sold with the understanding that the publisher is not engaged in giving spiritual, legal, medical, or other professional advice. If authoritative advice is needed, the reader should seek the counsel of a competent professional

---

Copyright © 2002, 2006, 2011 TEACH Services, Inc.
ISBN-13: 978-1-57258-097-8 (Paperback)
ISBN-13: 978-1-57258-956-8 (E-book)
Library of Congress Control Number: 97-80515

Published by
TEACH Services, Inc.
P U B L I S H I N G
www.TEACHServices.com

Table Contents

Foreword v
Introduction 7

Chapter One
Galatians 1:3-5 17

Chapter Two
Galatians 1:6-2:14 19
Galatians 2:17 34
Galatians 2:18, 19 36
Galatians 2:20 38
Galatians 2:21 40

Chapter 3
Galatians 3:1 42
Galatians 3:1 42
Galatians 3:2-5 44
Galatians 3:6-9 46
Galatians 3:6-9 49
Galatians 3:10 53
Galatians 3:10-12 55
Galatians 3:10-12 58
Galatians 3:15 63
Abraham Did Pass Through 67
Galatians 3:16, 17 68
Galatians 3:16, 17 71
Galatians 3:18 75
Galatians 3:19 78
Galatians 3:19 80
Galatians 3:19 83
Galatians 3:19 86
Galatians 3:19 89
Galatians 3:19 91
Galatians 3:21, 22 98
Galatians 3:23 101
Galatians 3:21-23 103
Galatians 3:24,25 105
Galatians 3:24-26 108
Galatians 3:27-29 113

Chapter Four

Galatians 4:1-7	115
Galatians 4:8-11	117
Galatians 4:12-20	118
The Two Covenants	121
Galatians 4:21-31	121
Galatians 4:21-24	122
Galatians 4:21-25	125
Galatians 4:21-25	129
The Epistle To The Galatians	133
Galatians 4:21-31	136
Galatians 4:21-24	139
Galatians 4:21-31	143
Galatians 4:21-24, 28	146
Galatians 4:21-31; 5:1	149

Chapter Five

Galatians 5:2-4	155
Galatians 5:3	157
Galatians 5:5	160
Galatians 5:6	163
Galatians 5:7-15	165
Galatians 5:16-18	167
Galatians 5:19-21	170
Galatians 5:22-26	173

Chapter Six

Galatians 6:1	178
Galatians 6:2	180
Galatians 6:3	182
Galatians 6:4-10	185
Galatians 6:11-18	188

Foreword

All italicized words were italicized by Jones. Any time Jones used Greek characters, we have used the exact equivalent in English letters (using Strong's Concordance).

There are so many gems of truth contained herein that we are sure you will find enjoying and uplifting.. These studies should be an excellent companion to "Glad Tidings" by E. J. Waggoner, (which is also a series of studies on the entire book of Galatians). Both of these men, we are told by the Spirit of Prophecy, had a very precious message for the church in their time. Seeing how their message was to prepare a people for the imminent return of Jesus Christ, and He has not yet come, their message is, we believe, just as relevant for us today. Should these studies bring you into an ever deeper "abiding in Christ" experience, the time and effort taken to reproduce them will be insignificant in comparison.

Thanks to Mary M. Cleveland and the James White Library at Adventist Heritage Center.

—The Publisher

Introduction

July 25, 1899

Several letters have been received asking what law is the subject of consideration in the book of Galatians.

The answer is: Not any law at all; it is *the gospel* that is the subject, and the whole subject, under consideration in the book of Galatians.

So emphatically is this so, that in the very first part of the first chapter it is declared and repeated, "Though we, or an angel from heaven, preach any other gospel unto you than that which we have preached unto you, *let him be accursed.* As we said before, so say I now again. If any man preach any other gospel unto you than that ye have received, *let him be accursed*." Verses 8, 9.

"I certify you, brethren, that *the gospel which was preached of me* is not after man. For I neither received it of man, neither was *I* taught it, but by revelation of Jesus Christ." Verses 11, 12.

In Galatians it is not a question of one law or another, the sole question is *the truth of the gospel;* for in telling what he had done, Paul says that he did it, "that *the truth of the gospel* might continue with you." Gal. 2:5. He withstood Peter to the face at Antioch, because he and those who followed his example "walked not uprightly according to *the truth of the gospel*." Verse 14.

It is not a question of one *law* or another, but of one *gospel* or another. See, the first words in the book, after the salutation, are these: "I marvel that ye are so soon removed from him that called you into the grace of Christ unto *another gospel;* which is not another; but there be some that trouble you, and would pervert the gospel of Christ. But though we, or an angel from heaven, preach any *other gospel* unto you than *that which we have preached* unto you, let him be accursed. As we said before, so say I now again, If any man preach *any other gospel* unto you than *that ye have received,* let him be accursed."

In the book of Galatians, therefore, the question under consideration is not at all a question of two laws; but altogether a question of *two gospels,*—the true gospel of Christ, as against a perversion of that gospel.

Now we ask you who are interested in the book of Galatians, to read that book *through* seven times with this thought in mind; then you will be prepared for some studies of that book, which we may give in these columns soon. Even at slow reading you can easily read the book of Galatians through in half an hour.

August 1, 1899

The subject in the book of Galatians is the gospel. Gal.1:8, 9.

In the way the subject is discussed, however, it is *two* gospels,—the true gospel as against a false one,—the true gospel as against a perversion of that gospel. Verse 6, 7.

Now the true gospel is the gospel of the true way of salvation from sin. And as the subject in Galatians is the true gospel as against a false one, therefore the subject of the book of Galatians is the true way of salvation from sin as against a false way,—the true way of salvation as against a perversion of that way.

Accordingly, we there read that when Peter and others "walked not uprightly *according to the truth of the gospel*," and Paul withstood Peter to the face on account of it, these are the words with which he withstood him: "Knowing that a man is not justified by *the works of the law*, but by *the faith of Jesus Christ,* even we have believed in Jesus Christ, *that* we might be justified by *the faith of Christ,* and *not* by *the works of the law;* for by the works of the law shall no flesh be justified…I do not frustrate the grace of God: for if righteousness come by the law, then Christ is dead in vain." Gal. 2:16, 21.

And when his appeal is made directly to the Galatians themselves, it is in these words: "This only would I learn of you, Received ye the Spirit by *the works of the law,* or by *the hearing of faith*?" Gal. 3:2.

Again: "Are ye so foolish? having *begun* in *the Spirit,* are ye now *made perfect* by *the flesh*?" Verse 3.

Again: "He therefore ministereth to you the Spirit, and worketh miracles among you, doeth he it by the *works of the law,* or by the *hearing of faith*?" Verse 5.

Again: "That no man is justified by *the law* in the sight of God, it is evident: for, The just shall live by *faith*." Verse 11.

And again: "Christ is become of no effect unto you, whosoever of you are justified by *the law;* ye are fallen from grace." Gal. 5:4.

It is therefore perfectly plain that the subject of the book of Galatians is the true gospel—the gospel of salvation, of justification, of righteousness, by FAITH—as against a false gospel; as against a perversion of the gospel of Christ,—a gospel of salvation, of justification, of righteousness, *by works,* by LAW, by THE FLESH.

The question in the book of Galatians is solely the question of salvation by *grace,* not by *law;* by *faith,* not by *works;* by the *Spirit,* not by the *flesh;* by *Christ,* not by *self.*

Now let all who are interested in "the law in Galatians," or in the gospel in Galatians or anywhere else, read the book of Galatians through seven times with this thought in mind, and they will be better prepared for some studies in Galatians, which we may give in these columns soon.

August 8, 1899

Though it is true that the great subject in the book of Galatians is the true gospel as against the false gospel, salvation by faith of Jesus Christ and not by works of the law, still the question is asked, "What law is referred to in the phrase 'works of the law,' which is several times used?"

The answer is: It is not *any particular law* exclusive of all other laws; it is any law at all, all laws, in the general idea of law. Accordingly the Revised Version puts in the margin each time, "works of the law," and other translations render it directly "works of law," as of the idea of law in general.

The Greek also sanctions this; for in each place where the expression, or a kindred one, is used, it is written without any article ergon nomos—works of law, or nomos—law (Gal. 2:16 three times; 3:2, 5, 10); while in other instances, such as Gal. 3:12, 13, 19, 21, 24, it is written each time with the definite article to tou nomos—of the law, or ho nomos—the law.

The expression, then being that of the general idea of law, that men are justified by faith of Christ and not by works of law, in the nature of the case any law and all law would be comprehended, and therefore the highest of all law—the law of God—as well as all other: that there is no justification, no righteousness, no salvation, by any law whatever, nor by the works of any law whatever; but only by the faith of Jesus Christ.

And that more than one law is included in the argument is evident from the text itself.

    a. In chapter 5:14 it is written: "All the law is fulfilled in one word, even in this: Thou shalt love thy neighbor as thyself," which is unquestionably a direct reference to the law of God, while in the same chapter, and even all through the book, the question, the law, of circumcision—the law of Moses (John 7:23)—is involved.

    b. In chapter 6:13 it is written, "For neither they themselves who are circumcised keep the law." Here plainly both the law of Moses and the law of God, the ceremonial law and the moral law, are referred to; because it says that they who are circumcised do not keep the law. Now their being circumcised was in itself to keep the law of circumcision—the law of Moses. Therefore if only the one law were referred to, it could not be said that they who are circumcised do not keep the law. But when it is borne in mind that circumcision, both in the mind of God (Deut. 30:6) and in the scheme of these controversialists, was the sign that the law of God was kept, and these who were so tenacious of circumcision did not keep the law, then it is perfectly plain that both the law of circumcision and the law of God are referred to in the words, "Neither they themselves who are circumcised keep the law."

c. The same thing is shown also in chapter two, verses 12–14 with 17–19.

d. All this shows that in Galatians there is involved the same matter that was raised by the "Pharisees which believed," and that was considered in Acts 15: "Except ye be circumcised after the manner of Moses, ye cannot be saved." Verse 1. They must be circumcised *to be saved!* They "must be circumcised and keep the law" to be justified, to be righteous, to be saved! Justification, righteousness, salvation, must be *by works* of law!

But there Peter showed that God had already settled the matter, saying, "Men and brethren, ye know how that a good while ago *God made choice* among us, that the Gentiles by my mouth should hear the word of *the gospel,* and *believe.* And *God,* which knoweth the hearts, *bare them witness,* giving them the Holy Ghost, even as he did unto us; and put no difference between us and them, purifying their hearts *by faith.* Now therefore *why tempt ye God,* to put a yoke upon the neck of the disciples, which neither our fathers nor we were able to bear?" Verses 7–10.

And when the sentence was pronounced by James and the decree was framed and sent forth, it showed that it was the general idea of law—including all law—that was involved, rather than any specific law, exclusive of all others; for the sentence was that "they abstain from pollutions of idols [the moral law], and from fornication [the moral law] and from things strangled [the ceremonial law] and from blood [the ceremonial law]." Verse 20.

And that it is not the merit of any law in itself, not even of the ceremonial, nor the relative merit of certain laws, that is involved; but solely of law *as a means of justification,* of righteousness, of salvation, is doubly emphasized by this fact:

When certain in Jerusalem wanted Titus circumcised in accord with their views of justification, Paul would give "place by subjection, no, not for an hour; *that the truth of the gospel* might continue." Gal. 2:4, 5. Yet when the question had been settled, and the decree proclaimed, and Paul and Silas went through the cities of Syria and Cilicia, and "delivered them decrees for to keep, that there were ordained of the apostles and elders which were at Jerusalem;" when they came to Derbe and Lystra and found there Timothy, whose father was a Greek, and whom Paul would have to go forth with him, Paul "took and circumcised him, because of the Jews that were in those quarters." Acts 15:40, 41; 16:1–4. That is to say: So long as people clung to circumcision as essential, or as a means, *to justification,* Paul would not countenance such a thing for a moment. But when there was in it no question of justification, he would do it when entrance for the gospel could the better be gained by it. So long as law was held up as essential, or as a means, *to justification,* or as having any part in it, Paul would not recognize it at all. But when it was acknowledged that justification is by faith alone, without any deeds of any law whatever, then he would recognize and consider the merit, the purpose, and the place of any law and of every law.

Thus the subject of the book of Galatians is salvation by the gospel, not by law; it is justification, righteousness, life, by faith of Christ, not by *works of law.* It is to show that as a means of justification, of righteousness, of salvation, any law of any kind, and all law of every kind, is absolutely excluded. "If righteousness come by law, then Christ is dead in vain." Gal. 2:21.

As to what law is referred to, whether the moral, the ceremonial, or law in the abstract, in particular verses, this is easily discovered in and by the details of the argument, when the *great thought* —the two gospels—is held constantly in mind.

Now let all who are interested in the book of Galatians, read that book through seven times with the thought of this article in mind, and they will be prepared for some studies in Galatians, which we hope to begin next week.

August 13, 1899

On the book of Galatians a question has been asked that calls for another preliminary study before beginning the study of the book in detail.

The inquiry is: Since the ceremonial law, the moral law, and the general idea of law, are all involved in the argument, what then becomes of the view that has been so long held, and that seems to rest upon authority, that the ceremonial law is the chief subject *as to law* in the book of Galatians?

The answer is, *It is true.* Yet in this answer there must be borne in mind what

Studies in the Book of Galatians

is comprehended in the term "ceremonial law," and especially the ceremonial law involved in the book of Galatians. This is worth studying.

That it is *not* the ceremonial law, as expressed in sacrifices and offerings, that is particularly the subject, is evident from the fact that from the beginning to the end of the book, neither sacrifice nor offering is even once referred to.

That it *is* the ceremonial law, *as expressed in circumcision and it's meaning among the "Pharisees which believed,"* is evident from the fact that, over and over, circumcision is named.

What, then, was the meaning of circumcision among the "Pharisees which believed?" How much did circumcision cover that Pharisaic ceremonial system?—Rabbi Jehuda Hakkadosh declared, "So great is circumcision that but for the Holy One, blessed be he, would not have created the world;" and that "but for circumcision, heaven and earth could not exist." "It is as great as all the other commandments." "How great is circumcision, since it is *equivalent to all the commandments of the law*!"—*Farrar's "Life of Paul," chap. 15, note to par. 4 from end; and chap. 22, note to par. 5.*

By this it is evident that with those "false brethren" (Gal. 2:3–5) who are answered in the letter to the Galatians, circumcision comprehended all the commandments of the law—even all the commandments of the moral law, equally with any other. So that one who was circumcised, in that bore the certificate that he was a keeper of the law. This is also evident from their demand, "Ye must be circumcised, and *keep the law*;" and from the expression, in Gal. 6:13, "For neither they themselves who are circumcised *keep the law*."

Now, it is true that in the mind of God true circumcision did signify the full and perfect keeping of the law. But true circumcision was, and is always, "that of the heart, in the spirit, and not in the letter," of which the outward circumcision in the flesh was only the sign. Therefore it is written, "The Lord thy God will circumcise thine heart, and the heart of thy seed, *to love the Lord thy God* with *all thy heart,* and with *all thy soul.*" Deut. 30:6. And to love the Lord with all the heart and with all the soul, is the keeping of all the commandments.

Wherein, then, were the people wrong, who were bothering the Galatians and all other people to whom Paul preached, in insisting that "ye must be circumcised and keep the law," and that circumcision comprehended all the commandments?—They were wrong in this, that with them it was all of *works;* it was all done to be justified, to be saved—except ye do so, "ye can not be saved."

On the other hand, while in the mind of the Lord circumcision also

Introduction

comprehended all the commandments, here it was all of *faith*. With the Lord, the sign of circumcision was a seal of the righteousness of faith (Rom. 4:11; Gal. 3:5–7)—"faith which worketh by love." Gal. 5:6. And as "this is the love of God that we keep his commandments," it was a faith that keeps all the commandments.

With the "Pharisees which believed," those "false brethren," men must perform these works of circumcision and keeping the law in order to be justified. With the Lord and Paul, men are justified *by faith* without any deeds of any law.

With the "Pharisees which believed," men must *work* in order to be *justified*. With the Lord and Paul, men must be *justified* in order to *work*.

With the "Pharisees which believed," everything was of works, of the flesh, outward, and formal. With the Lord and Paul, everything must be of faith, of the Spirit, inward, and spiritual; and outward only as the manifestation of the new life within.

With the "Pharisees which believed," everything was ceremonial; because it was outward, of works, of the flesh, of self; everything was done and must be done, in order to be justified by it, in order to be righteous by it, in order to be saved by it. In this way the moral law itself was made merely ceremonial—the moral law, the ceremonial law, *all law*, was thus reduced to one vast system of ceremonialism. And of this vast system of ceremonialism, circumcision was the very nucleus.

And it is this system, and this spirit, of ceremonialism, that is combated and repudiated in the book of Galatians. And *this* is the ceremonial law which, over all and through all, is the great subject *as to law* in the book of Galatians; and which as a false gospel, subverted souls, and perverted and opposed the true gospel.

Bear in mind, however, that this is not by any means to say that such is the true ceremonial law. There was nothing true about it; it was ceremonialism entire: circumcision was perverted; the moral law was perverted; everything as to law was perverted by it; and it fought hard to pervert even the gospel. But it could not prevail: the book of Galatians was written to set the ceremonial law, the moral law, and the gospel, in their true and relative positions; and to annihilate ceremonial*ism,* forever.

All this will be plainly seen, as we shall study the book of Galatians in detail. In the meantime, let all read the book of Galatians through seven times, with this thought in mind, and they will be the better prepared for the study in detail as it shall be given next week.

STUDIES IN GALATIANS

August 22, 1899

"Paul, an apostle (not of men, neither by man, but by Jesus Christ, and God the Father, who raised him from the dead), and all the brethren which are with me, unto the churches of Galatia."

The first two chapters of the book of Galatians are an explanation and defense of Paul's apostleship and of the gospel that he preached. This first verse is a defense of his apostleship. This is the cause of the words in parenthesis, saying that he was an apostle, "not of man, neither by man, but by Jesus Christ, and God the Father, who raised him from the dead."

Another translation is, "Paul, an apostle, not from men, nor by the instrumentality of any man, but by Jesus Christ and God our Father who raised him from the dead."

Another is, "Paul, an apostle, not by man, nor through a man, but appointed by Jesus Christ and his Raiser from the dead, God the Father."

The Revised Version is, "Paul, an apostle, (not from men, neither through man, but through Jesus Christ, and God the Father, who raised him from the dead)."

The defense shows that his true apostleship was denied, and that he was opposed and denounced as being only an apostle of men, appointed and sent only by a man or by men.

Nor was this opposition sown only among the churches of Galatia. It was sown everywhere, especially in the churches that Paul had raised up. There were "false, skulking brethren," who made it their business and their message, even to follow up Paul, and sow these seeds of distrust and of evil; as the council at Jerusalem described it, "digging up from the foundations" the souls of those who believed his preaching.

These evil seeds were sown at Corinth. After Paul's departure from there, these false brethren had told the brethren that he was not an apostle; and cited as proof that he had not seen Jesus; that he was only a tent-maker, who went about working for a living; and even that he was not an apostle because he had no wife!

In his letter to the Corinthians he makes answer thus (we use Conybeare and Hawson's translation, as this, *with* our common version, makes the matter plain): "Is it denied that I am an apostle? Is it denied that I am free from man's authority? Is it denied that I have seen Jesus our Lord? Is it denied that you are the fruits of my labor in the Lord? If to others I am no apostle, yet at least I am such to you; for you are yourselves the seal which stamps the reality of my apostleship, in the Lord; this is my answer to those who question my authority. Do they deny my right to be maintained [by my converts]? Do they deny my right to carry a believing wife with me on my journeys, like the rest of the apostles, and the brothers of the Lord, and Cephas? Or do they think that I and Barnabas alone have no right to be maintained, except by the labor of our own hands?…If I have sown for you the seed of spiritual gifts, would it be much if I were to reap some harvest from your carnal gifts? If others share this right over you, how much more should I? Yet *I have not used my right,* but *forego every claim,* lest I should by any means hinder the course of Christ's Glad-tidings… The Lord commanded those who publish the Glad-tidings to be maintained thereby. *But I have not exercised any of these rights,* nor do I write this that it may be practiced in my own case. For I had rather die than suffer any man to make void my boasting." 1 Cor. 9:1–15.

They circulated also the slanderous report, and really themselves affirmed, that Paul had held and taught the pernicious doctrine, "Let us do evil, that good may come." Rom. 3:8.

These are only *some* of the "perils among false brethren," which Paul cites with the many other perils among which he so constantly moved that his Christian life has been not inaptly termed a "long martyrdom." And it was false brethren such as these who, as at other places, had crept in among the churches of Galatia, and were perverting the gospel, which they had received, dragging them from liberty to bondage, from the Spirit to the flesh, from justification by faith to justification by works, and so "digging up from the foundation" their very soul's salvation.

Of Paul it has also been truly said: "It was, throughout life, Paul's unhappy fate to kindle the most virulent animosities; because, though conciliatory and courteous by temperament, he yet carried into his arguments that intensity and forthrightness which awaken dormant opposition. A languid controversialist will always meet with a languid tolerance. But any controversialist whose honest belief in his doctrines makes him terribly earnest, may count on a life embittered by the anger of those on whom he has forced the disagreeable task of reconsidering their own assumptions. No one likes to be suddenly awakened. The Jews were indignant with one who disturbed the deep slumber of decided opinions. Their accredited teachers did not like to be deposed from the papacy of infallible ignorance…If arguments are such as can not be refuted, and yet if those who hear them will not yield to them, they will inevitably excite a bitter rage.

Thus it was, not only with the Jews who did not believe, but also with those "Pharisees which believed,"—those Jews who, not knowing true faith, thought to bind Christianity in the hard bands of their ceremonialism. And thus it is ever with those who insist that all new wine must be put into old bottles. But Christianity demands always that the old bottles shall be made altogether new, that they may receive and hold the new wine.

Chapter One

Galatians 1:3-5

August 29, 1899

"Grace be to you and peace from God the Father, and from our Lord Jesus Christ, who gave himself for our sins, that he might deliver us form this present evil world, according to the will of God and our Father: to whom be the glory forever and ever. Amen."

"Grace be to you and peace from God the Father, and from our Lord Jesus Christ." Such is the salutation in every epistle by Paul, except that to the Hebrews; and, slightly varied, in both by Peter.

Yet it is not by any means a mere form. These epistles have come to us as the word of God, which they are in truth. This salutation, then, though often repeated,—yea, even *because* often repeated,—comes to us as the word of God in greeting and full assurance of his favor and peace everlastingly held forth to every soul.

Grace is favor. This word of God, then extends his favor to every soul who ever reads it, or who hears it.

His very name is Gracious—extending grace. His name is only what he *is*. And what he is, he is "the same yesterday, and today, and forever." With him is "no variableness, neither shadow of turning." Therefore by him grace, boundless favor, is always extended to every soul. Oh, that all would only believe it!

"And peace." He is the "God of peace." There is no true peace, but that of God. And "there is no peace, saith my God, to the wicked." The wicked are like the troubled sea, which can not rest.

But all the world lieth in wickedness, yet the God of peace speaks peace to every soul. For Christ the Prince of peace, "our peace, hath made both God and man one, having abolished in his flesh the enmity, to make in himself of two—God and man—one new man, *so* making peace—making peace through the blood of his cross." Eph. 2:14,15; Col. 1:20. "And, having *made* peace through the blood of his cross," he "came and *preached* peace to you which were afar off, and to them that were nigh:" peace to you all. Therefore, always and forevermore, his salutation to every soul is, Peace to thee. And all from God the Father and from our Lord Jesus Christ!

Oh, that every one would believe it; so that the peace of God, which passeth all understanding, could keep his heart and mind through Christ Jesus.

"Let the peace of God rule in your hearts." *Let* it; that is all he asks of you. Don't refuse it, and beat it back; *let it.*

"Who gave himself *for our* sins." O brother, sister, sinner, whosoever you be, laden with sins though you be, Christ gave himself for your sins. Let him have them. He bought them—your sins—with the awful price of his crucified self. Let him have them.

He does not ask you to put all your sins away before you can come to him and be wholly his. He asks you to come, *sins and all,* and be wholly his, *sins and all;* and he will take away from you, and put away forever, *all your sins.* He gave himself for you, *sins and all;* he bought you, *sins and all;* let him have what he bought, let him have his own, let him have *you, sins and all.*

He "gave himself for our sins, *that he might deliver us from this present evil world.*" Notice that to deliver us from this present evil world, he gave himself for our *sins.* That shows that all that there is of this present evil world to each one of us, *is in our sins.*

And they were "*our* sins." They belonged to us. We were responsible for them. And so far as we were concerned, this present evil world lay in our own personal selves, in our sins. But, bless the Lord, he gave himself for us, sins and all; he gave himself for our sins, ourselves and all; and this he did in order that he might deliver us from this present evil world.

Would you like to be delivered from this present evil world?—Let him have yourself, sins and all, which he bought, and which therefore by full right belong to him. Please do not rob him of what is his own, and so still remain in this present evil world, when at the same time you would like to be delivered from this present evil world. Please do not commit the additional sin of keeping what does not belong to you.

As they were *our* sins, and he gave himself for them, it follows plainly enough that he gave himself *to us* for our sins. Then, when he gave himself for *your* sins, your sins became *his;* and when he gave himself *to you* for your sins, *he* became *yours.* Let him have your sins, which are *his,* and take for them *him,* who is *yours.* Blessed exchange; for in him you have, as your very own, all the fullness of the Godhead bodily; and all "according to the will of God." Thank the Lord.

Why should there not be to him "glory forever and ever"? And why should not you and all people say, Amen?

Chapter Two

Galatians 1:6-2:14

Sepetmber 5, 1899

As THE "Pharisees which believed" said that Paul was not a true apostle, so also they said that the gospel which he preached was not the true gospel. And as the first verse of the epistle is a defense of his apostleship as true, so chapters 1:6 to 2:14 is a defense of the gospel that he preaches as the true, and the *only* true, gospel.

Therefore he writes: "I marvel that ye are so soon removed from him who called you into the grace of Christ unto *another gospel:* which is *not another:* but ["simply a contrivance of some people to disturb you."—Fenton] there be some that trouble you, and would *pervert the gospel of Christ.* But though we, or an angel from heaven, preach any other gospel unto you than that which we have preached unto you, let him be accursed. As we said before, so say I now again. If any man preach any other gospel unto you than that ye have received let him he accursed."

And as those "false brethren" had reported that he preached, and was ever ready to shift his ground only to please men, he now interjects the words, verse 10, "Well, am I NOW trying to be plausible to men, or to conciliate God himself? Had I still been trying to be a man-pleaser, I should not have been what I am—a slave of Christ."—Farrar's Translation.

Again, he turns to the defense of the gospel which he preached, verses 11, 12: "Now I declare to you, brethren, as to the gospel preached by me that it is not a mere human gospel. For neither did I myself receive it from man, nor was I taught it but by revelation from Jesus Christ."—Ibid.

And that he could not possibly have received it from merely man, he proves—verses 13, 14—by the fact that "you have heard of my former behavior in the days of my Judaism, how I persecuted beyond measure the church of God, and strove to root it out, and outran in Judaism many of my own age and nation, being more exceedingly zealous of the traditions of my fathers."—Conybeare and Hawson's Translation. That is to say: As when he was a Pharisee, he was ahead of many of his own day and nation, was more exceedingly zealous of the traditions of the fathers than were others, and was far beyond them in persecuting the church of God, and in striving to root it out as wild boars uproot a vineyard,—since all this was true, there was no mere man from whom he could have possibly received what he was now preaching.

But the false brethren were saying that even though he had not received his gospel merely from man, at the very most he had received it *only from the true apostles,* and *not from the Lord direct,* as had the true apostles. This he confutes by a series of indisputable facts:—

1. Verses 15-17: "But when he who set me apart even from my mother's womb and called me by his grace thought good to reveal his Son in me that I should preach him among the Gentiles, immediately I *did not confer with mere human teachers,* nor did I go away *to Jerusalem to those who were apostles before me,* but I went away into Arabia, and returned to Damascus."—Farrar's Translation. And these very false brethren who had now disconcerted the Galatian Christians, knew that at Damascus he had preached the gospel, and confounded the Jews who dwelt there, "proving that this is very Christ," that this he had done many days at Damascus; and that he was driven away from Damascus by the Jews who sought to kill him—all this before he had ever met personally a single one of those who were apostles before he became an apostle.
2. Verses 18-20: "Next, after three years, I went up to Jerusalem to visit Kephas, and I stayed at his house fifteen days; but not a single other apostle did I see, except James, the Lord's brother. Now in what I am writing to you, see, before God, I am not lying."—Ibid.
3. Verses 21-24: "Next I came into the regions of Syria and Cilicia: and was quite unknown by person to the churches of Judea which were in Christ, only they were constantly being told that our former persecutor is now a preacher of the faith which once he ravaged. And they glorified God in me."—Ibid.
4. Chapter 2:1-5: "Then fourteen years after, I went up again to Jerusalem with Barnabas, and took Titus with me also. At that time I went up in obedience to a revelation, and I communicated to the brethren in Jerusalem the glad-tidings [the gospel] which I proclaim among the Gentiles; but to the chief brethren I communicated it privately, lest perchance my labors, either past or present, might be fruitless. Yet not even Titus, my own companion (being Greek), was compelled to be circumcised. But this communication [with the apostles in Judea] I undertook on account of the false brethren who gained entrance by fraud, for they crept in among us to spy out our freedom (which we possess in Christ Jesus) that they might enslave us unto their own yoke. To whom I yielded not the submission they demanded;

no, not for an hour; that the truth of the glad-tidings might stand unaltered for your benefit."—Conybeare and Hawson's Translation.

In this citation of fact there are several facts, each of which disproves the charge that he had received his gospel from the apostles at Jerusalem:—

    a. He communicated *to them* the gospel which he preached, instead of their having communicated it to him.

    b. And this he did, not especially to teach the apostles anything, but because of the false reports of the false brethren, so that the apostles might understand the truth of the matter.

    c. He took Titus with him, whom, with him, the apostles received, and did not compel him to be circumcised; thus the apostles at Jerusalem themselves utterly disregarded the claim of the "Pharisees which believed," that "except ye be circumcised. . . ye can not be saved."

    d. He gave not an hour's subjection to the demands of the false brethren; this in the very presence of the apostles at Jerusalem; and the apostles did not require him to yield.

    e. Not only did the apostles not require him to yield anything; but "James, Cephas, and John, who seemed to be pillars," actually gave to him and Barnabas "the right hands of fellowship." Verse 9.

    f. And more than this, those who were the chief in reputation, he says, "added nothing to me"—"gave me *no new instruction.*" Verse 9.

All this was positive and conclusive confutation of the claim that he had received his gospel from the apostles. But he does not stop even here; that which is already conclusive, he makes overwhelming by the citation of—

5. (Verses 11-14) "When Peter was come to Antioch, I *withstood him to the face,* because he was to be blamed. For before that certain came from James, he did eat with the Gentiles: but when they were come, he withdrew and separated himself, fearing them which were of the circumcision. And the other Jews dissembled likewise with him; insomuch that Barnabas also was carried away with their dissimulation. But when I saw that they walked not uprightly according to the truth of the gospel, *I said unto Peter,* BEFORE THEM ALL.," "If thou, being born a Jew, art wont to live according to the customs of the Gentiles, and not of the Jews, how is it that thou constrainest the Gentile to keep the ordinances of the Jews? We are Jews by birth, and not unhallowed Gentiles: yet, knowing that a man is not justified by the works of the law, but by the faith of Jesus Christ, *we ourselves also* have put our faith in Christ Jesus, that we might be justified by

the faith of Christ, and not by the works of the law; for by the works of the law shall no flesh be justified."

When he had publicly withstood to the face even Peter, and had called him back to the truth of the gospel, and through him even James, for it was "certain which came from James" who caused Peter to swerve, nothing more needed to be said, and indeed what more *could* be said, to settle it forever that the gospel which he preached was not received from men, not from the Lord through men, not even through the first apostles, but from the *Lord himself* DIRECT.

Thus in the book of Galatians is set forth the only true gospel, in its perfect purity, direct from the Lord himself by the hand of Paul. And whosoever misses this perfect gospel in the Book of Galatians misses the whole book of Galatians.

September 19, 1899

The opposition that those of "the sect of the Pharisees which believed," carried on against Paul and the true gospel, and the difficulty and confusion that they were able to create, were the stronger and more perplexing because of the encouragement they found in the attitude of the apostles themselves, especially of Peter and James the Lord's brother. We say, "the encouragement *they found,"* for no encouragement was really and intentionally given by these brethren to the work and course of the Pharisees who believed. Yet while no encouragement was intentionally *given* by the apostles, nor even by Peter and James the Lord's brother, the temporizing and compromising attitude held by these was such that "the Pharisees which believed" *found* in it encouragement, made a handle of it, and used it to the fullest possible extent in making their efforts effective.

These brethren, in their intended kindness of heart, thought to *harmonize* the two elements by occupying an intermediate position. They did not at once clearly discern the true and all-important issue that was really involved. They did not perceive the difference between Paul's teaching and that of "the Pharisees which believed" was one of *principle,* essential and vital; they therefore thought to find a middle ground upon which—each side, especially Paul, modifying some of their "strong statements," and yielding some of their "extreme positions"—there would be found a harmony. They did not at first discern that the two things were *not* so much alike that they gradually shaped into each other and would allow a new one to be formed, or developed, from both. They did not perceive that the two were of absolutely antagonistic principles: that they had no kinship to any extent whatever; and that therefore

Galatians 1:6-2:14

the only true course must be the utter abandonment of the old and the complete espousal of the new.

As Peter and James are both involved in the matter of the letter to the Galatians, and at least incidentally in the events that called it forth, it is essential to an intelligent study and understanding of the book of Galatians that this phase of the subject should be understood.

All know that as late as several years after Pentecost it required a special vision, and that the substance of the vision should be *three times shown,* to break down traditionalism in the mind of Peter and to open his eyes to the divine truth that God is no respecter of persons (see Acts 10). And that this was the object and the necessity of the vision, is made certain by the words of Peter himself, speaking directly on that subject. For when, in obedience to the word of the Lord, he had gone to the house of Cornelius and begun to speak to the "many that were cone together" there, and the very first words that he said were these: "Ye know how that it is an unlawful thing for a man that is a Jew to keep company, or come unto one of another nation; *but God hath showed me* that I should not call any man common or unclean." Acts 10:28. The Interlinear Greek, the word-for-word translation, gives Peter's words thus: "Ye know how unlawful it is for a man, a Jew, to unite himself, or come near, to one of another race." Not simply, ye know that it is an unlawful thing; but, "Ye know how unlawful it is."

But the truth is that it never was an unlawful thing at all, except by their pharisaic inventions and traditionalism. Those pharisaic inventions and tradition, and that traditionalism, were never entitled to any recognition whatever as law or obligation. And so far as they were so recognized, their only effect was to make void the whole word and Spirit of God both in the law and in the gospel of God. How unlawful it really was, however, by that Pharisaic ceremonialism, is worth stating here, and is seen in this piece of teaching of the rabbis: "He who eats with an uncircumcised person, eats, as it were, with a dog; he who touches him, touches, as it were, a dead body; and he who bathes in the same place with him, bathes, as it were, with a leper."—Farrar's "Life and Work of Paul," chap. 15, note to par. 4 from end.

In view of this, how expressive is the statement that when Cornelius fell down at his feet, and worshipped him "Peter *took* him up. . . and as he talked with him, he went in;" showing that Peter both touched him and walked and talked familiarly with him as with a brother. and the explanation of it all was that "God hath showed me that I should not call any man common or unclean." In truth, God had never showed anything else: it was only the traditionalism and ceremonialism of pharisaism that had ever showed otherwise.

But that was not the last of it. "The apostles and brethren that were in Judea heard that the Gentiles also received the word of God." And not only this, but the news reached there of the awful thing that Peter had done in associating with Gentiles. "And when Peter was come up to Jerusalem, *they that were of the circumcision CONTENDED* with him, saying, *Thou wentest in to men uncircumcised, AND DIDST EAT WITH THEM."* That the word of God's salvation had been preached to lost men, and that *they had received it* was nothing, yea, was worse than nothing, in presence of the awful fact that a Christian should have associated with men uncircumcised, and had even eaten with them! "But Peter rehearsed the matter from the beginning, and expounded it in order unto them; "and after giving the full account, he appealed to themselves; "Forsomuch then as God gave them the like gift as he did unto us, who believed on the Lord Jesus Christ; what was I, that I could withstand God?" And "when they heard these things, they held their peace, and glorified God, saying, Then hath God also to the Gentiles granted repentance unto life." Acts 11:1-18.

Yet, though for that particular occasion they acknowledged the truth and the propriety of Peter's course, they did not hold fast to the truth. For when the gospel began to spread among the Gentiles, it was some of these men of Judea who went to Antioch and "taught the brethren, and said, Except ye be circumcised after the manner of Moses, ye can not be saved." Acts 15:1. In the council, Peter stood firmly and openly for the truth, as he had been instructed in the vision and by the Holy Spirit, and as he had stood when called to account by those at Jerusalem. The controversy thus urged by the Pharisees who believed caused the council at Jerusalem. He said the same thing now as before. Acts 15:7-11. The council decided the same way and published to all the churches their decision accordingly.

Yet after all this, still the pharisaic ones nursed their traditionalism and ceremonialism, and soon began again to urge it, especially against Paul. However, when, after the council, Peter went to Antioch, he still stood firmly and openly in the truth, and "did eat with the Gentiles." But presently "certain came from James" and from Jerusalem, and so strongly urged their traditionalism and ceremonialism that Peter actually abandoned his instruction in the vision; surrendered his firm and consistent stand at Jerusalem when called to account, and when in the council; and forsook brotherhood with the Christians who were from the Gentiles—the uncircumcised. Gal. 2:12.

This was caused, says the record, by "certain which came," not from

Galatians 1:6-2:14

Judea nor from Jerusalem alone, but *"from James."* This shows that before reaching Peter they had affected James; and then, coming from James, had used the prestige of James to affect Peter and to draw him away. James, too, had stood firmly and openly for the truth in the council. It was his sentence that had settled the question in the council. The very words of his decision were adopted by the council, and were published as the decision of the council. And yet even him the pharisaic traditionalists and ceremonialists "which believed" had succeeded in dragging back from the truth.

The real position of James at this time, and indeed to a much later time, is shown in the record of Paul's last visit to Jerusalem—his last visit just because of this attitude of James; even long after the letter to the Galatians was written. The account is in Acts 21:18-26. This visit was made especially to win the brethren in Jerusalem. Paul and his company arrived at Jerusalem, and the brethren received them gladly. "And the day following Paul went in with us *unto James,* and all the elders were present." This shows that James was a chief one who was the object of the visit. Though all the elders were present, yet Paul and his companions "went in. . . unto James."

And what did they meet there?—When Paul "had saluted them, he declared particularly what things God had wrought among the Gentiles by his ministry. And when they heard it, they glorified the Lord, and said unto him"—what, think ye?—They begin at once to try to drag even him away from the truth of the gospel to a compromise on traditionalism and ceremonialism.

"Instead of doing justice to the one whom they had injured, they still appeared to hold him responsible for the existing prejudice, as if he had given them cause for such feelings. They did not nobly stand in his defense, and endeavor to show the disaffected party their error; but they threw the burden wholly upon Paul, counseling him to pursue a course for the removal of all misapprehension."—*Sketches from the Life of Paul,* pp. 211, 212. And this even from James, who had stood so straight and true in the council, and who, after hearing from Paul a full statement of the gospel that he preached, could add nothing to it, and therefore had given him his right hand in fellowship!

They said unto him, "Thou seest, brother, how many thousands of Jews there are which believe; and they are all zealous of the law: and they are informed of thee, that thou teachest all the Jews which are among the Gentiles to forsake Moses, saying that they ought not to circumcise their children, neither to walk after the customs. What is it therefore? The multitude must needs come together: for they will hear that thou art come. *Do therefore this* that we say to thee: We have four men which have a vow on them; them take, and purify *thyself with them,* and be at charges with them, that they may shave their heads: and *all may know* that those things, whereof they were informed concerning thee, *are nothing;* but that thou thyself also walkest orderly, and keepest the law. As touching the Gentiles which believe, we have written and concluded that they observe no such thing, save only," etc., etc.

"The brethren hoped that by this act Paul might give a decisive contradiction of the false reports concerning him. But while James assured Paul that the decision of the former council (Acts 15) concerning the Gentile converts and the ceremonial law still held good, the advice given was not consistent with that decision which had also been sanctioned by the Holy Spirit. The Spirit of God did not prompt this advice. It was the fruit of cowardice."—Ibid., pg. 212.

These facts throw a strong light upon the expression that when "certain came from James," Peter withdrew from the Gentiles and "separated himself, fearing them which were of the circumcision." This also gives a better idea of the powerful influence that was exerted to draw Peter back from the truth—the influence which was indeed so powerful that even "Barnabas also was carried away with their dissimulation."

But Paul knew the gospel that he was sent to preach. He knew that it was the truth. And though thus left to stand alone against, to him, the most powerful human influence in the world, he cared not for this. "But when I saw that they walked not uprightly according to the truth of the gospel, I said unto Peter before them all, If thou, being a Jew, livest after the manner of Gentiles, and not as do the Jews, why compellest thou the Gentiles to live as do the Jews? We who are Jews by nature, and not sinners of the Gentiles, knowing that a man is not justified by the works of the law, but by the faith of Jesus Christ, even we have believed in Jesus Christ, and not by the works of the law; for by the works of the law shall no flesh be justified."

Both Peter and James did finally come to clear faith; but it took time for them to do it: and while they were coming to it, their course had no little influence in creating the condition that called forth the letter to the Galatians.

September 26, 1899

In a previous study on this subject—the fourth one—we remarked that while it is true that "the ceremonial law is the chief subject, *as to law,* in the book of Galatians," yet even then it is not the ceremonial law as given by the Lord; that even where the ceremonial law as given by the Lord is involved it is such a perversion of it as to make it altogether another thing than what it was in truth; and consequently that the great subject, as to law, as to works,

Galatians 1:6-2:14

is more ceremonialism—ceremonialism entire—than it is the true ceremonial law itself in any phase of it.

That *traditionalism* was an essential part of the teaching of those who had driven back the Galatian Christians is certain from the fact that Paul cites it as a thing in his own experience, and shows how he had been delivered from it by the gospel, which he preached. "Ye have heard of my conversation [manner of life] in time past in the Jews' religion. . . and profited in the Jews' religion above many my equals in mine own nation, being more exceedingly zealous of *the traditions of my fathers,* BUT when it pleased God, who separated me from my mother's womb, and called me by his grace, *to reveal his son in me,* THAT I MIGHT PREACH HIM among the brethren; immediately I conferred not with flesh and blood." Gal. 1:13-16.

That is to say: This very thing that these disturbers are trying to fasten upon you, I myself once held even more zealously than they; for "beyond measure I persecuted the church of God, and wasted it." But from that I was delivered and redeemed by the revelation of the Son of God in me. I have preached to you, and am now preaching to you, simply what I know through my own heart's experience and the revelation of the gospel of Christ. I *know* that the gospel of Christ, the gospel which I preach, delivers the soul from all the burden and the toil of the traditions of a perfect righteousness. I *know* that all that they seek by the many toilsome exactions of their traditions is found unto perfect and soul-rejoicing fulness in Jesus Christ, and that is obtained simply by faith alone in him.

But that is not all: the thing which brought the crisis at Antioch in the case of Peter, and which is the crisis in the introduction to the real subject in the book of Galatians, was the question of *eating with the Gentiles,* with men uncircumcised. This, too, was the thing which marked the crisis in the work of Peter as to Jew and Gentile, as is shown in his experience in the vision at Joppa, and at the home of Cornelius; and which he himself summed up in the words, "Ye know how that it is an unlawful thing for a man that is a Jew to keep company or come unto one of another nation; but God hath showed me that I should not call any man common or unclean." Acts 10:28.

But eating with the Gentiles was not an unlawful thing at all, *except by their own traditionalism.* This exclusiveness was never enjoined nor inculcated by anything which the Lord had ever committed to the Jews. The Scriptures, which they themselves had, were against it. That exclusiveness was altogether of their own construction, built up from their own exclusive self-righteousness. Yet this was a vital point and an essential element in the contention of the

"Pharisees which believed," that called forth the letter to the Galatians. And this being so, it is certain that the *traditional* ceremonial law of the Jews was an essential part of the ceremonial law that is the chief subject, *as to law,* in the book of Galatians.

It is true that the ceremonial law that God gave is also included in the controversy that called forth the letter to the Galatians; and yet even that, *as God gave it,* is not included. Circumcision is included; but so far perverted from its true intent and meaning as God gave it, and so laden with traditionalism, as to be only another phase of sheer pharisaic ceremonialism.

From the history of James in this connection, especially in Acts 21, it is plain that the rest of the true ceremonial law was also included—even to self-contradiction in the offering of sacrifices for sin while professing to believe in Christ. For one of the offerings made in purification of the Nazarite was a "lamb of the first year without blemish *for a* SIN OFFERING." Num. 6:14. And when Paul, out of deference to the brethren at Jerusalem, especially to James the brother of Jesus, had yielded so far for *appearance's sake* as to accompany some men who were actually practicing this, to a believer in Jesus, self-contradictory, ceremony, it was *while "he was conversing with the priest concerning the sacrifices to be offered, t*hat the mob broke loose: the truth is that just then God *let loose* the mob to save Paul from the effect of his deference to the ill advice of the compromising brethren.

"When we consider Paul's great desire to be in harmony with his brethren, his tenderness of spirit toward the weak in faith, his reverence for the apostles who had been with Christ, and for James the brother of the Lord, and his purpose to become all things to all men as far as he could do this and not sacrifice principle,—when we consider all this, it is less surprising that he was constrained to deviate from his firm, and decided course of action. But instead of accomplishing the desired object, these efforts for conciliation only precipitated the crisis, hastened the predicted sufferings of Paul, separated him from his brethren in his labors, deprived the church of one of its strongest pillars, and brought sorrow to Christian hearts in every land.

"The Saviour's words of reproof to the men of Nazareth apply in the case of Paul, not only to the unbelieving Jews, but *to his own brethren in the faith.* Had the leaders in the church fully surrendered their feelings of bitterness toward the apostle, and accepted him as one specially called of God to bear the gospel to the Gentiles, the Lord would have spared him to them still to labor for the salvation of souls. He who sees the end from the beginning, and who understands the hearts of all, saw what would be the result of the envy and

Galatians 1:6-2:14

jealousy cherished toward Paul. God had not in his providence ordained that Paul's labors should so soon end; but he did not work a miracle to counteract the train of circumstances to which their own course gave rise.

"The same spirit is still leading to the same results. A neglect to appreciate and improve the provisions of divine grace, has deprived the church of many a blessing. How often would the Lord have prolonged the life of some faithful minister had his labors been appreciated. But if the church permit the enemy of souls to pervert their understanding, so that they misrepresent and misinterpret the words and acts of the servant of Christ: if they allow themselves to stand in his way and hinder his usefulness, the Lord removes from them the blessing which he gave.

"Satan is constantly working through his agents to dishearten and destroy those whom God has chosen to accomplish a great and good work. They may be ready to sacrifice even their own life for the advancement of the cause of Christ, yet the great deceiver will suggest doubts, distrust, jealousy, concerning them, which, if entertained, will undermine confidence in their integrity of character, and thus cripple their usefulness. Too often he succeeds in working through their own brethren, to bring upon them such sorrow and anguish of heart that God graciously interposes to give his persecuted servants rest. After the hands are folded upon the pulseless breast, after the voice of warning and encouragement is silent, then death may accomplish that which life has failed to do" Then the obdurate may be aroused to see and prize the blessings they have cast from them.—*Sketches from the life of Paul,* pp. 214, 231, 232.

On the part of the Pharisees who believed, the "false skulking brethren" who confused the Galatian Christians, and even weakened Peter and James, the moral law was not included, except incidentally. But the infinite variety of ceremonial observances, which by "oral tradition" had been invested and set up as hedges about the law, and which were more to them than the God-given law itself,—these *were* included, and were an essential part of *their* side of the controversy. Simply to neglect the washing of hands, etc., as referred to in Mark 7, "was as bad as homicide [murder],and involved a forfeiture of eternal life." Farrar's *Life of Christ,* chap. 31.

However, in the book of Galatians, in Paul's setting forth of the only true gospel, the moral law is included, both in showing that it is impossible to he justified by any law whatever, even the moral law, and in showing that the very object of faith in Christ, the very object of the true gospel, is to accomplish in men the righteousness of that law, perfect obedience to the ten commandments.

If anything is needed to make plainer or more certain that ceremonialism altogether is the ceremonial law involved in the book of Galatians, here it is:—

"Tidings had been received at Corinth from the churches in Galatia, revealing a state of great confusion, and even of absolute apostasy. Judaizing teachers were opposing the work of the apostle, and seeking to destroy the fruit of his labors.

"In almost every church there were some members who were Jews by birth. To these converts the Jewish teachers found ready access, and through them gained a foot hold in the churches. It was impossible, by Scriptural arguments, to overthrow the doctrines taught by Paul; hence they resorted to the most unscrupulous measures to counteract his influence and weaken his authority. They declared that he had not been a disciple of Jesus, and had received no commission from him; yet he had presumed to teach doctrines directly opposed to those held by Peter, James, and the other apostles. Thus the emissaries of Judaism succeeded in alienating many of the Christian converts from their teacher in the gospel. Having gained this point, they induced them to return to the observance of the ceremonial law as essential to salvation. Faith in Christ, and obedience to the law of ten commandments, were regarded as of *minor importance.* Division, heresy, and sensualism were rapidly gaining ground among the believers in Galatia.

"The *doctrines which the Galatians had received* could not in any sense be called the gospel; they *were the teachings of men,* and were directly opposed to the doctrines taught by Christ. . . In the Galatian churches, open, unmasked error was supplanting the faith of the gospel. Christ, the true foundation, was virtually renounced for the obsolete ceremonies of Judaism.

"The apostle urged upon the Galatians, as their only safe course, to leave the false guides by whom they had been misled, and to return to the faith which they had received from the Source of truth and wisdom. Those false teachers were hypocritical, unregenerate men, unholy in heart, and corrupt in life. Their religion consisted in a round of ceremonies, by the performance of which they expected to receive the favor of God. They had no relish for a doctrine which taught, "Except a man be born again, he can not see the kingdom of God." Such a religion required too great a sacrifice. Hence they clung to their errors, deceiving themselves, and deceiving others.

"To substitute the external forms of religion for holiness of heart and life, is still as pleasing to the unrenewed nature as in the days of the apostles. . . Paul. . . describes the visit which he made to Jerusalem to secure a settlement of *the very questions which are now agitating the churches of Galatia,* as to whether the Gentiles should submit to circumcision and keep the ceremonial law."—*Sketches from the Life of Paul,* pp. 188-193.

And of the question considered at Jerusalem, we read:—"They [certain Jews from Judea] asserted, with great assurance, that none could be saved without being circumcised and keeping *the entire ceremonial law.* Jerusalem was the metropolis of the Jews, and there were found the greatest exclusiveness and bigotry. The Jewish Christians who lived in sight of the temple would naturally allow their minds to revert to the peculiar privileges of the Jews as a nation. As they saw Christianity departing from *the ceremonies and the traditions* of Judaism, and perceived that the peculiar sacredness with which the Jewish customs had been invested would soon be lost sight of in the light of the new faith, many grew indignant against Paul, as one who had, in a great measure, caused this change. Even the disciples were not all prepared willingly to accept the decision of the council. Some were zealous for the ceremonial law, and regarded Paul with jealousy, because they thought his principles were lax in regard to the obligation of the Jewish law."—*Ibid.,* pp.63, 71.

Thus the ceremonial law that is the chief subject, *as to law,* in the book of Galatians, is the ceremonial law both divine and human, but with the divine so perverted as in its perversion to be only human, and is, in a word, *ceremonialism* entire—a dead formalism against a living faith.

October 3, 1899

As we have now passed the preliminaries, and have come to the study of the real substance of the book of Galatians, the first thing to be noted is the surpassing value of what is here to be studied. This is made known in chapter 1, verses 8, 9, in those remarkable words, "Though we, or an angel from heaven, preach any other gospel unto you than that which we have preached unto you, let him be accursed. As we said before, so say I now again, if any man preach any other gospel unto you than that ye have received, let him be accursed."

This shows that if there could be any distinctions made among books of the Bible, then of all places in the Bible, the gospel, in its perfect sincerity, would be found in the book of Galatians. It would be found that whatever might be done with other books of the Bible, it must stand that in the book of Galatians the gospel is presented in such truth that even an angel from heaven could not alter it without incurring the curse. This being so, surely a study of the book of Galatians should enlist the most earnest attention and the deepest interest of every one who loves the gospel of Christ.

In our studies we have reached chapter 2:15. And, after the introduction, here, in Paul's appeal to Peter upon principle, is where the real consideration of the gospel upon its merits is first entered upon. So much so is this, that it is impossible to tell just where Paul's speech to Peter ends and definite word to the Galatians begins. This indeed is natural enough; because Paul's address to Peter was an argument and an appeal for "the truth of the gospel" (verse 14), and the letter to the Galatians is the same identical thing. Therefore as his address and appeal to Peter was in very substance what his address and appeal must be to the Galatians, there was no need of any definite break to mark the point at which his direct word to Peter ceased and that to the Galatians began. Accordingly, after the introduction, chapter 2:15 is where is begun the direct re-presentation of the gospel to the Galatians.

"We who are Jews by nature, and not sinners of the Gentiles, *knowing* that a man *is not justified* by the works of the law, *but by* the *faith* of Jesus Christ, *even* we have believed in Jesus Christ, *that we might be justified by the faith of Christ,* and not by the works of the law: for by the works of the law shall no flesh be justified."

The word "law," as used in these two verses is not any particular law demanding the definite article, *"the* law;" but in Greek is simply the word "law"—*nomos*—without any article. The word-for-word rendering is thus;— *"We, Jews by nature,* and not sinners of [the] nations, *knowing* that a man is *not justified* by works of law [*nomos*]: *but through faith* of Jesus Christ, also we on Christ Jesus *believed, that we might be justified by faith* of Christ, and not by works of law [*nomos*]: because shall not be justified by works of law [*nomos*] any flesh."

By this it is plain that it is law in general, the idea of law, that is considered in this text: that men are not justified by any law at all, nor by all law together; but solely by faith of Jesus Christ without any works of any law whatever. Evidently it could not be otherwise. For to specify some particular law, and assert that men were not justified by *that* law, would leave the question open to the implication that men might be justified by some other law. But "the truth of the gospel" is that man can not be justified by any law at all, nor by all laws together; but only by the faith of Christ: simply by believing in Jesus.

The vital point in this appeal to Peter is not discerned without careful attention. It is this: We who are Jews by nature, who have all the advantages that pertain to the Jews, whose are the fathers, and the covenants, and the laws, and the ordinances, all given by the Lord himself directly to the Jews— we who are thus Jews by nature, not sinners of the Gentiles: *"even we* have believed in Jesus Christ *that we might be justified by the faith of Christ,* and not by works of law: for by the works of law shall no flesh be justified." The very fact that we Jews, with all the native advantages of all the laws of the Jew, have believed in Jesus Christ that we might be justified by faith,—this in itself is open confession and positive evidence that there in no justification in law.

And when this is so with us Jews who have all these advantages, what else can possibly be the hope of the Gentiles who have no shadow of any such advantage? When "even we" must be justified by faith, how much more must the Gentiles be justified by faith? When we who have all these laws can not be justified by them, but must be justified by faith, without them, what shall the Gentile do who has none of these laws at all, if he is not to be justified by faith without them? And when we have confessed that we can not be justified by these laws, how can we ask the Gentiles to think of being justified by these same laws? Why put a yoke upon the necks of the Gentiles, which we ourselves were not able to bear, and which, by the liberty of the faith of Christ, we have thrown off? Therefore, "if thou, being a Jew, livest after the manner of Gentiles, and not as do the Jews—If you have abandoned the ground of the Jews, which, in order to be justified, is the right thing to do, and have gone over to the ground of the Gentiles, why will you require the Gentiles to abandon their ground, and go over to that of the Jews, which we have confessed must be abandoned?

All this was simply, in other words, the very argument that Peter himself had made in his statement of the truth of the gospel in his own experience, in the council at Jerusalem. "Men and brethren, ye know how that a good while ago *God made choice* among us, that *the Gentiles* by *my mouth* should hear *the word of the gospel* and believe. *And God,* which knoweth the hearts, *bare them witness,* giving them the Holy Ghost, even as he did unto us; and put no difference between *us* and *them* [note: not between them and *us;* but "between *us* AND THEM], purifying *their* hearts by faith. Now therefore why tempt ye God, to put a yoke upon the neck of the disciples, which neither our fathers nor we were able to bear? But we believe that through the grace of the Lord Jesus Christ *we shall be saved,* EVEN AS *THEY."* Note again: not, *they* shall be saved *even as* WE; but we shall be saved, *even as THEY.* And "THEY" were justified by FAITH without the deeds of any law—they *must* be; for they didn't have any; and "WE," the Jews, being saved *even as* THEY, must be justified by faith without the deeds of any law, even though "we" had all the laws that ever were.

Thus by the instruction of God and demonstration of the Holy Spirit, it was made plain to all that Jew and Gentile are saved in precisely the same way—by a common faith in Jesus Christ, without any deeds of any law; and that by this faith of Jesus Christ the middle wall of partition between them is annihilated, and all are made one with God and with one another in the blessedness, the righteousness, and the joy of the glorious gospel of the blessed God, who is blessed, and shall be blessed forevermore. Amen.

Galatians 2:17

October 10, 1899.

"But if, while we seek to be justified by Christ, we ourselves also are found sinners, is therefore Christ the minister of sin? God forbid."

Having abandoned all law *as a means of justification,* have we abandoned all law *altogether?*—God forbid. For while seeking to be justified by Christ, it is possible that we might be found sinners. And what is a sinner?—*"Whosoever committeth sin* transgresseth also *the law;* for *sin is* THE TRANSGRESSION OF THE LAW." 1 John 3:4.

And what law is it, the transgression of which is sin?—"I had not known sin, *but by the law;* for I had not known lust except *the law* had said, Thou shalt not covet." Rom. 7:7. That word then—"Thou shalt not covet"—belongs in a law; it is a part of a law.

It is not simply the *commandment,* but *THE LAW,* that says, "Thou shalt not covet." It is not, I had not known sin but by *the commandment;* it is not, I had known lust except the commandment had said, Thou shalt not covet. But it *is,* "I had not known sin, but by *THE LAW."* It is, "I had not know lust, except *THE LAW* had said, Thou shalt not covet."

Now *that law* which says, "Thou shalt not covet," says also, Thou shalt not kill, Thou shalt not steal, Thou shalt have no other gods before me, Thou shalt not take the name of the Lord thy God in vain. It is the Ten Commandment law: It is the law of God, which he spake from heaven, and wrote *twice* with his own hand on tables of stone, and which he writes with his own Spirit on the tables of the heart of the believer in Jesus.

That is *the law* by which is the knowledge of sin. That is "THE LAW," the transgression of which is *"sin."* And that is the law, and the only law, by which, while seeking "to be justified by Christ," we *could* be "found sinners." And as this word in Galatians recognizes the possibility that, while seeking to be justified by Christ we might be found sinners; and as there is no knowledge of sin without the law of Ten Commandments, this is therefore conclusive evidence that, while it is true that all law must be abandoned *as a means of justification,* all law is *not* abandoned *altogether.* It is conclusive evidence that THAT LAW by which is the knowledge of sin, the law of Ten Commandments, is NOT abandoned *as the means of the* KNOWLEDGE OF SIN.

That law, the law of Ten Commandments, while it, with all other law, must never be used as a *means of justification* is *NOT* abandoned altogether; because *that* would make *Christ* THE MINISTER OF SIN. And against any such suggestion as that the Lord plunges his emphatic "God forbid." Thus the Lord has set his everlasting "God forbid" against all idea that the law of Ten Commandments is abolished or in any sense "loosed down" or done away.

The Lord Jesus did not come into the world to minister to sin, but altogether to save from sin. Sin is the transgression of the law of Ten Commandments; and as the Lord Jesus came to save men from sin, in the nature of the case he came to save men from the transgression of that law. By that law is the knowledge of sin; and as Jesus came to save men from sin, his mission would be completely nullified and altogether vain if the law were taken away: for to take away the law would take away the knowledge of sin and the very means of the knowledge of sin; and this in itself would make it impossible to save men from sin. And to make the coming of the Lord Jesus create a condition of things in which it would be impossible to save men from sin, would be nothing else than to make Jesus the minister of sin. It would make Christ confirm sin upon the world forever; and that is precisely what would satisfy Satan forever. And why should not God cry out against it forever, "God forbid"? And to this everlasting "God forbid" who that would not play directly into the hands of Satan can ever say anything but Amen?

Therefore "if, while we seek to be justified by Christ, we ourselves also are found sinners," transgressors of the law of Ten Commandments, does Christ sanction that?—"God forbid." Does he justify men in order that they may be free to transgress the law?—"God forbid." Does he save men from sin in order that they may continue in sin?—"God forbid." Do we believe in Jesus in order that we may continue to be sinners?—"God forbid." Do we "seek to be justified [made righteous] by Christ" in order that we may continue to sin?—"God forbid." And let all the people forever say Amen.

Let it be borne in mind and upon the heart forever by every soul, that justification (being made righteous) by faith of Jesus Christ, means, in itself, in every sentiment of it, the total abandonment of sins, and the destruction of the body of sin in order that henceforth we should not serve sin. Otherwise I build again in works what I destroyed by faith: and "if I build again the things which I destroyed, I make myself a *transgressor.*" Faith will never justify sin. The two are eternal opposites; for *"whatsoever* is NOT of faith *is sin."* And in Christ Jesus nothing avails but faith, which worketh by love that keeps the commandments of God.

Galatians 2:18, 19

October 17, 1899.

"For if I build again the things which I destroyed, I make myself a transgressor. For I through the law am dead to the law, that I might live unto God."

What is it that is referred to in the words, "If I build again the things which I destroyed"? There are at least two special thoughts involved in the words.

1. The one great idea of those who had turned back the Galatian Christians was justification by *LAW.* Whereas the truth of the gospel, which Paul had preached to the Galatians, and which even "an angel from heaven" could not contradict is justification by *FAITH.*

Paul has already shown, in verses 15, 16, that even they who were Jews by nature, and so had all the laws that the Lord had given, had believed on Christ in order that they might be justified by *faith* and not by works of *law;* and this for the accepted reason that by works of law no flesh can be justified.

This was the utter abandonment and destruction of all idea of justification by *law.* And having abandoned all idea of justification by *law,* in order, by believing in Jesus, to be justified by the *faith of* Christ, now, being justified by *faith,* shall I set up again the idea and the hope of being justified by *law?* Having abandoned the idea of justification by *law,* in order to find justification by *faith,* having *found* justification by *faith,* shall I again adopt the idea of justification by law?—God forbid; for when to be justified by faith, I must abandon all idea of justification by *law,* if I now adopt again the idea of justification by *law,* I must abandon all idea of justification by *faith.* But when I abandon justification by faith I make myself a transgressor; for "whatsoever is not of faith is sin." Therefore, if I build again the structure of justification by *law,* which I destroyed by justification by *faith,* I make myself a transgressor; because by the law is the knowledge of sin.

2. That which I destroyed by abandoning all idea of justification be law,

and adopting justification only by the faith of Christ, is "the old man," "the body of sin." And to build again that which I destroyed is only to bring back from the dead that old man, is only to make alive the body of sin, *and that* can only make me a transgressor.

Justification by the faith of Christ means *in itself* the total abandonment of all sins committed, the remission of all "sins that are past," and also the *destruction of the body of sin, so that "henceforth* we should not serve sin." Therefore while seeking to be justified by faith, we must not be found sinners. For if I build again the body of sin which I destroyed, I make myself a transgressor. And in again adopting the idea of justification by law, I do build again, in *works,* what I destroyed by faith, because all seeking of justification by *law,* is seeking justification by *our own works,* and our own works are simply the works *of the flesh,* which are all sin; for "the works of the flesh are manifest, which are these: Adultery, fornication, uncleanness, lasciviousness, idolatry, witchcraft, hatred, variance, emulations, wrath, strife, seditions, heresies, envying, murders, drunkenness, revelings, and such like."

And in building again the structure of justification by *law,* which I abandoned in order to be justified by *faith,* I make myself a transgressor, because "for I through the law am *dead to the law,* that I might live unto God." Since abandoning the idea of justification by *law* and adopting justification by *faith* caused me to become *dead to the law* and *alive unto God,* the adopting again the idea of justification by *law,* which, in itself, is the abandonment of justification by faith, would cause me to become *alive to the law* and *dead unto God.* But to be dead unto God is nothing but to be dead *in trespasses and in sins.* And as to be dead unto God is to be dead in trespasses and in sins, and to be dead unto God is to be alive unto the law, then to be alive unto the law is only to be a transgressor.

Therefore, my brethren, justification by faith forever, without any works of any law of any kind whatever,—this is the only ground of hope of salvation.

Galatians 2:20

October 24, 1899.

"I am crucified with Christ; nevertheless I live, yet not I, but Christ liveth in me: and the life which I now live in the flesh I live by the faith of the Son of God, who loved me, and gave himself for me."

It may not be amiss to emphasize what this scripture does say, by noting what it does not say.

It does *not* say, I want to be crucified with Christ. It does *not* say, I wish I were crucified with Christ that he might live in me. It *does* say, "I am crucified with Christ."

Again: it does *not* say, Paul was crucified with Christ; Christ lived in Paul, and the Son of God loved Paul, and gave himself for Paul. All that is true; but that is *not* what the scripture *says,* nor is that what it means; for it means just what is says. And it *does* say, "I am crucified with Christ: nevertheless I live; yet not I, but Christ liveth in me, and the life which I now live in the flesh I live by the faith of the Son of God, who loved me, and gave his life for me."

Thus this verse is a beautiful and solid foundation of Christian faith for every soul in the world. Thus it is made possible for every soul to say, in full assurance of Christian faith, "He loved *me.*" "He gave himself for *me.*" "I am crucified with Christ." "Christ liveth in *me.*" Read also 1 John 4:15.

For any soul to say, "I am crucified with Christ" is not speaking at a venture. It is not believing on a guess. It is not saying a thing of which there is no certainty. Every soul in this world can say, in all truth and all sincerity, "I am crucified with Christ." It is but the acceptance of a fact, the acceptance of a thing that is already done, for this word *is* the statement of a fact.

It is a fact that Jesus Christ was crucified. And when he was crucified, *we* also were crucified; for he was one of *us.* His name is Immanuel, which is 'God with us—not God with *him,* but "God with *us."* When his name is *not* God with *him,* but "God with *us:"* and when God with *him* was *not* God with him , but God with *us,* then who was he but *"us"*? He had to be *"us"* in order that God with *him* could be not God with him, but "God with *us."* And when he was crucified, then who was it but *"us"* that was crucified?

This is the mighty truth announced in this text. Jesus Christ was *"us."* He was of the same flesh and blood with us. He was of our very nature. He was in all points like us. "It behooved him to be made in all points like unto his brethren." He emptied himself, and was made in the likeness of men. He was "the last Adam," and precisely as the first Adam was ourselves, so Christ, the last Adam, was ourselves. When the first Adam died, we being involved in him, died with him. And when the last Adam was crucified,—*he* being ourselves and we being involved in him—we were crucified *with him.* As the first Adam was in himself the whole human race, so the last Adam was in *himself* the whole human race; and so when the last Adam was crucified, the whole human race—the old, sinful, human nature—was crucified with him. And so it is written: "Knowing this, that *our old man* is CRUCIFIED *WITH HIM, that the body of sin* might be *destroyed,* that henceforth we should not serve sin."

Thus every soul in this world can truly say, in perfect triumph of Christian faith, "I am crucified with Christ;" my old sinful human nature is crucified with him, that this body of sin might be destroyed, that henceforth I should not serve sin. Rom. 6:6. Nevertheless I live; yet not I, but Christ liveth in me. Always bearing about in my body the dying of the Lord Jesus,—the crucifixion of the Lord Jesus, for I am crucified with him,—that the *life also of Jesus* might be made manifest in my body. For I who live am always delivered unto death for Jesus sake that the life also of Jesus might be made manifest in my mortal flesh. 2 Cor. 4:10, 11. And therefore the life which I now live in the flesh I live by the faith of the Son of God, who loved *me,* and gave himself for *me.*

In this blessed fact of the crucifixion of the Lord Jesus, which was accomplished for every human soul, there is not only laid the foundation of faith for every soul but in it there is given the *gift of faith TO* every soul. And thus the cross of Christ is not only the wisdom of God displayed from God to us, but is the *very power of God* manifested to deliver us from all sin, and bring us to God.

0 sinner, brother, sister, believe it, Oh, receive it. Surrender to this mighty truth. *Say* it, say it in full assurance of faith, and say it forever. "I am crucified with Christ: nevertheless I live; yet not I, but Christ liveth in me: and the life which I now live in the flesh I live by the faith of the Son of God, who loved *me,* and gave himself for *me."* Say it; for it is the truth, the very truth and wisdom and power of God, which saves the soul from all sin.

Galatians 2:21

October 31, 1899.

"I do not frustrate the grace of God: for if righteousness come by law [*nomos*—: not *ho nomos*—the law] then Christ is dead in vain.

This is one of those mighty, universal statements of eternal principle so frequently found in the writings of Paul. It is the climax of the argument begun in his protest to Peter when "before them all" Paul withstood him to the face because he "walked not uprightly according to the truth of the gospel." It will therefore make plainer to the reader of this climacteric, if we recall the issue as it was begun in Paul's words to Peter:—"When I saw that they walked not uprightly according to the truth of the gospel, I said to Peter before them all, if thou, *being born a Jew,* art want to live according to the customs of the Gentiles and not of the Jews, how is it that thou constrainest the Gentiles to keep the ordinances of the Jews? *We who are Jews by nature,* and not sinners of the Gentiles, *knowing* that a man is not justified by works of law, but by the faith of Jesus Christ, *even we* have believed in Jesus Christ, that [in order that] we might be justified by the faith of Christ and *not by works of law:* for by works of law shall no flesh be justified."

That is to say: We who are Jews by nature, who have all the advantages that pertain to the Jews, whose are the fathers, and all the covenants, and the laws, and the ordinances, all given by the Lord himself directly to the Jews,—we who are Jews by nature and not sinners of the Gentiles, *EVEN WE* have believed in Jesus Christ, that we might be justified by *the faith of Christ* and *not by works of law:* for by works of law shall no flesh be justified." The very fact that *we Jews,* with all the native advantages of all the laws of the Jews, have believed in Christ in order that we might be justified by faith—this in itself is open confession that there is no justification by law. When even we can not be justified by all these laws, laws which even the Lord gave to us, but must be justified by *faith in Christ,* that is both confession and demonstration that there is no possibility of justification by law.

Nor in this is there any denial or frustration of the grace of God. It is true that it was the grace of God that gave to us all these laws, which are indeed all advantages; but these laws—any of them, or all of them together—were not given that we should be justified or find righteousness *by them.* The one great object of all these laws was and is *Christ.* In his great grace God gave to us all these laws that we might more plainly see, more clearly discern, and more fully know, *Christ.* They were all given that we should be justified—not by *the laws* but—by *Jesus Christ;* that we should find righteousness—not by *doing the laws,* but—by *believing in Jesus.*

Therefore when we who are Jews by nature, and who, as such, have all the advantages of all the laws ever given to the Jews,—when even we have believed in Jesus in order that we might find righteousness by faith of Jesus Christ and not by works of law, *in so doing* we do not *frustrate the grace of God;* for this is the very purpose of all these laws which themselves were given by the grace of God. And since Christ, and righteousness by faith in Christ, was and is the very object of all these laws, then "if righteousness come by *law, Christ is dead in vain."*

And, finally, since Christ has died for our offences, and is risen again for our justification, *now* for anybody to seek to be justified by *law* and not by *faith of Christ,* is to deny that Christ *ever was* the object of the laws, and so is to assert that justification is and always was by *works* and *not* by *faith,* and so is, in a word, the utter repudiation of Christ now and *ever;* because he is "the Lamb slain from the foundation of the world," and "who *verily* was foreordained *before* the foundation of the world."

Consequently it is an eternal and universal principle that "if righteousness come by law, then Christ is dead in vain."

"And let all the people say, Amen and Amen."

Chapter 3

Galatians 3:1

November 7, 1899[1]

Lately a pilgrim in India, making his way to a shrine, was so loaded with chains and iron bands that, when he decided to make part of his journey by railroad, the company demanded that he pay for his passage both regular fare and freight. It was estimated that there was on his body about two hundred pounds of iron; and at night, in his journey on foot, he would stake himself out like an animal. The object of all this was to do penance, to make atonement, for his sins. In relating the occurrence, the Interior very justly remarks: "What is Lent, throughout three fourths of Christendom, but an attempt by personal sacrifice to propitiate God? The same thought which lay at the basis of the Indian fakir's conduct lies at the basis of Lent's abstention. It is that man must pay at least part of the penalty of his sin in bodily pains. It is that he must atone, in part at least, for that sin which the Bible says was completely blotted out by the one sufficient Redeemer. 'Old Dan Chaucer' struck the keynote of the Reformation in his pre-Reformation line, when he wrote, 'Either he forgives us every whit or not a dele.' But direct as that lesson is taught in the holy Gospels, it has not yet been mastered by the Greek, Romanist, or Protestant." The "Studies In Galatians" now being conducted in the REVIEW AND HERALD will help on this subject, everybody should read them.

Galatians 3:1

"O foolish Galatians, who hath bewitched you, that ye should not obey the truth, before whose eyes Jesus Christ hath been evidently set forth, crucified among you?"

Christ having been set forth, crucified among them, it was easy for the Galatians to understand the words of chapter 2:20: "I am crucified with Christ." When he was set forth, crucified among them, it was easy enough for all who

---

1 This paragraph appeared on the editorial page just prior to the beginning of this week's study in Galatians. It is included because reference is made to the study.

were willing, to be crucified with him.

Paul preached only "Christ, and him crucified." This he preached wherever he went. And wherever he went, he preached Christ crucified among the people *in that place*. That is, when he was in Galatia, he preached not only Christ crucified down in *Judea,* but also *in Galatia.* When he was in Corinth, he preached not only Christ crucified away over at *Jerusalem,* but also Christ crucified there in Corinth.

In other words, Christ crucified at Jerusalem in Judea, was also Christ crucified wherever there is a man on the earth. And the preaching of Christ crucified at Jerusalem in Judea, to be the true preaching of that fact must be also the preaching of Christ crucified *wherever the fact is preached.* It is simply the preaching of the universal and ever-present Christ the Saviour.

The preaching in Galatia, in Corinth, in Rome, in Britain, in the United States, of Christ crucified *only at Jerusalem in Judea,* is too far away both in distance and in time for the people readily to grasp it as a power in their own lives. But the preaching of Christ crucified at Jerusalem in Judea, and also wherever there is a human soul,—this brings to each soul, *just where that soul is,* Christ, the crucified, the risen, and the ever-living Saviour. And then and there each soul who hears the preaching can be crucified with him (Rom. 6:6), can rise with him (Eph. 2:5, 6), and can *live with him* (Rom. 6:8), as the ever-crucified, ever-risen, and ever-living Saviour.

Such preaching, and such alone, is the true preaching of Christ and him crucified. Such preaching, and such alone, is the true preaching of the cross of Christ. Such preaching of the cross of Christ is the preaching of "the power of God;" and such preaching of Christ crucified is "Christ the power of God, and the wisdom of God." 1 Cor. 1:17, 18, 23, 24.

We can do no better than to say again, in this connection, what we said two weeks ago, on chap. 2:20: Jesus Christ was *"us."* He was of the same flesh and blood with us. He was of our very nature. He was in all points like us. "It behooved him to be made in all points like unto his brethren." He emptied himself, and was made in the likeness of men. He was "the last Adam." And precisely as the first Adam was ourselves, so Christ, the last Adam, was ourselves. When the first Adam died, we, being involved in him, died with him. And when the last Adam was crucified,—*he* being ourselves, and we being involved in him,—*we* were crucified *with him. As* the first Adam was in himself the whole human race, *so* the last Adam was in *himself* the whole human race; and *so* when the last Adam was crucified, the whole human race— the old sinful human nature—was crucified with him. And so it is written:

"Knowing this, that *our old man* IS CRUCIFIED *WITH HIM, that the body of sin* might be *destroyed,* that henceforth we should not serve sin."

Thus every soul in this world can truly say, in the perfect triumph of Christian faith, "I am crucified with Christ:" my old sinful human nature is crucified with him, that this body of sin might be destroyed, that henceforth I should not serve sin. Rom. 6:6. Nevertheless I live; yet not I, but Christ liveth in me. Always bearing about in my body the dying of the Lord Jesus—the crucifixion of the Lord Jesus, for I am crucified with him—that *the life also of Jesus* might be made manifest in my body. For I who live am always delivered unto death, for Jesus' sake, that the life also of Jesus might be made manifest in my mortal flesh. 2 Cor. 4:10, 11. And therefore the life which I now live in the flesh I live by the faith of the Son of God, who loved me, and gave himself for me.

In this blessed fact of the crucifixion of the Lord Jesus, which was accomplished for every human soul, there is not only laid the foundation of faith *for* every soul, but in it there is given the *gift of faith TO* every soul. And thus the cross of Christ is not only the wisdom of God displayed from God to us, but it is the *very power of God* manifested to deliver us from all sin, and bring us to God.

0 sinner, brother, sister, believe it. Oh, receive it. Surrender to this mighty truth. Say it, say it in full assurance of faith, and say it forever. "I am crucified with Christ: nevertheless I live; yet not I, but Christ liveth in me: and the life which I now live in the flesh I live by the faith of the Son of God, who loved me, and gave himself for me." Say it; for it is the truth, the very truth and wisdom and power of God, which saves the soul from all sin.

Galatians 3:2-5

November 14, 1899.

"This only would I learn of you. Received ye the Spirit by the works of the law, or by the hearing of faith? Are ye so foolish? Having begun in the Spirit, are ye now made perfect by works of law [*nomos*] or by the hearing of faith? Are ye so foolish? Having begun in the Spirit, are ye now made perfect by the flesh? Have ye suffered so many things in vain? If it be yet in vain. He therefore that ministereth to you the Spirit, and worketh miracles among you, doeth he it by works of law [*nomos*], or by the hearing of faith?"

Galatians 3:2-5

In these verses is revealed the deep secret of the difficulty with the Galatians, and especially with those who had bewitched them, which called forth the letter to the Galatians.

That secret is that they held that men are justified, *not* by faith in Christ, *BUT* by faith in Christ *AND works of law,* that men are saved, *not* by faith in Christ, *BUT* by faith in Christ *and something else.* That these who have never yet believed in Christ may be justified by faith in Christ; but those who *believe* in Christ must be justified by works of law: that a man who is only a sinner must be justified by faith; but when he has been justified, and has become a Christian, then he must be justified by works of law: that righteousness is *obtained* by faith, but it must be *kept* by works: that the righteousness of Christ must be received in place of all our sins, and to *set* us in the way of right; but our own righteousness *keeps* us in the way of right: that Christ avails in all the we can not do; but in all that we *can* do *we ourselves* avail: that we *begin* the Christian course by faith; but we must complete it by works: in short, and in the words of Inspiration, that we begin "in the Spirit." but are *"made perfect by the flesh."*

That this analysis is correct is shown in other words that are a material part of the story of the controversy that called forth the letter to the Galatians.

Note, it was not the Pharisees alone, but "the Pharisees *which BELIEVED,"* who started this controversy, and continued it, and carried it into Galatia, and planted it among the Galatian Christians. It was these professed believers in Christ who said to *believers in Christ,* "Except ye be circumcised,. . . *ye can not be saved."* It was these professors of faith in Christ who insisted that those who had *faith in Christ* must be also circumcised and keep the law, *in order to be saved.* Thus with those "Pharisees which believed," faith in Christ is not enough to save: it must be faith in Christ and something else. It required what Christ had done, with what we can do added to that.

This is further confirmed by the fact, which some time ago we pointed out, that the controversy, so far as circumcision was concerned, was not as to the merits of circumcision itself; but altogether as to whether believers in Christ must be circumcised *in order to be saved.* This is certain because that after the question had, in council, been decided *against circumcision,* Paul *circumcised Timothy.*

It was also as to the keeping of the law of God: it was not a question of keeping or not keeping the law of God on its merits, but altogether the question of keeping the law *in order to be saved by the keeping of the law.*

And the most singular phase of this whole story is that those people thought that *that* was the true gospel, that *that* was righteousness by faith! They thought that *they* were the ones who held the true faith in Christ, and that Paul was an innovater, the chief enemy of the true faith, that he was making void the law of God, and undermining all righteousness. But the truth is that they did not know what is righteousness by faith. They had no true idea of faith, and so *could* not know truly what is righteousness by faith.

Now the letter to the Galatians was written to correct this fearful error, and to show to them and to all people forever what righteousness by faith is in the very truth of the gospel. It was written to make plain that the faith of Jesus Christ, *and that alone,* saves the soul, at the beginning and at the end and all the way between: that what is begun by faith is kept only by faith: that what is begun by faith is completed only by faith: that faith alone sets us in the right way, and faith alone keeps us in the right way: that *"In Christ Jesus* neither circumcision availeth anything, nor uncircumcision; but *faith* which *worketh,"* not faith *and* works, but "faith *WHICH* worketh by love." And as love is the fulfilling of the law, then in Christ nothing avails but faith which fulfills the law—not faith *and* the fulfilling of the law, but faith *which* fulfills the law. The law is kept, *not* in order to be saved, but *because we are saved.* It is only the saved, the righteous, man that *can* fulfill the law; therefore he fulfills the law only because he is saved; and he is saved only by grace through faith. The power, the virtue, to fulfill the law is in the *faith,* which is received as the free gift of God through Jesus Christ. And this neither frustrates the grace of God nor makes void the law of God. On the contrary, it magnifies the grace of God, and establishes the law of God. It is the true righteousness by faith.

Galatians 3:6-9

November 21, 1899.

"Even as Abraham believed God, and it was so counted to him for righteousness. Know ye therefore that they which are of faith, the same are the children of Abraham. And the scripture, forseeing that God would justify the heathen through faith, preached before the gospel unto Abraham, saying, 'In thee shall all nations be blessed.' So then they which be of faith are blessed with faithful Abraham."

The great contention of those who had confused the Galatians was that the Gentiles who believed in Christ must be circumcised *in order to be saved.* In the

Galatians 3:6-9

nature of the case, they carried back to Abraham the obligation of circumcision; because in his family circumcision was instituted. They disconcerted the Galatian Christians by presenting to them this fallacious argument :—

The promise of inheriting the world, and, indeed, all the promises, was made to Abraham. Abraham and all his family were circumcised. Now it is perfectly proper to believe in Jesus *for the forgiveness of sins:* but in addition to this you must be circumcised, and so become children of Abraham, in order that, *as children of Abraham,* you can be heirs to the inheritance, the world to come, that was promised to Abraham. None but true children can inherit from the father. Therefore do you not see that if you would inherit from Abraham, you must be children of Abraham? That is plain enough. *BUT Abraham,* to whom the property belongs, *was circumcised.* You can be children of his only by circumcision; because all his children must be circumcised. Therefore do you not see that while it is proper and even necessary to believe in Jesus *for the forgiveness of sins,* it is *essential* that in addition to that you shall be circumcised *in order to be saved,* and *so* to *inherit the land* and all the promises *given to Abraham,* the *father?* Do you not now see how Paul is robbing you of your inheritance, and shutting you out from all the blessings of Abraham our father, by telling you that you need not be circumcised?

Now, that argument is wholly fallacious, and is shown to be fallacious in the double fact that Abraham received the promise of the inheritance and, indeed, all the promises, and also that which makes sure the inheritance, *before* he was circumcised. In other words, it was while Abraham was a Gentile that he received the promises; and he received them altogether by faith. Then, whosoever are of faith, *these* are the children of Abraham.

Righteousness is that which makes sure the inheritance; and it is written: "Abraham believed God, and it [his believing God] was accounted to him for righteousness." Thus Abraham obtained the righteousness of God by believing God. Righteousness is that which makes sure the inheritance; and it is written: "Abraham believed God, and it [his believing God] was accounted to him for righteousness." Thus Abraham obtained the righteousness of God by believing God. He obtained the inheritance, the world to come, also by believing God. Thus both the inheritance and the righteousness that makes it sure were received by Abraham by faith alone.

So, then, *all* that are of faith are the children of Abraham; and, being children of Abraham, are heirs of the inheritance, which is the world to come.

It was also while Abraham was yet uncircumcised, while in that respect he was yet "a heathen," that God gave to him the promise that he would "justify the heathen," in the words: "In thee shall all nations be blessed." Therefore, again, as it was while he was yet a heathen that Abraham was justified, and justified wholly by faith; and, as it was then too that God promised to Abraham that he would justify *all the heathen* exactly as he had justified Abraham, it follows inevitably that all the heathen must be justified by faith, in order to be children of Abraham. And, so, being thus by faith children of Abraham, they are "heirs according to the promise" given to Abraham. "So then they which be of faith are blessed with faithful Abraham."

And this justifying, saving faith is not faith *and circumcision;* but faith *without* circumcision. For "cometh this blessedness then upon the circumcision only, or upon the uncircumcision also? For we say that faith was reckoned to Abraham for righteousness. How was it then reckoned? When he was in circumcision, or in uncircumcision? Not in circumcision, but in uncircumcision. And he received the sign of circumcision, a seal of the righteousness of the faith which he had yet being uncircumcised."

And it was so in order "that he might be the father of *all them* that *BELIEVE though they be NOT* circumcised; that righteousness might be imputed unto them also; and the *father of circumcision* to them who are not of the circumcision only, but who also walk in the steps of *that faith* of our father Abraham, which he had being yet uncircumcised."

That is to say that even though they were children of Abraham by natural birth confirmed by circumcision, yet he was *their* father, and they were really his children *only* when they were *justified* by *that faith* which *he* had, and when they *walked* in the steps of that faith which *he* had while he was yet, as regards circumcision, a Gentile. And now when He had come in whom Abraham while a Gentile had believed and had been justified and had obtained the promises, and these Gentiles had believed in him, just as had Abraham when he was a Gentile, for those who were circumcised to insist that those believing Gentiles must be circumcised in order to be the children of Abraham and to be saved, was simply to show themselves altogether behind the times, and sadly lacking in understanding of the very truths which they themselves professed, and of which they bore the mark.

Therefore it is faith in Christ, and faith alone, that avails: it is faith in Christ that avails to obtain forgiveness of sins: it is faith in Christ that obtains the inheritance; it is faith in Christ that obtains the righteousness which, alone can make the inheritance sure. And it is faith in Christ, and that alone, that can enable the one whose sins are forgiven, to enter, in full and assured heirship, upon the inheritance that was given to Abraham and his seed, through the righteousness of faith.

Galatians 3:6-9

December 5, 1899.

The Galatians and other Gentiles were justified by faith in Christ without circumcision. They thus became children of Abraham, because Abraham was justified by faith in Christ without circumcision. They thus became heirs also of the inheritance promised to Abraham, because Abraham received the promise of the inheritance by faith, without circumcision. Therefore, since they were children of Abraham, and heirs according to the promise to Abraham, and had the righteousness which fully entitles them to the inheritance,—all without circumcision,—and since in all this they were exactly as Abraham was, and were walking in the steps of that faith of our father Abraham which he had being yet uncircumcised, what possible need could there be of circumcision?

This is the answer that was made to the demands of the Pharisees who believed, who insisted that Gentiles who believe in Christ must be circumcised in order to be saved. This is the answer, in both Romans and Galatians, to the contention of the Pharisees who believed. This is the Christian argument.

But to this they came back with the question, What profit was there *ever* in circumcision? What was circumcision for? How did it ever come in? And why *should* it ever have come in? And they argued, even admitting that Abraham had all this before he was circumcised, and the Gentiles now coming in and finding it all by faith without circumcision, just as Abraham did, the fact is that after Abraham got it all by faith, *he was circumcised.* Then, admitting that these have it all by faith, as he got it, why should not these be circumcised after they have it by faith, just as Abraham was circumcised after he got it by faith? Thus, claimed the Pharisees, it is not enough to say that Abraham received this by faith without circumcision, and that the Gentiles have gone far enough when they have received it all without circumcision, as did Abraham; because, when Abraham had received it without circumcision, *he was afterward circumcised.* Then the Gentiles have not gone far enough in the way of Abraham unless they, having what Abraham had without circumcision, also, as did Abraham, go yet farther, and *be circumcised.*

This was the claim of the Pharisees who believed, and who went everywhere in opposition to the work of Paul, insisting that all the Gentiles who believe in

Christ must be circumcised in order to be saved.

And this same question is raised, even to this day, by many persons. Even today there are large numbers of people who ask the question, Why should not Christians be circumcised, because surely Abraham was circumcised, and he is the father of all them that believe? So that, though the same contention is not still carried on that was started by the Pharisees of Jerusalem in the days of the apostles, yet really the same query abides. And Romans and Galatians—Galatians particularly—is, even today, present truth; not only because of its insisting upon the everlasting truth that those who are justified by faith, as was Abraham, without circumcision are the children of Abraham, and heirs of the promise without circumcision.

Why, then, was Abraham circumcised after he received the righteousness and the promises, and yet his true children—his children by faith—now be not circumcised? The answer is: For the simple reason that circumcision was not in the original plan. It *was* no part, and *is* no part, of the original order of God in justification or salvation. The truth is that if Abraham had continued to walk in the faith in which he walked before he was circumcised, he *never would have been circumcised,* nor any of his children.

Why, then, was Abraham circumcised? It is important to know. And in order to know, it is important to look at the record in the Bible; for it is all there, and it is all plain. Notice, in Gen. 11:29-32 is the record of Abram's leaving his native country. Then Gen. 12:1 tells us that the Lord *"had said"* unto Abram, "Get thee out of thy country, and from thy kindred, and from thy father's house, unto a land that I will show thee." This shows that it was in obedience to the call of the Lord that Abram left his country, though his father's house and his kindred were with him in this. And it was *at that time,* when God "had said" to him thus, that God also showed that he would justify the heathen through faith; for then it was that he preached the gospel unto Abram, saying, "In thee shall all families of the earth be blessed." Gen. 12:3; Gal. 3:8.

After his father died, Abram came into the land of Canaan, and *then* it was that "the Lord appeared unto Abram and said, Unto thy seed will I give this land," Gen.12:7. But Abram's kindred were yet with him; and though the Lord had now *promised* him the land, he had not yet *showed* it to him as he had said he would do, and he could not show it to him until he had become separated from his kindred as well as from his country and from his father's house. But in the thirteenth chapter, Lot and his people, the only kindred that were with him, did separate from him; and just then, "after that Lot was separated from him," the Lord said unto Abram, "Lift up now thine eyes, and *look* from the place where thou art northward, and southward, and eastward, and westward: for all the land which thou *seest,* to thee will I give it, and to thy seed forever." And the land which Abram then saw, and which was then promised to him, included "the world;" for this promise was "the promise, that he should be the heir of the world." Rom. 4:13.

Then in Genesis 15, Abram said to the Lord "Behold, to me thou hast given no seed: and, lo, one born in my house is mine heir. And, behold, the word of the Lord came unto him, saying, This shall not be thine heir; but he that shall come forth out of thine own bowels shall be thine heir. And he brought him forth abroad, and said, Look now toward heaven, and tell the stars, if thou be able to number them: and he said unto him, So shall thy seed be. And he believed in the Lord; and he counted it to him for righteousness." Verses 3-6.

At the same time the Lord said to him: "I am the Lord that brought thee out of Ur of the Chaldees, to give thee this land to inherit it." And Abram asked, "Lord God, whereby shall I know that I shall inherit it?" In answer the Lord made a covenant with Abram,—a covenant of sacrifice—pledging his own life to the fulfillment of all that he had promised and spoken; for he told Abram to take "an heifer of three years old, and a she goat of three years old, and a ram of three years old, and a turtle dove, and a young pigeon." And when Abram had divided them all in the midst except the birds, and had laid the pieces one against another upon the altar in sacrifice to God, and watched the sacrifices until the going down of the sun, then "a deep sleep fell upon Abram; and lo, an horror of great darkness fell upon him,'" and "when the sun went down, and it was dark, behold a smoking furnace, and a burning lamp that passed between those pieces." And "the Lord made a covenant with Abram, saying, Unto thy seed have I given this land." Gen. 12:7-18.

Thus Abram had received the blessing of God, which was to make him a blessing to all nations; he had received the promise of the world for an inheritance; he had received the promise of the seed in whom all nations should be blessed; he had received the righteousness of God; and God had made his covenant with him, in which he pledged himself: and all this by faith alone, utterly without circumcision, and with no mention or even hint of circumcision, or of any necessity for it. Thus the Lord had given to Abram, and by faith Abram had received, all that the Lord has to give anybody, and all that anybody ever can receive. And it was, and is, altogether of faith, and faith alone—faith without works, without circumcision.

In the sixteenth chapter of Genesis, "Sarai said unto Abram. Behold now, the Lord hath restrained me from bearing: I pray thee, go in unto my maid; it may be that I may obtain children by her. *And Abram hearkened to the voice of Sarai."* Gen. 16:2. Hagar conceived and bare Ishmael. And we know, from the other scriptures, that this whole arrangement was altogether a scheme of the flesh, springing wholly from distrust of the promise of God, springing from unbelief; and Abraham had to repudiate it all, and bear the fearful test of the offering of his only son Isaac, on Mount Moriah, before he recovered his true standing in faith alone. It was an effort of themselves to fulfill the promise of God, which, in the nature of things, God alone could fulfill. It was an effort of the flesh to do the works of the Spirit, and so was a lapse by Abram from the true faith and work of God, into unbelief and the plans of self and the works of the flesh. *Then it was* that circumcision came in. And it was *because of this* that circumcision did come in. It was a mark made in the flesh as a reminder, a humiliating reminder, of Abram's resort to the flesh; and thus also a reminder that every one who bore it must not make the same mistake that Abram did, but must remain true to the faith and work of God.

Consequently, it is written: "Circumcision verily profiteth if thou keep the law, but if thou be a breaker of the law, thy circumcision is made uncircumcision." And Abraham was "the father of circumcision" to them who are of the circumcision, *when*, and *only* when, they walked "in the steps of that faith of our father Abraham, which he had being yet uncircumcised." Thus it was "a token that God had cut them out and separated them from all nations as his peculiar treasure."—*Spirit of Prophecy* Vol. 1, pg. 262. This must be so until the seed should come in the line of Abraham, in whom alone all these things can be fulfilled.

Thus it is perfectly plain that if Abraham had been faithful to that which he received from God by faith, he never would have been circumcised. And it is equally certain that when any one, receiving by faith in Christ alone, as Abraham received it, that which Abraham received, he needs not to be circumcised.

Since the Seed has come who is the giver of all the promises, who is the pledge of the covenant, who is the one from whom must come all that was promised to Abram, and which Abraham received by faith alone, then, whosoever *believes in Him* and walks by faith alone in him, as did Abram before he was circumcised, in the nature of things he needs not be circumcised. For the fruit of this faith was, in Abram, and is in every one who believes, the keeping of the commandments of God. Gen. 26:5; Gal. 6:1; Cor. 7:19. And so it is written: "If man had kept the law of God, as given to Adam after his fall, preserved by Noah, and observed by Abraham, there would have been no necessity for the ordinance of circumcision.—*Patriarchs and Prophets,* page 364.

And since the faith of Jesus brings to the believer in Jesus, and gives to the believer in Jesus, the perfect keeping of the law of God, the perfect righteousness of God, there *is* "no necessity for the ordinance of circumcision." And let all the people say, Amen.

This is the mighty truth that Paul saw. This is the mighty truth that Stephen saw. And though it is made so plain in the Scriptures, and is now so plain to us, yet to the carnally minded Jews and the formalistic "Pharisees which believed," it seemed but the uprooting of all religion, and as fairly an attack upon the very foundations of the Throne.

Galatians 3:10

December 12, 1899.

"For as many as are of the works of the law are under the curse: for it is written, Cursed is every one that continueth not in all things which are written in the book of the law to do them."

The reason that all who are of the works of the law are under the curse is that "by the law is the knowledge of sin."

Since "by the law is the knowledge of sin," who ever by the law is of the works of the law, his works are only of works of sin; and of course he is under the curse, because he is only under sin, and sin brings only the curse.

All that the law *of itself* ever says, or ever can say, to any man is that he is a sinner. As it is written, "Now we know that what things *soever* the law saith, it saith to them who are under the law: that every mouth may be stopped, and all the world may become guilty before God." Rom. 3:19.

Then how could it be expected that that which in all things whatsoever declares a man guilty, could of itself by any possibility declare him innocent? But when he is guilty, he is under the curse. And, as in whatsoever works he does the law still declares him guilty, even though it be in endeavor to do the works of the law, he is still under the curse.

"Therefore" it is that "by the deeds of the law there shall no flesh be justified in his sight: for by the law is the knowledge of sin." Rom. 3:20.

In order for any man who is of the works of the law, any man by the works of the law, to be anywhere but under the curse, there would have to be by the law the knowledge of righteousness. But if by the law were the knowledge of righteousness. then, though all the world has gone overwhelmingly into sin and is laden with iniquity, none could ever know it; and the law, bringing to *such* persons the knowledge of righteousness, would ruin the universe, because in so doing it would be only declaring *sin* to be *righteousness*.

But sin is not righteousness; and no variance from true righteousness can ever be sanctioned in any degree whatever. Therefore as this world has wholly gone so far out of the way that "there is none righteous, no, not one," "*all* have sinned," it is all-essential that they should know that they are in sin, and lost, so that they may be saved. "Moreover the law entered, *that the offense might abound* [to make sin appear, "that sin by the commandment might become exceeding sinful"]. But where sin abounded, grace did much more abound: that as sin hath reigned unto death, even so might grace reign through righteousness unto eternal life by Jesus Christ our Lord." Rom. 5:19-21.

But it may be asked, Does not the law in giving the knowledge of sin, and in condemning sin, give by contrast the knowledge of righteousness?—The answer still is, No. In this way of contrast the law does indeed convey, or impress, the idea that there is *such a thing* as righteousness; but as for righteousness itself, *what* it really is, and the knowledge of it *in the life,* which is the only true knowledge—none of this is, and none of it can be, conveyed by the law. The reason of this is that the only true righteousness that there is, is the righteousness of God. Anything that does not meet in full measure the standard of God's righteousness is not righteousness at all; but is sin. Now it is the truth that the utmost measure of righteousness that any man can see or find in the law of God, comes far short of the true measure of God's righteousness. But just so far as it does come short of God's righteousness, it is sin. It is, in fact, simply the man's own measure of righteousness according to the measure of his own powers of comprehension. And though lived up to by himself in complete measure, it is only his own righteousness instead of the righteousness of God; because it is according to his own measure instead of the measure of God; it is simply self-righteousness instead of God's righteousness, and so is sin. Consequently by the law is only the knowledge of sin.

Yet it is also true that the very righteousness of God is in the law; because the law is but the expression of the will of God, it is only the transcript of his character. And since this is so, it follows in the nature of the case that nobody can see in the law the righteousness of God, nobody can find in the law the righteousness of God, but God *himself.* And this only emphasizes the mighty truth that all that *anybody,* whether God or man, *can ever see or find in the law is* HIS OWN righteousness. On the part of man, this is sin; because it comes short of the righteousness of God. But on the part of God, it is righteousness; because it is the very righteousness of God in all perfection.

And this makes clear and emphasizes the mighty and eternal truth that the righteousness of God that is in the law can never come to anybody by the law: but must come as the gift of God, from God alone, "without the law." Therefore it is written, "If righteousness come by the law, then Christ is dead in vain." Gal. 2:21. "But now the righteousness of God *without the law* is manifested, . . even the righteousness of God which is *by faith of Jesus Christ* unto all and upon all them that believe: for there is no difference: for all have sinned, and *come short* of the glory of God." Rom. 3:22, 23.

By the law is the knowledge of sin; by the gospel is the knowledge of righteousness, "for therein is the righteousness of God revealed." Rom. 1:17. As many as are of the works of the law are under the curse, because by the law is the knowledge of sin; as many as are of the faith of the gospel are delivered from the curse, because "therein is the righteousness of God revealed from faith to faith: as it is written, The just shall live by faith."

Galatians 3:10-12

December 19, 1899.

"For as many as are of the works of the law are under the curse: for it is written, Cursed is every one that continueth not in all things which are written in the book of the law to do them. But that no man is justified by the law in the sight of God, it is evident: for, The just shall live by faith. And the law is not of faith: but, The man that doeth them shall live in them."

Note the proof that is given that "as many as are of the works of the law are under the curse." It is this: "Cursed is every one that continueth *not* in all things which are written in the book of the law to do them."

Now, since the proposition is that "as many as are of the works of the law are under the curse," why does not the proof of that proposition read, Cursed is every one that *continueth* in all things which are written in the book of the law to do them?—Well, the simple reason is that the fault which brings the curse is not in *the law,* but in *those who would be the doers of the law:* not in the *law, but* in the *people.*

No curse could ever possibly come to any who *really* do the law. But all who "are of the works of the law are under the curse" simply because their works are not truly the works of the law, but are their own works, which they themselves have shaped by their own blurred and imperfect conception of what the law really is; and are therefore sin. Therefore the curse is upon all who "are of the works of the law," simply because they have *not* continued "in all things which are written in the book of the law to do them;" but have *all* sinned.

If they had *begun* and had continued *truly* "in all things which are written in the book of the law to do them," there never could have been any curse. However, mark this: though they had begun and had continued *truly* in all things which are written in the book of the law, or in the law, to do them, *even then* their righteousness would not have been *of the law;* because they would necessarily have had to be righteous before they could begin in righteousness to do the righteousness of the law. As it is written: "He that *doeth* righteousness *is* righteous."

He *has to be* righteous, in order to *do* righteousness. For, in the nature of things, it is impossible for one who is unrighteous to do righteousness: it is impossible for a sinner, while he is a sinner, to do good. The law is perfect with the very perfection of God. Therefore, in the very nature of things, it is impossible for an imperfect person to do the law. Therefore every man must *be* righteous *to begin with,* in order to do righteousness. And he must *remain* righteous *in the same way that he became righteous to begin with,* in order to continue to do righteousness. And this righteousness, which every soul must have *to begin with* in order to *do* righteousness, is "the righteousness of God without the law" (Rom 3:21); that is, it is a righteousness which he obtains from God, and not at all from the law. Accordingly, it is written: "He that doeth righteousness is righteous, *even as HE is righteous.*"

Every soul must be righteous to begin with, before he can, by any possibility, do righteousness. There is no true righteousness except the righteousness of God. Therefore every soul must have the righteousness of God to begin with, before he can ever do righteousness; which is simply to say that every soul must *have* the righteousness of God before he can *show* it: it must be *in* him before it can *appear.*

The only true righteousness of the *law* of God is the righteousness of *God.* But nobody *but God* can see *in the law* the righteousness *of God.* Consequently, nobody but God can find in the law the righteousness of God. Everybody else can find only *his own* righteousness, which comes as far short of the righteousness

Galatians 3:10-12

of God as the individual differs from God. Therefore the righteousness that every soul must have before he can ever do the righteousness that is in the law of God, must be the righteousness of God. And as nobody but God can see or know this righteousness that is in the law of God, it follows inevitably that it is *from God alone* that every soul must obtain the righteousness which he must have *to begin with,* and which he must have *always,* in order to manifest *at any time* in his life the righteousness of the law,—the true keeping of the commandments of God.

And this righteousness that every man must have to begin with, before it can possibly be manifest in his life,—this righteousness which he must have in his life to begin with, before the righteousness that is *in the law* can appear in his life,—this righteousness which is the righteousness of God, and which comes only from God—in the nature of things, can come only as *the gift of God,* and can be received only *by faith.* It never can come to any soul by the law, but only by faith. Therefore it is written "that no man is justified by the law in the sight of God, it is evident." And what is the evidence?—Ah! the evidence is precisely that, and *because,* "the just shall live by faith." That is, God's word that "the just shall live by faith" is the evidence, conclusive and universal, that no one is justified by the law in the sight of God. "The just shall live *by faith,* not by *the law;* by the law *is* to attempt to live by himself: as all the law he can thus have is *his own* conception of the law, and not God's at all, which is the only true one. "And the law is not of faith: but, The man that doeth them shall live in them."

And it is with *life* as it is with righteousness: for "in the way of righteousness is life;" and in the way of life—true life—is righteousness. Every man must live before he can possibly do anything. And every man must live from God, before there can be found in his life any of the doing of the things of God. And the life can come only as *the gift of God,* and is received *by faith.* And having *received* the *life of God,* which, in itself, is able to manifest the righteousness of God that is in the law, *then* the man that doeth these things is righteous. In the doing of them there is no sin; consequently, no curse: therefore, no death; and so, in such doing *he lives;* and so long as the righteousness of the law is fulfilled in him, so long *he lives.*

Thus, he that doeth those things "shall live in them;" but even then he does not *get* life *by* the doing of these things: he has to *get* life *from God* to begin with, before he can possibly do; and this life can come only from God as the gift of God, and can be received only by faith. And so it is forever written, "The just shall *live* by faith."

Therefore, as all have sinned, all are under the curse, and all are dead; because "the wages of sin is death." But now, bless the Lord, *Christ,* the Gift of God, *has come,* and "hath redeemed us from the curse of the law, being made a curse for us." Therefore "the gift of God is eternal life through Jesus Christ our Lord." And "Christ liveth in me: and the life which I now live in the flesh I live by *the faith* of the Son of God, who loved me, and gave himself for me." And in all this "I do not frustrate the grace of God: for if righteousness come by the law, then Christ is dead in vain.

"But now the righteousness of God without the law is manifested, being witnessed by the law and the prophets; even the righteousness of God which is *by faith of Jesus Christ* unto all and upon all them that believe: for there is no difference: for all have sinned, and come short of the glory of God; being justified *freely* by *his grace* through the redemption that is in Christ Jesus: whom God hath set forth to be a propitiation *through faith in his blood,* to declare *his righteousness* for the *remission of sins that are past,* through the forbearance of God; to declare, I say, *at this time* his righteousness: that he might be just, and the justifier of him that believeth in Jesus. Where is boasting then? It is excluded. By what law? *Of works? Nay:* but by the law of faith."

Bless the Lord! Believe, only believe, in the Lord Jesus Christ; and thou shalt be saved. And "this is the *work* of God, that ye *believe* on him whom he hath sent."

Galatians 3:10-12

December 26, 1899.

"Christ hath redeemed us from the curse of the law, being made a curse for us: for it is written, Cursed is everyone that hangeth on a tree: that the blessing of Abraham might come on the Gentiles through Jesus Christ; that we might receive the promise of the Spirit through faith."

The curse of the law, all the curse that ever was or ever can be, is simply because of sin. This is powerfully illustrated in Zech. 5:1-4. The prophet beheld a "flying role; the length there of. . . twenty cubits, and the breadth thereof ten cubits." Then the Lord said to him: "This is the curse that goeth forth over the face of the whole earth." That is, this roll represents all the curse that is upon the face of the whole earth.

And what is *the cause* of this curse over the face of the whole earth?—Here it is: "For every one that *stealeth* shall be cut off as on this side according to it; and every one that *sweareth* shall be cut off as on that side according to it." That is, this roll is the law of God, and one commandment is cited from each table, showing that both tables of the law are included in the roll. Every one that stealeth—everyone that transgresseth the law in the things of the second table—shall be cut off as on this side of the law according to it; and every one that sweareth—everyone that transgresseth in the things of the first table of the law—shall be cut off as on that side of the law according to it.

Thus the heavenly recorders do not need to *write out* a statement of each particular sin of every man; but simply to indicate on the roll that pertains to each man, the particular commandment which is violated in each transgression. That such a roll of law does go with every man wherever he goes and even abides in his house, is plain from the next words: "I will bring it forth, saith the Lord of hosts, and it shall enter into the house of the thief, and into the house of him that sweareth falsely by my name: and it shall remain in the midst of his house." And unless a remedy shall be found, there that roll of the law will remain until the curse shall consume that man, and his house, "with timber thereof and the stones thereof;" that is, until the curse shall devour the earth in that great day when the very elements shall melt with fervent heat. For "the strength of sin" and the curse "is the law." 1 Cor. 15:56.

But, thanks be to God, "Christ hath redeemed us from the curse of the law, being made a curse for us." All the weight of the curse came upon him, for "the Lord hath laid on him the iniquity of us all." He was made "to be sin for us, who knew no sin." And whosoever receives *him,* receives freedom from all sin, and freedom from the curse because free from all sin.

So entirely did Christ bear all the curse, that, whereas, when man sinned, the curse came upon the ground, and brought forth thorns and thistles (Gen. 3:17, 18), the Lord Jesus, in redeeming all things from the curse, wore the *crown of thorns,* and so redeemed both man and the earth from the curse. Bless his name. The work *is done.* "He *hath* redeemed us from the curse." Thank the Lord. He *was made* a curse for us, because he *did hang* upon the tree.

And since this is all *an accomplished thing,* freedom from the curse by the cross of Jesus Christ is *the free gift* of God to every soul on the earth. And when a man receives this free gift of redemption from all the curse, that roll still goes with him; yet, thank the Lord, not carrying a curse any more, but *bearing witness* to "the righteousness of God which is by faith of Jesus Christ unto all and upon all them that believe; for there is no difference." Rom. 3:21, 22. For the very object of his redeeming us from the curse is "that the blessing of Abraham might come on the Gentiles through Jesus Christ." That blessing of Abraham is the righteousness of God, which, as we have already found in these studies, can come only from God as the free gift of God, received by faith.

And as "as many as are of *the works of the law* are under the curse;" and as "Christ hath redeemed us from the curse of the law," then he has also redeemed us from the works of the law, which, being only *our own works,* are only sin; and has, by the grace of God, bestowed upon us *the works of God,* which, being the works of faith, which is the gift of God, is only righteousness, as it is written: "This is the work of God, that ye believe on him whom he hath sent." John 6:29. This is rest indeed—heavenly rest—the rest of God. And "he that is entered into his rest, he also hath ceased from his own works, as God did from his." Heb. 4:10.

Thus, "Christ hath redeemed us from the curse of the law," and from the curse of our own works, that the blessing of Abraham, which is the righteousness and the works of God, "might come on the Gentiles through Jesus Christ." And all this in order "that we might receive the promise of the Spirit through faith." And "there is therefore now no condemnation to them which are in Christ Jesus who walk not after the flesh, but after the Spirit. For the law of the Spirit of life in Christ Jesus hath made me free from the law of sin and death." And "what the law could not do, in that it was weak through the flesh, God, sending his own Son in the likeness of sinful flesh, and for sin, condemned sin in the flesh: that the righteousness of the law might be fulfilled in us, who walk not after the flesh, but after the Spirit." Rom. 8:1-4.

Thanks be unto God for the unspeakable gift of his own righteousness in place of our sins, and of his own works of faith in place of our works on the law, which had been brought to us in the redemption that is in Christ Jesus, who "hath redeemed us from the curse of the law, being made a curse for us."

There is not a single RULE in the Bible. Not one. You are never to look for one there; and you are never to turn into a rule anything that is in the Bible. The Bible is simply a set of *principles,* which, when received into the heart, make our life. The Lord wishes you to live by *principle,* not by *rule.*[2]

January 2, 1900

So far in our studies in Galatians we have reached the end of the fourteenth verse of the third chapter. And in this study we have been brought about five

---

2 *This paragraph followed the study in Galatians. It has been included here as it fits in with the over all thought of these studies by Jones.*

Galatians 3:10-12

times, by different lines of reasoning, to the fact that the coming of Christ—the sacrifice of Christ, and the work of Christ—brings salvation to the Gentiles just *where the Gentiles are,* and *not* where *the Jews are;* that the special claims of the Jews are now passed, and that, instead of the Gentiles being required to meet Christ in the field of the Jew, even the Jew himself must now meet Christ in the field of the Gentile, and not in the field of the Jew.

Over and over it has been seen that the Jews claimed justification by *law,* while the truth of the gospel is, and always was, justification by *faith.* Laws were given to the Jews by the Lord; yet the object of these never was that those to whom they were given should be justified by the laws: the giving of those laws was but the consequence of their transgression and their unbelief, and that they might the better attain to righteousness by faith. As they went further into darkness by unbelief and transgression, God in mercy followed them with further means that, if by *any* means, he might bring them to a true and clear faith in Jesus Christ.

Consequently, if they had maintained the true faith which Abraham had before he was circumcised,—faith which works the works of God, and which, therefore, keeps the commandments of God,—the keeping of the commandments of God and the faith of Jesus,—none of these other laws, not even the *written form* of the law of God, would ever have been added. They would have kept the commandments of God and the faith of Jesus. For "if man had kept the law of God, as given to Adam after his fall, preserved by Noah, and observed by Abraham, there would have been no necessity for the ordinance of circumcision. And if the descendants of Abraham had kept the covenant, of which circumcision was a sign, they would never have been seduced into idolatry, nor would it have been necessary for them to suffer a life of bondage in Egypt. They would have kept God's law *in mind,* and there would have been no necessity for it to be proclaimed from Sinai, or engraved upon the tables of stone. And [even when God's law had been engraved upon the tables of stone] had the people practiced the principles of the ten commandments, there would have been no need of the additional directions given to Moses."—*Patriarchs and Prophets* pg. 364.

But the sole object of all these laws *when they were added,* was *faith in Christ,* and not *works of law.* And, therefore, when Christ had come, who was the sole object, aim, and purpose of all the laws and statutes that had been given by the Lord—when these had all met and found their purpose *in him,* and he had showed the grand glory of the true and clear faith of God, it is, of all things, extravagant to claim justification by law, as did "the Pharisees which believed," and who had *confused* the Galatians *who believed in Christ,* by insisting that, in order to be saved, they must be circumcised and keep the law.

This was made clear by Paul in his appeal to Peter before them all, when he said, "If thou, being a Jew, livest after the manner of Gentiles, and not as do the Jews, why compellest thou the Gentiles to live as do the Jews?" That is, if you have abandoned the ground of the Jews, which, in order to be justified, is the right thing to do, and have gone over to the ground of the Gentiles, how can it be required of the Gentiles to abandon their ground and go over to that of the Jews, which, as we ourselves have confessed, must be abandoned by even us who by nature belong on the ground?

Next he followed this thought back to Abraham himself, and showed that even Abraham was justified by faith, and received all the promises, and became heir to the inheritance, by faith alone, without circumcision, or any other of the laws which were given to the Jews.

He next showed that even to those who were circumcised and had all these laws, these things were of no profit, and availed, *only* when they walked "in the steps of that faith of our father Abraham, which he had being yet uncircumcised." So that, even with themselves, and through all their day, and forever, "they which are of faith are blessed with faithful Abraham."

Next he demonstrates by the Scripture that those who are of the works of law, those who go about by the law to be saved, and to be justified by law, are under the curse; and that Christ is come, and "hath redeemed us from the curse of the law," from the curse of our own works; and that *he did this* in order "that the blessing of Abraham might come *on the Gentiles."*

In all this it has been shown over and over that the Gentile meets Christ in the field of the Gentile, and not in the field of the Jew. It is also demonstrated over and over that the Jew meets Christ *not* in the field of the Jew, but also in the field of the Gentile; exactly where the Gentile meets him, where Abraham met him, and where all, alike, and forever, must meet him—in the glorious field of "the commandments of God, and the faith of Jesus."

All this, too, gives added emphasis, and sets in a fuller light, those two expressions in the word of Peter at the council in Jerusalem on this question, when he, telling the assembly that God had made choice of him among the apostles that the Gentiles by his mouth "should hear the word of the gospel, and believe," and then said: "God, which knoweth the hearts, bear them [the Gentiles] witness, giving them the Holy Ghost, even as he did unto us; and put no difference between us and them [note, not between them and *us,* but "between *us* and them"] purifying their hearts by faith." He then appealed to them: "Now therefore why tempt ye God, to put a yoke upon the neck of disciples, which neither our fathers nor we were able to bear? But we believe that through the grace of our Lord Jesus Christ we shall be saved, *even as they.*" Note again that Peter by the Holy Spirit, said *not* that *they* shall be saved even as we, but "WE shall be saved *even as THEY.*" The means of salvation to the Gentile, and not to the Jew, is *the supreme standard* of salvation. We, Jews, shall be saved even as they, the Gentiles, *are saved.* And they were saved by being justified, *by faith;* not by *law,* but without law. They must be so justified; for they did not have any of these laws, as had the Jews, by which to be justified, if that had been the way. And so we, the Jews, must be justified *even as they* must be justified—by faith without any works of any law, even though we had all the laws that ever were.

There was a time when the Gentile could meet Christ in the field of the Jew; but that time is past. It passed by the fact of the Jews rejecting Christ, even though it had not passed by any other means. But it also passed by the coming of Christ as the object, purpose, aim, completion, and fullness, of all these laws that must of necessity be given to the Jews because of their unbelief and transgression. And since that time is doubly past, in which the Gentile could meet Christ in the field of the Jews: and since it is more than doubly so that now the Jew must meet Christ in the field of the Gentile there is no other name, nor other means, by which either Jew or Gentile must be saved but by the name of Jesus Christ through faith in his name.

It must be borne in mind always that in all this there was no question raised nor any point made as to the value of any law *in itself;* the sole question was, and is, as to any value or use of any law *in justification.* Justification is by faith, not by law; by faith which is of God, and so, which works by the love of God, which is the keeping of the commandments of God. And so of all who catch the thought of God as it is in the book of Galatians, it can truly be written, "Here are they which keep the commandments of God, and the faith of Jesus."

Galatians 3:15

January 9, 1900

"Brethren, I speak after the manner of men: Though it be but a man's covenant, yet if it be confirmed, no man disannulleth, or addeth thereto."

Though it be but a man's covenant, yet if it be confirmed, no man disannulleth, or addeth thereto. How much more, then, shall it be so with God's covenant? Then, since the making of God's covenant with Abram, there has never been, and never could be, anything added to it, nor anything taken from it. Let us notice God's covenant with Abram, and what it included.

In Gen. 11:29-32 is recorded Abram's leaving his native country because that "the Lord had said unto Abram, Get thee out of thy country, and from thy kindred, and from thy father's house, unto a land that I will shew thee." At that time God also said to Abram: "I will make of thee a great nation, and I will bless thee, and make thy name great; and thou shalt be a blessing." Gen. 12:2. At that time also God preached the gospel unto Abram, saying: "In thee shall all families of the earth be blessed." Gen. 12:3; Gal. 3:8.

After Abram had lived in the land of Haran, and had come into the land of Canaan, God said to him: "Unto thy seed will I give this land; and there builded he an altar unto the Lord, who appeared unto him." Gen. 12:7.

The Lord had said that he would show to Abram the land which was to be his. And, though he was in the land of Canaan, yet the Lord had not showed to him the land that he said he would give to him: and he could not yet show it to him, because Lot, of his kindred, was yet with him; and the first condition of the promise was, "Get thee out of thy country, and from thy kindred, and from thy father's house." Abram was separated from his father's house, but so long as Lot was with him, he was not yet separated from his kindred: and so long as that was so, God could not show him the land.

But after a while, their flocks and herds increased so that "the land was not able to bear them, that they might dwell together;" and so, by mutual agreement, and as "brethren" they separated, Lot choosing "all the plain of Jordan." *Then,* "after that Lot was separated from him," the Lord said to Abram, "Lift up now thine eyes, and look from the place where thou art northward, and southward, and eastward, and westward: for all the land which thou seest, to thee will I give it, and to thy seed forever. And I will make thy seed as the dust of the earth: so that if a man can number the dust of the earth, then shall thy seed also be numbered." Gen. 13:14-16.

And the land which Abram then saw, and which was promised to him, included the world; for this promise was "the promise that he should be the heir of the world." And since that is a world that includes "a city which hath foundations, whose builder and maker is God" (Hebrews 11), and which God "hath prepared" for him and his children; and since it is "a better country" than any on the earth, even "an heavenly," it is certain that the land which Abram then saw, and which included the world, was, and is, *"the world to come."*

Galatians 3:15

And more: since this was promised to Abram and his seed—to neither without the other, but to both together; since this promised seed "is Christ;" and since while Abram was in this world, he never received any inheritance in it," no, not so much as to set his foot on (Acts 7:5), it is certain that the inheritance then promised to Abram, and which he then saw, and which included the world, is *only* "the world to come."

This is further confirmed by that which Abram next met in his experience; for it is written that when Abram had returned from the slaughter of Chedorisomer and the kings that were with him, he met "Melchisedec king of Salem," who "brought forth bread and wine: and he was the priest of the most high God." "And he [*Melchisedec*] blessed him [Abram], and said, "Blessed be Abram of the most high God, possessor of heaven and earth." Gen. 14:18, 19. Thus the priest of the Most High, Melchisedec, who "was the voice of God in the world," recognized Abram.

In this connection there is another important element to be noticed, that is, that Abram now meets and recognizes "Melchisedec," "the priest of the most high God," and in him recognizes *the Melchisedec priesthood.* He received blessing from this priest of the Melchisedec priesthood; and yet further recognized this priesthood in that "he gave him tithes of all."

Several times, now, in Abram's experience, the Lord has referred to that "seed" of Abram. And now Abram makes definite inquiry about this "seed," saying to the Lord: "Behold, to me thou hast given no seed: and lo, one born in my house is mine heir. And, behold, the word of the Lord came unto him, saying, This shall not be thine heir; but he that shall come forth out of thine own bowels shall be thine heir. And he brought him forth abroad, and said, Look now toward heaven, and tell the stars, if thou be able to number them: and he said unto him, so shall thy seed be. And he believed in the Lord; and he counted it to him for righteousness. And he said unto him, I am the Lord that brought thee out of Ur of the Chaldees, to give thee this land to inherit it." Gen. 15:3-7.

Abram had now received from God, in promise, the blessing of God which would make him a "blessing to all nations;" he had received the promise of the world for an inheritance; he had received the promise of a seed in whom all nations should be blessed; he had received the benefit of the priesthood of the most high God; and he had received the righteousness of God, fitting him to enter of right into that eternal inheritance.

And now Abram asks: "Lord God, whereby shall I know that I shall inherit it?" And here and now, *in pledge to Abram that he shall inherit all that has been promised,* God made a covenant with Abram: "And he said unto him,

Take me an heifer of three years old, and a she goat of three years old, and a ram of three years old, and a turtle dove, and a young pigeon. And he took unto him all these, and divided them in the midst, and laid each piece one against another: but the birds divided he not. And when the fowls came down upon the carcasses, Abram drove them away. And when the sun was going down, a deep sleep fell upon Abram; and, lo, a horror of great darkness fell upon him. . . And it came to pass, that, when the sun went down, and it was dark, behold a smoking furnace, and a burning lamp that passed between those pieces. In the same day the Lord made a covenant with Abram, saying, Unto thy seed have I given this land, from the river of Egypt unto the great river, the river Euphrates." Gen. 15:9-12, 17, 18.

Now it is a truth laden with meaning that in these animals and birds which he brought and offered, there was included every animal sacrifice that was ever allowed or commanded to be offered to God. And when Abram, as directed, had divided all these except the fowl, and had laid them in their pieces, one against another, "behold a smoking furnace, and a burning lamp that passed between those pieces." And "In the same day the Lord made a covenant with Abram, saying, Unto thy seed have I given this land."

The Lord did this because in ancient times "it was the custom of those who entered into a covenant with each other to take a heifer and cut it in two, and then the contracting parties passed between the pieces." And the reason of this was that the contracting parties agreed, and thus expressed the agreement, that if either of them broke that covenant, he submitted himself to be cut in two just as was the sacrifice between the parts of which they passed.

But *Abram did not pass between the parts of these victims: ONLY GOD PASSED THROUGH.* This because this is not a covenant of agreement between two persons in which each is equally responsible; but it is a covenant *of promise* from God, in which *he alone* is the responsible party. Consequently, God *alone passed* between the parts of the slain victims, in the making of this covenant. And, in that act, God agreed, and thus expressed his agreement, that that covenant could no more fail than that he himself could be severed in twain. Thus the Lord pledged *himself,* in his very life, that all the promises which he had made to Abram should be fulfilled, and that not one of these promises could fail; that this covenant to fulfill the promises could not fail any more than that God should cease to live.

Thus, that covenant of God with Abram was confirmed *even there,* by the sacrifice of Him who made the covenant. And when Abram, not yet fully comprehending the greatness of the blessed promises of this covenant, slipped, the Lord, in his mercy, even repeated himself, and again pledged himself,—"interposed himself"—swearing by himself, and thus by his oath confirmed his covenant that his promises should not fail. Heb. 8:17. And thus *again* that covenant was "confirmed."

Therefore, since "though it be but a man's covenant, yet if it be confirmed, no man disannulleth, or addeth thereto," how much more shall this be so of God's covenant with Abram, which is doubly confirmed? Therefore, that covenant could never be disannulled, nor could anything ever be added to it. In that covenant *at that time* was all that ever has been since, or that *ever can be* to anybody. And whoever has that covenant, has everything in heaven and earth,—everything in the wide universe, to all eternity.

That is the Abrahamic covenant, "And if ye be Christ's, then are ye Abraham's seed, and heirs according to the promise" which is made sure by that covenant.

Abraham Did Pass Through[3]

January 23, 1900

That statement was wrong that I made two weeks ago in connection with God's covenant with Abraham in saying that *"only God passed through"* between the parts of the sacrifices offered by Abraham. Abraham *also* passed through.

This fact, however, is not stated in Genesis. It is given in Jer. 34:18: "I will give the men that have transgressed my covenant, which *they made before me,* where *they cut the calf in twain, and passed between the parts thereof,* the princes of Judah and the princes of Jerusalem, the eunuchs, and the priests, and all the people of the land, which *passed between the parts of the calf."*

This was spoken to the people in the days of Zedekiah; and the only way in which it was possible for them to *have passed* "between the parts of the calf" was in the fact of Abraham's having passed through; just as in Heb. 7:9, 10 it is said that *Levi,"* who receiveth tithes, *paid tithes in Abraham."* I have many a time used Jer. 34:18 to show that the people in the days of Zedekiah were included in God's covenant with Abraham; I do not know how it slipped my mind in the article of two weeks ago, unless it was that my mind was just then

---

3   Two weeks after the last study A.T. Jones comments upon a statement he had made. It has been included to keep the context.

absorbed in discovering and describing what *God* had put into that blessed covenant.

This is the more singular, too, from the fact that many a time I have read, even in the galley-proofs, the words in *Patriarch and Prophets*, to which a brother in Illinois has just now called my attention, that, when Abraham had arranged the sacrifices according to the divine direction, "This being done, he reverently passed between the parts of the sacrifice making a solemn vow to God of perpetual obedience;" and "as a pledge of this covenant of God with men, a smoking furnace and a burning lamp, symbols of the divine presence, passed between the severed victims, totally consuming them." page 137.

Since writing this article, I have found the following account of an incident in the journey of General Grant around the world which more fully, and in great beauty, illustrates the meaning of the "passing between the pieces." The General was to be entertained at the house of an official, Wassel Khayai, at Assiout in Egypt; and the account says: "When General Grant alighted at the consul's house he was detained from entering until a beef, beautifully garlanded with flowers, had been brought out. It was killed, and cut into two pieces which were laid on either side of the doorway. Then the consul invited General Grant to enter his home with him. They stepped over the blood on the threshold, and *between the pieces.* By this act they entered into the most solemn covenant known to the Oriental,—the blood covenant,—and thus became 'blood brothers' a relation which outranks every other relation in life. One blood brother can not ask anything that the other will refuse."

These things show that Abraham "passed between the pieces;" that when he did so, all his children also passed between them, and that since we, *being Christ's are Abraham's seed, WE* PASSED BETWEEN THE PIECES, and thus became "blood brothers" with the Lord; that we can not ask of him anything that he will refuse, and that he can not ask anything of us that we will refuse. John 14:13, 14; 15:7, 16.

Galatians 3:16, 17

January 16, 1900

"Now to Abraham and his seed were the promises made. He saith not, And to seeds, as of many; but as of one. And to thy seed, which is Christ. And this I say, that the covenant, that was confirmed before of God in Christ, the law,

Galatians 3:16, 17

which was four hundred and thirty years after, can not disannul, that it should make the promise of none effect."

God's covenant with Abraham was not a covenant of law, but of promise: not of works, but of faith. This covenant, as we have seen, and as is even here said, was not only confirmed, but was even doubly confirmed, *"in Christ,"* at the time of the making of the covenant. Then, since the covenant, even though a man's, once confirmed, can not be disannulled, neither can anything be added to it, it is perfectly plain that the law, which entered four hundred and thirty years afterward, was never intended to change the character of the covenant. The law did not enter in any sense to take the place of the promise. In the entering of the law there was never any purpose in the mind of God that the works of the law should take the place of righteousness by faith.

But just here was the great mistake that was made by Israel: they utterly mistook their own standing, and the meaning of what the Lord gave to them, and his purpose in the giving of all that came after that covenant was confirmed. If the covenant with Abraham had been held in faithfulness, nothing else would have ever been needed to enter. But, when the real truth and virtue of that covenant were not discerned, and men went further into unbelief and darkness, the Lord followed them, and employed means and gave instruction to bring them from unbelief and darkness to the faith, light, and blessing of the covenant that he had made.

For, "if man had kept the law of God, as given to Adam after his fall, preserved by Noah, and *observed by Abraham,* there would have been no necessity for the ordinance of circumcision. And if the descendants *of Abraham* had *kept the covenant* of which circumcision was a sign, they would never have been seduced into idolatry, nor would it have been necessary for them to suffer a life of bondage in Egypt. They would have kept God's law in mind, and there would have been no necessity for it to be proclaimed from Sinai, or engraved upon the tables of stone. And had the people practiced the principles of the ten commandments, there would have been no need of the additional directions given to Moses.

"The sacrificial system, committed to Adam, was also perverted by his descendants. Superstition, idolatry, cruelty, and licentiousness corrupted the simple and significant service that God had appointed. Through long intercourse with idolaters, the people of Israel had mingled many heathen customs with their worship; therefore the Lord gave them at Sinai definite instruction concerning the sacrificial service."—*Patriarchs and Prophets*, pg. 364.

The law entered in written form, ordinances were established, and all only because of their unbelief and transgression. None of these things were ever necessary to the covenant, nor were they parts of the covenant: the covenant was complete in itself when it was confirmed, and being confirmed, nothing could possibly be added to it.

Therefore nothing that ever came afterward was essential *to the covenant.* But because of their unbelief and transgression, these things were essential *to them,* to help them to the place where they could discern the truth, the light, and the purpose of the covenant; and where in faith they could enjoy all its blessings and its power. In other words, these things were all to help them to an enlightened faith—the true faith of the covenant—the faith of Christ. Accordingly, in another place, it is written: "The law entered that the offense might abound [to make sin appear "that sin by the commandment might become exceeding sinful"]. But, where sin abounded grace did much more abound, that, as sin hath reigned unto death, even so might grace reign through righteousness unto eternal life, by Jesus Christ our Lord." Thus the object of the entering of the law was to bring men to Jesus Christ. And the object of all that came in after the covenant was made and confirmed was to help them to a true knowledge of that covenant.

But instead of receiving all these things in this light, and using them for this purpose,—the purpose only of coming to the full faith of the covenant of God—Israel made the mistake of putting all these things *in the place of the covenant,* and using *these,* instead of God's covenant, *as the way of salvation.*

Thus *the law of God* which, as we have seen, entered to give the knowledge of sin, and so impress the need of the Saviour provided in the covenant with Abraham, Israel turned into the way of salvation by their own endeavors to do the law.

The *law of the Levitical priesthood,* which was instituted to instruct them with respect to the true,—the Melchisedec priesthood of the covenant with Abraham,—Israel turned from this purpose, and made it the final priesthood, and expected salvation and perfection by it. Heb. 7:11.

The *earthly sanctuary and its services,* which were given in connection with the Levitical priesthood, and which were given to instruct them concerning the true,—the heavenly sanctuary and its services, in which Christ was to be priest after the order of Melchisedec,—this Israel also perverted, and made it the final service, and expected salvation by this service. Ps. 110:4; Heb. 6:13-20; 7:9-22, 28; 8:1-5; 9:2-28; 10:1-17.

Thus they lost sight altogether of the covenant with Abraham,—the true way of salvation,—and all these things which were given to them in their unbelief and transgression to lead them to the light and to instruct them unto the covenant with Abraham and the true way of salvation, they put in the place of that. And this was only to put their own perverse views in the place of the truth of God; to pervert to the inventions of their own carnal minds, the sacred ordinances which the Lord had given to lead them to spiritual mindedness, it was only to make themselves their own saviors, it was to put themselves in the place of God.

But when these things which, in his love, God had given to help them to faith, were thus perverted to their own carnal views, all life was taken out of them, and they found in them no help whatever to righteousness. And, as in this way which they had gone, everything depended upon *their own doing,* this caused them to go yet further, and add to these things that God had given, that vast multitude of fine-spun distinctions, legal exactions, and pharisaic traditions, which was manifested in the ceremonialism of the Jews in the days when Jesus came, and which "the Pharisees which believed" thought to fasten upon Christianity, by which they confused the Galatians. And this it was which called forth from the Lord the epistle to the Galatians, to show to both Jews and Gentiles the truth of God's everlasting covenant and the true relation of the law, both moral and ceremonial, to that covenant. And this instruction is needed today just as well as then, or ever; because it is the bane of human nature to be ever ready to put its own views in the place of the truth of God; to put its own works in the place of the righteousness of God; to put ordinances and ceremonies in the place of faith; to put the inventions of the carnal mind in place of the work of God; to put self in the place of God.

Galatians 3:16, 17

January 23, 1900

"Now to Abraham and his seed were the promises made. He saith not, And to seeds as of many; but as of one, And to thy seed, which is Christ. And this I say, that the covenant that was confirmed before of God, in Christ, the law, which was four hundred and thirty years after, can not disannul, that it should make the promise of none effect."

We have seen that Israel made the mistake of putting in the place of God's covenant the things which the Lord gave to them to aid them in arriving at the full light and blessing of the covenant. There is another great mistake that Israel made, and the same mistake is made today by thousands of persons *concerning Israel;* and that is that the things which God gave to them were *for them alone,* not for the people of the world in general.

Israel, thinking thus, naturally shut herself away from the nations, and made all these things specially her own. Thus she separated herself from all the nations, and held herself aloof from, and above, the nations, as being holier than they, and because of this special holiness, as more highly regarded by God than were the other nations. Yet this whole conception of things was an utter mistake, and was a perversion of the intent of the things that God had given.

Everything that the Lord gave to Israel was for the benefit of *the whole world.* Israel was to be *the missionary people* who should extend to all nations the light and blessing given to her, in order that all nations might enjoy the light and blessing of God, as revealed in the Abrahamic covenant, to the full knowledge of which all these things that were given were to lead Israel, and *all people.*

We again set down here, for study, the passage from *Patriarch and Prophets*, which was quoted in last week's article:—"If man had kept the law of God, as given to Adam after his fall, preserved by Noah, and observed by Abraham, there would have been no necessity for the ordinance of circumcision. And if the descendants of Abraham had kept the covenant, of which circumcision was a sign, they would never have been seduced into idolatry, nor would it have been necessary for them to suffer a life of bondage in Egypt. They would have kept God's law in mind, and there would have been no necessity for it to be proclaimed from Sinai, or engraved upon the tables of stone. And had the people practiced the principles of the ten commandments, there would have been no need of the additional directions given to Moses.

"The sacrificial system, committed to Adam, was also perverted by his descendants. Superstition, idolatry, cruelty, and licentiousness corrupted the simple and significant service that God had appointed. Through long intercourse with idolaters, the people of Israel had mingled many heathen customs with their worship; therefore the Lord gave them at Sinai definite instruction concerning the sacrificial service."—pg. 364.

It was the apostasy of mankind in general that was the cause of God's calling Abraham, and setting him as a light to the nations. It was the unfaithfulness of the descendants of Abraham that caused them "to suffer a life of bondage in Egypt." In Egypt, amid its darkness of every sort, the ideas that they had received in descent from Abraham were more and more obscured until they

Galatians 3:16, 17

were practically lost. And thus "in their bondage the people had, to a great extent, lost their knowledge of God, and of the principles of the Abrahamic covenant."

As they had thus lost the law of God from their *minds,* all this must be renewed. But, having no true conception of the law of God as in the Abrahamic covenant, this had to be taught them. Therefore God proclaimed his law with his own voice to all the people, then gave it in written form, that they might under his guidance, discern its deep, spiritual principles. And that this might the better be done in their obscurity of mind, the principles of the ten commandments were drawn out in detail, in the writings of Moses, which the people had in their hands, and which they were to study constantly until these words of God and these holy *principles* should be engraved upon their hearts, imbedded in their souls and written in their minds; that is, until they had attained to the glory of the covenant with Abraham.

Now, since all this was necessary to Israel because of her unfaithfulness and the confusion of Egypt, it is certainly plain enough that all these things were necessary to *the people of Egypt and the other nations* that were in darkness, as she was, that these might find the knowledge of God and his salvation. Then, in the very nature of things, all these things, and all this teaching that came to Israel to bring them to the light of God, were intended by the Lord to be passed on by Israel to the other nations, that these also might be brought to where *they* should walk in the light of God.

Thus it is perfectly plain that the law of God in all its forms—as spoken from heaven, as written on the tables, and as drawn out in detail in the writings of Moses—was just as much for the nations of the world as it was for the people of Israel. And both Israel and the nations made the mistake of thinking that it was only for Israel,—Israel thinking so, and confining it to herself, and shutting it away from the nations; and the nations thinking so, and therefore despising it. And the nations were, indeed, helped in *their* mistake by the attitude that was assumed by Israel in *her* mistake. For when, in her self-righteousness, Israel shut herself away from the nations, despising them, this only resulted in the nations seeing her *as shut away* from them in self-righteousness, and despising them, and consequently, further resulted in their *despising her,* and all that was given to her *for their benefit.* And that same thing continues to this day concerning those things *in the Bible* which were given to Israel for all the nations.

This is true, not alone of the moral law, but of the ceremonial law—the sacrificial system—as well. Before Adam left Eden, the sacrificial system was instituted. By Noah it was observed. Thus the sacrificial system pertained to all mankind; it was simply the means of expressing faith in God's sacrifice, which *he* had made to save man from sin. As God has given the firstling of his flock, the best that he had, so every soul who accepted that gift of God, and would show his faith therein, would, in very gratitude to God, offer the firstling of his flock, the best of all that he had. That was true faith in God, and in the Lamb that he had given. "By faith Abel offered unto God" his sacrifice, "the firstlings of his flock," "by which he obtained witness that he was righteous." Thus Abel's righteousness was true righteousness by faith. And that was the way for all mankind.

But as the nations apostatized, and came more and more under the darkening influence of Satan, they began to look upon God as, like themselves, a stern, forbidding, exacting judge, who was angry with them, and waiting only for the opportunity to punish them for their evil doing. Therefore they thought they must offer sacrifices to *appease* him, and the more precious and costly the sacrifice, the more favor they should gain, and so they were led to sacrifice their own sons and daughters.

Thus the sacrificial system, which God had given to Adam, and which was observed by Noah, and which was included in the covenant with Abraham, was altogether perverted and lost sight of in this apostasy of the nations. And the descendants of Abraham, in their unfaithfulness, through their association with the nations, and amid the darkness of Egypt, also lost sight of the true, the simple, and the significant service that God had given to Adam, and had continued with Abraham. Accordingly, when they came out of Egypt, the Lord renewed to Israel the sacrificial system, with definite instruction in it, that they might, according to his own direction, offer his sacrifices in purity, and according to truth; that they might see in these the true meaning that God put there at the beginning, which was the sacrifice that he had made,—the offering of his only begotten Son,—the firstling of his flock,—the best of all that he had.

Thus it is plain that the sacrificial system that was given to Israel was for the enlightenment and instruction of all the people of the world as certainly as it was for Israel; because it was Israel's likeness to all the other nations in their darkness that made it necessary that this should be given to them.

God has no favorites, and never had any. All that he ever had is free to all people. All that he ever gave to anybody is free to all others, and he gives to any only that they may pass it on to all others. And those who receive, and do not pass it on to all others, but confine it to themselves, *lose* that which God has in truth given, and can cling only to the empty *form* of the truth, absolutely dry and barren.

This principle is present truth today, to the people of the Third Angel's Message. There is positive danger, and there has been for years, that *these* shall repeat the history of the Jews.

Galatians 3:18

January 30, 1900

"For if the inheritance be of the law, it is no more of promise, but God gave it to Abraham by promise.

The Greek words are "*o nomos*" "of law," not "*tou nomos*" "of the law," signifying law in general rather than any particular law. Thus the inheritance, exactly as justification, is received altogether by faith, and not at all by the works or deeds of any law.

It can not possibly be otherwise, because the inheritance is the first and grand object in the call of Abraham. *For, first of all,* God said to Abram: "Get thee out of thy country and from thy kindred, and from thy father's house, *unto a land that I will show thee."* Gen. 12:1. And in this "he was called to go out into a place which he should after receive *for an inheritance;*" and when so called he "obeyed, and he went out not knowing whither he went." Heb. 11:8.

And since this inheritance is altogether in *the world to come,* and includes the *whole* world to come, it is absolutely impossible for any one ever to obtain it by works. It was and is impossible for Abraham or any other man ever to work enough to earn it; and so, since the inheritance is so utterly beyond all possible reach of the works of any man, in the nature of things it must come only as the gift of God, and can be received by men only by faith, altogether as the gift of God.

And since the inheritance is the one great object in the call of Abraham, everything else that came from God to Abraham was only contributory to this great object; it was only to fit Abraham to enter upon and enjoy in all its fullness that wondrous inheritance which is the original and settled object of the call to him. For instance, God said to Abraham: "I will bless thee." This blessing is essential to entering upon the inheritance; for no one who is under the curse can possibly have any part in the inheritance. Therefore, to be relieved from the curse, and to be put under the blessing, of God, is an essential to any one's ever having any part in the inheritance. And this blessing upon Abraham, relieving him from the curse, and preparing him for the inheritance, was to be extended, through him, to all the families of the earth, that these also might be relieved of the curse and receive the *blessing,* and thus have a part in the grand inheritance.

Again, we have found that in the covenant with Abraham there was sacrifice and a priesthood—the Melchisedec priesthood. This also was essential to the entering upon the inheritance, because "all have sinned," and "without shedding of blood is no remission." Therefore every one who will enter upon that grand inheritance must be absolutely cleansed and purified from all sin. But this can be done only by that great sacrifice which God made in the gift of his Son, and by the ministration of that priest and priesthood of Christ unto which he was ordained by God alone, "after the order of Melchisedec." Thus the sacrifice and service of the priesthood are also essential in behalf of every soul who shall enter into that inheritance, and are essential in order that he may enter into that inheritance.

Righteousness is essential to the entering upon that inheritance. It is an eternal inheritance; the righteousness, which alone can fit anyone to enter upon the inheritance, must be eternal righteousness. But the only righteousness that is eternal is the righteousness of God. To this no man can possibly attain by works, or anything that he can do. It is only the righteousness of God, and it can come to man only as the free gift of God, and can be received by man only by faith.

Again, as this inheritance is an eternal inheritance, whosoever enters upon it must have eternal life in order to possess it. But all have sinned and "the wages of sin is death." How then can these who are subject only to death ever obtain eternal life by any works that they can do?—It simply can not be done. This life, therefore, being eternal life, must come from him who is eternal—the only source of eternal life, which is God. It can, therefore, come to men in no conceivable way except as the gift of God, and can be received only by faith. And since only in the way of righteousness is life, only in the way of eternal righteousness can be eternal life. And these both being essential to entering upon the inheritance, every soul who will ever enter upon that inheritance must have these. And they can come only as the gift of God, received only by faith.

Thus the inheritance being the great and original object of the call of Abraham; that inheritance being altogether the gift of God; and it being impossible for man ever to have obtained it otherwise, it follows that everything that can help man unto that inheritance, and fit him for the inheritance, must also be altogether from God, as the gift of God, received by men only by faith. And since the blessing of God, the sacrifice and priesthood of Christ, eternal righteousness, and eternal life, are the essentials to receiving the inheritance; and since all these are utterly beyond any possible reach of man by anything that he can do, it follows that these all, in the nature of things, come as the gift of God, and are obtained by men only by faith in God.

And, thank the Lord, he *has given* all these:

He has given the blessing; for it written: "Blessed be the God and Father of our Lord Jesus Christ, who *hath blessed us* with all spiritual blessings in heavenly things in Christ;" and "sent him to bless you, in turning away every one of you from his iniquities."

He has given his only begotten Son, the "Lamb of God, which taketh away the sin of the world." He has made him our great high priest, who "ever liveth to make intercession" for us.

He has given his righteousness, the free gift of God "unto all and upon all them that believe, for there is no difference." To every creature he has sent his gospel, wherein is "the righteousness of God revealed from faith to faith."

He has given eternal life; for it is written: "This is the record, that God hath given to us eternal life, and this life is in his Son. He that hath the Son hath life; and he that hath not the Son of God hath not life." 1 John 5:11, 12. And the Son of God says: "Verily, verily, I say unto you, He that heareth my word, and believeth on him that sent me, *hath everlasting life,* and shall not come into condemnation; but *is passed* from death *unto life."* John 5:24.

Therefore the inheritance can not possibly be of law—of any kind of law, nor of all kinds of law,—"for if the inheritance be of law, it is no more of promise; but God gave it to Abraham by promise. And everything that God ever gave or ordained after this promise, is, in the nature of things, contributory to the promise. And whoever would use anything God ever gave after the promise, at any time or in any way, without, in such use, holding the promise in view, frustrates every purpose of God in the giving of those things.

Therefore even though it had been a man's covenant, yet, once confirmed, no man could disannul it nor add thereto. Much more, being God's covenant, and being even doubly confirmed, it could not possibly be disannulled, neither could anything be added thereto. And since "to Abraham and his seed were the promises made," and that seed "is Christ;" and since that covenant "was confirmed before of God in Christ, anything that came afterward can not take the place of the covenant, neither can it be added to the covenant.

Galatians 3:19

February 6, 1900

It will be noticed that the word "serveth" is a supplied word. It really adds nothing to the sense. The question stands just as strong and just as plain to read. "Wherefore then the law?" Another translation is, "Why then the law?"

This was the ready argument of "the Pharisees which believed," against all the gospel which was presented by Paul. And this, because the gospel presented justification by faith of Christ, and not by works of law. And wherever this was presented, "the Pharisees which believed," who had no conception of justification in any other way than by works of law, raised this inquiry, "Wherefore then the law?" "What is the use of the law?" In their estimation, this objecting question was a sufficient refutation of all that might ever be said as to justification by faith, without any deeds of any law.

And, indeed, this same argument, in this same superior, self-assertive way, is used for this same purpose by "the Pharisees which believe" today. Let the claims of the law of God, precisely as God wrote it, be presented today in any part of this whole land, or even in any other land, and immediately professed ministers of the gospel will arise, all bristling with objections, and will oppose every claim of the law of God upon them, because it "never could justify anybody." They will single out, and search out, every expression they can find in the Scriptures, such as, "By the deeds of the law shall no flesh be justified;" and, "Whosoever of you are justified by the law; ye are fallen from grace," etc.; and with strong voice will ring forth and then vigorously demand, "What is the use of such a law? What is it good for? It can not justify anybody."

The scene here described is perfectly familiar to thousands upon thousands of the readers of the *REVIEW AND HERALD*, and especially to the preachers of the gospel, in the Third Angel's Message, which calls all people to the keeping of "the commandments of God, and the faith of Jesus."

It is worthy of notice, however, that in the ancient days this objection was never raised by the Gentiles, but only by "the Pharisees which believed:" never by the plain, simple sinner, who knew that his works could not justify him, and who therefore longed for justification indeed; but only by those who professed to know God, and to know justification, but who knew only justification by their own works of law. And so it is even now.

Therefore, this inquiry—"Wherefore then the law?"—is *present* truth, and will be present truth forever. To a person whose conception of justification is altogether justification by works, such an inquiry, presented in objection, is a sufficient refutation of all the claims of the law of God; and no stronger proof could ever be given by any one that his only conception of justification is altogether by works, than that he should raise against the law of God, this objecting inquiry, "Why then the law?" "What is the use of the law?" This because such an objection certifies that in his estimation, there can be no possible use for law of any kind unless it will justify a man, even the transgressor.

But every one who knows justification in truth, which is justification by faith, knows full well, and can see with perfect plainness, that there may be abundant use for law, altogether apart from any idea of justification by it. And thus there is a place for this question, in sober inquiry.

"Why then the law?" The answer is—

1. "By the law is the knowledge of sin:" "that sin by the commandment might become exceeding sinful," in order that men, knowing the enormity of sin, may be able to appreciate the greatness of the salvation that God has sent in the gift of his Son.

Even so, it is said in another place. "The law entered, that the offense might abound. But where sin abounded, grace did much more abound: that even so might grace reign through righteousness unto eternal life by Jesus Christ our Lord."

2. When the sinner, having learned by the law the greatness of his sin, and having found in the Lord Jesus a salvation so great as to save him from all sin, and a righteousness so complete as to reign in him against all the power of sin, he still finds a *second* grand use for the law *in its witnessing,* in his behalf, to the righteousness of God, which he obtained without the law. And so, it is written: "By the deeds of the law shall no flesh be justified in his sight; for by the law is the knowledge of sin. "But now the *righteousness of God WITHOUT THE LAW* is manifested, being *witnessed BY THE LAW* and the prophets; even the righteousness of God which is by faith of Jesus Christ unto all and upon all them that believe; for there is no difference." Such, and so far, is, Wherefore then the law?

Galatians 3:19

February 13, 1900

"Wherefore then the law?"

This inquiry of "the Pharisees which believed" was not limited to the law of God, although that, being the chief of all laws, was of course the principal thought in the inquiry. But from the beginning of this study of the book of Galatians we have found that there was involved not only the moral law, but also the ceremonial law—indeed all that God had given. And this, because all the service of the Pharisees was a service merely of law; since their only idea of justification was justification altogether by law, and their only idea of salvation was salvation together by works.

Therefore with "the Pharisees which believed" this inquiry extended also to, Wherefore the Levitical law? Wherefore the sacrificial system? Wherefore circumcision? What was the use of all these, if salvation were not attained by any of them? Such was the only use *they* had ever made of any of these things: indeed, this was the only conception that they had of them. They expected perfection by the Levitical priesthood; the same by circumcision; and the same by all that was given by the Lord. Their only idea of their use was that justification, salvation, came to them in the doing of these things. *BY THE DOING* of them. But this was all error, and was a perversion of the true intent of all that God gave. Justification was not by any of these, nor by all of them together, any more than it was by the law of God. Justification was always by faith; and the sacrificial system, and all the services and ceremonies of the Levitical law, were only means which God gave, by which faith was expressed: the sacrifices were means of expressing faith that they already had in the great Sacrifice that God had made.

And this same query, and for the same reason, is raised today by thousands of "Pharisees which believe," in their enmity against the truth of the gospel. For this reason alone, "Wherefore then the law?" is a live question today, and always will be a live question wherever the truth of the gospel—righteousness by faith—is preached.

But there is a greater reason, than that, as to "Wherefore then the law?" being a live question today and always. It is a true and proper question always, in the inquiry after the truth as it is in Jesus. For in the whole divine economy of the times of Israel, there is precious truth, rich instruction, and glorious light, for all who would be taught of God. This was all there for the people

Galatians 3:19

of Israel of old; but through carnal-mindedness and its self-justification, they missed it. And because Israel did thus miss it, thousands of professed believers today, stumbling over Israel's failures, neglect and even reject all the great riches which Israel missed, but which were then and *are now* for all people. For to the people of the very last days it is written: "Remember ye the law of Moses my servant, which I commanded unto him in Horeb for all Israel, *with the statutes and judgments.*" Mal. 4:4. And "the Christian who accepts the truth, the whole truth, and nothing but the truth, will look at Bible history in its true bearing. The history of the Jewish economy from beginning to end, though spoken of contemptuously, and sneered at as 'the dark ages,' will reveal light, and still more light, as it is studied."

"Wherefore then the law" of Levitical priesthood, sacrifice, offering, burnt offering, and offering for sin, the sanctuary and its ministry?—It was all only the divinely appointed means of expressing the faith that they already had, and that had already brought to them the righteousness of God without any deeds of any law.

The Levitical priesthood was the means of expressing faith in that greater priesthood—the priesthood of the Son of God—announced in the words: "The Lord said unto my Lord. . . Thou art a priest forever after the order of Melchisedec. Ps. 110:1-4. The sanctuary and the services of this priesthood were but means of expressing faith in the sanctuary and the services of the priesthood that is in heaven. For, of all that system, "this is the sum: We have such an high priest, who is set on the right hand of the throne of the Majesty in the heavens; a minister of the sanctuary, and of the true tabernacle, which the Lord pitched, and not man." Heb. 8:1, 2.

And this whole story, as here outlined, is shown in the instruction given to the people, in the book of Leviticus. In Lev. 4:13-20 it is said that when the people had sinned through ignorance, and the thing was hid from their eyes in having "done somewhat against any of the commandments of the Lord concerning things which should not be done, and are guilty; when the sin, which they have sinned against it—against the law of God—was known, then the congregation should "offer a young bullock for the sin, and bring him before the tabernacle of the congregation."

And the elders of the congregation were to lay their hands upon the head of the bullock before the Lord, thus confessing the sin of the congregation, and laying it upon the bullock. Then the bullock must be "killed before the Lord." And the priest that was anointed brought "of the bullock's blood to the tabernacle of the congregation; and dipped his finger in some of the blood, and sprinkled it seven times before the Lord, even before the vail." And he "put some of the blood upon the horns of the altar," which was before the Lord, in the tabernacle of the congregation; and poured out "all the blood at the bottom of the altar of the burnt offering," which was "at the door of the tabernacle of the congregation." Thus the priest made "atonement for them," and the sin was "forgiven them."

There was the law of God, and by it the knowledge of sin, showing them guilty, Then there was the sacrifice, and the laying of the sin, in confession, upon the sacrifice as a substitute. Then there was the slaying of the sacrifice and the offering of its blood in their behalf, and by it atonement made and the forgiveness of sin to them. There was by the law the knowledge of sin, and by the gospel of sacrifice the forgiveness of sin and at-one-ment with God.

But "it is not possible that the blood of bulls and of goats should take away sins." Heb. 10:4. Wherefore then all this law, sanctuary, service, and ceremony? Ah! it was "a figure for the time then present" "until the time of reformation." But "Christ being come an high priest of good things to come by a greater and more perfect tabernacle, not made with hands, that is to say, *not* of this building; neither by the blood of goats and calves, but *by* his own blood he entered in once into the holy place, having obtained eternal redemption for us." Heb. 9:9-19.

And with Christ and in Christ we have this day, A.D.1900, the substance of which all that was the shadow. In the heavenly temple there is the ark of his testament, in which is the testament—his law. "By the law is the knowledge of sin." And by the gospel of the sacrifice of Jesus Christ and his priestly service, and the offering of his blood in the heavenly sanctuary, there is forgiveness of sin "to every one that believeth," and righteousness in his being made at one with God, in Jesus Christ, who is the atonement.

And the only difference between the times before Christ and these times after Christ, is that *then,* because Jesus had not yet come and offered himself, but was to come, faith in his coming and offering himself could be expressed only in this way; whereas, now that he *has come* and *has offered himself* a sacrifice, and *has entered upon his priesthood* and "ever liveth to make intercession for" us, faith is now expressed in the bread and wine—the body and blood—representing that which has actually been offered. To offer a sacrifice now, and to have a priesthood and a priestly ministry on earth would be to deny that Christ, the true Sacrifice, has yet been offered.

Thus, there was clear use, and intelligent use, for all the laws, both moral and ceremonial, which were given to Israel. And this without any purpose or thought of any justification coming by any of them, or all of them together; but that justification comes always and ONLY by faith.

And *this* is "Wherefore the law?" as to the ceremonial law. And from the considerable and careful study of the subject, we are thoroughly convinced that in the book of Galatians, *the book of Romans and the book of Hebrews MEET*. The letter to the Galatians was written before either the letter to the Romans or that to the Hebrews. In the controversy raised by "the Pharisees which believed," which had confused the Galatian Christians, both the moral and the ceremonial law were involved; and so both are involved in the letter to the Galatians, and the whole ground is briefly covered. Then afterward the book of Romans was written, enlarging, and dwelling wholly, upon that phase of Galatians which involves the moral law, and justification by faith; and the book of Hebrews was written, enlarging, and dwelling wholly, upon that phase of Galatians which involves the ceremonial law, and justification by faith. And we believe that as the whole subject is more and more carefully studied, the more it will be seen that in Galatians both Romans and Hebrews are comprehended.

Galatians 3:19

February 20, 1900

"Wherefore then serveth the law? It was added because of transgressions."

The Greek term that is here translated "added," is the same word that, in Heb. 12:19, is translated "spoken," in the clause referring to the voice of God speaking from Sinai, "which voice they that heard entreated that the word should not be *spoken* [for *added*] to them any more." It is the same word that is used also in Deut. 5:22 where it is translated "added," in the sentence, "These words the Lord spake unto all your assembly in the mount out of the midst of the fire, of the cloud, and of the thick darkness, with a great voice: and he *added* [for *spoke*] no more."

In both Hebrews and Deuteronomy the word is used with direct reference to the giving of the law of God, the ten commandments. This passage in Galatians, therefore, would certainly seem to suggest that the law here referred to would be the same law. And this is further sustained by the expression later, in this verse, that the law referred to was ordained *"in the hand of a mediator."* Now, since there is only "one Mediator between God and men, the Man Christ

Jesus," it was certainly Christ's hand in which this law was ordained. And Deut. 33:2, speaking of the same scene referred to in Deut. 5:22 and Heb. 12:20, says: "The Lord came from Sinai, and rose up from Seir unto them: he shined forth from mount Paran, and he came with ten thousands of saints: from *his right hand* went a fiery law for them."

Now the ten commandments were not only written by *the hand* of the Lord himself, but they were written on tables of stone, which "tables were *the work of God,*" as well as the writing, which was the writing of God. And these tables were given by *the hand* of the Lord, unto Moses. And even when Moses had broken these tables, and had been directed to make other tables, the Lord wrote again with *his hand* on *these tables* the *same law* that at first he had written on the tables that he himself had made.

But this is not true of any other law. It is true that the ceremonial law—the law concerning sacrifices, offerings, the sanctuary, the whole Levitical system—was also given by the Lord to Moses; but it was not given by *the hand* of the Lord to Moses. It did not come forth from *his hand,* either in writing by his own hand, or upon tables made with his own hand. It was given to Moses by the Lord, and was *written* altogether *by Moses,* and not at all by the Lord.

Some, taking the English word "added" in this clause in Gal. 3:19, and holding it in the restricted English sense of "added," have supposed that it is here taught that whatever law is referred to was necessarily added *to something* as a part of that thing, and so have held that it was added to *the covenant with Abraham.* But such a view as that would plainly be a mistake, because, in Gal. 3:15, it is positively stated that "though it be but a man's covenant, yet if it be confirmed, no man... *addeth* thereto." Thus it would be impossible for anything to be added to that covenant. The word translated "addeth," in Gal. 3:15, is not the same in Greek as that translated "added" in Gal. 3:19, nor are the words akin.

From the Greek word itself, in Gal. 3:19, and its use in connection with the law, in Heb. 12:20 and Deut. 5:22, as well as its further use in the Scriptures, it is plain that it is not necessarily implied that what is referred to should be literally added in the sense of a mathematical addition. One expression in which the Greek word is used is, "Seek ye first the kingdom of God, and his righteousness; and all these things shall be *added* unto you." Matt. 6:33. Here it is plain that the expression is equivalent to merely to "give"—"all these things shall be *given* unto you," or "ye shall *receive* all these things." Such is exactly its meaning in Mark 4:24, in which our translation is, "Unto you that hear shall more be given"—shall more be added. In Acts 12:3 our translation reads, "He *proceeded further* to take Peter also." This, translated as in Gal. 3:19, would be, "He *added* to take Peter." Thus the word in Gal. 3:19 could, with equal propriety be translated, "Wherefore then the law? It was *spoken* because of transgressions," or, "It was *given* because of transgressions." One translation of the clause is, "It was set because of transgressions." Another is, "It was introduced," etc.

True, to translate it, "It was added," is just as good, provided it be understood that the word "added" conveys these senses, and is not to be restricted to its special meaning of a mathematical addition, as of adding "one cubit unto his stature."

The law, then, was given, was spoken, was added, because of transgression. Will this statement that "it was added *because of transgressions"* hold in the case of the law of God, the ten commandments? With respect to that law as it is referred to throughout in the discussion in which the Galatian Christians were involved, that is, the law *in its written form,* the expression does certainly apply. This will not only be clearly seen, but it is positively stated, in a passage already several times quoted in these "Studies in Galatians;" and we here set it down again:—"If man had kept the law of God, as given to Adam after his fall, preserved by Noah, and observed by Abraham, there would have been no necessity for the ordinance of circumcision. And if the descendants of Abraham had kept the covenant, of which circumcision was a sign, they would never have been seduced into idolatry, nor would it have been necessary for them to suffer a life of bondage in Egypt; they would have kept God's law in mind, and there would have been no necessity for it to be proclaimed from Sinai, or engraved upon the tables of stone. And had the people practiced the principles of the ten commandments, there would have been no need of the *additional* directions given to Moses."—*Patriarch and Prophets,* page 364.

This corresponds exactly to the other expressions with reference to the entering of the law of God: "The law *entered,* that the offense might abound." Rom. 5:20. "That sin by the commandment might become exceeding sinful." Rom. 7:7, 13. "To bring transgressions to a head."—Farrar's translation of Gal. 3:19. "In order to bring about *as transgressions* the transgressions of it."—Alford. This will be followed further next week.

Galatians 3:19

February 27, 1900

"Wherefore then serveth the law? It was added because of transgressions."

From the evidences presented in last week's study in Galatians, it is perfectly plain that the law of God, the ten commandments, *in written form,* both in tables of stone and as drawn out in its principles in the statutes and judgments of the *"additional* directions given to Moses," was spoken, was given, was added, because of the transgressions of men. As men went further into darkness, the Lord followed them with added efforts, and with further details to bring them to the light. Indeed, they went so far into transgressions and darkness that the Lord actually followed them so far as to give them "statutes that were not good." The whole story is told in the following passage:—

"The law of God existed before man was created. The angels were governed by it. Satan fell because he transgressed the principles of God's government. After Adam and Eve were created, God made known to them his law. It was not then written, but was rehearsed to them by Jehovah.

"The Sabbath of the fourth commandment was instituted in Eden. After God had made the world and created man upon the earth, he made the Sabbath for man. After Adam's sin and fall, nothing was taken from the law of God. The principles of the ten commandments existed before the fall, and were of a character suited to the condition of a holy order of beings. *After the fall,* the *principles* of those *precepts* were *not changed,* but *additional precepts* were given to meet man *in his fallen state.*

"Adam taught his descendants the law of God which law was handed down to the faithful through successive generations. The continual transgression of God's law called for a flood of waters upon the earth. The law was preserved by Noah and his family, who for right-doing were saved in the ark by a miracle of God. Noah taught his descendants the ten commandments. The Lord preserved a people for himself from Adam down, *in whose hearts was his law.* He says of Abraham, 'He obeyed my voice, and kept my charge, my commandments, my statutes, my laws.'

"If the descendants of Abraham had kept separate from other nations, they would not have been seduced into idolatry.

"There were but a few families that first went down into Egypt. These increased to a great multitude. Some were careful to instruct their children in the law of God; but many of the Israelites had witnessed so much idolatry that they had confused ideas of God's law...

"To leave them without excuse, the Lord himself condescended to come down upon Sinai enshrouded in glory, and surrounded by his angels, and in a most sublime and awful manner made known his law of ten commandments. He did not trust them to be taught by any one, not even his angels, but spoke his law with an audible voice in the hearing of all the people. He did not, even then, trust them to the short memory of a people who were prone to forget his requirements, but wrote them with this own holy finger upon tables of stone. He would remove from them all possibility of mingling with his holy precepts any tradition, or of confusing his requirements with the practices of men.

"He then came still closer to his people, who were so readily led astray, and would not leave them with merely the ten precepts of the decalogue. He commanded Moses to write, as he should bid him, judgments and laws, giving minute directions in regard to what he required them to perform, and thereby guarded the ten precepts which he had engraved upon the tables of stone. These specific directions and requirements were given to draw erring man to the obedience of the moral law, which he is so prone to transgress.

"If man had kept the law of God, as given to Adam after his fall, preserved in the ark by Noah, and observed by Abraham, there would have been no necessity for the ordinance of circumcision. And if the descendants of Abraham had kept the covenant, of which circumcision was a token of pledge, they would never have gone into idolatry, nor been suffered to go down into Egypt; and there would have been no necessity of God's proclaiming his law from Sinai, and engraving it upon tables of stone, and guarding it by definite directions in the judgments and statutes given to Moses.

"Moses wrote these judgments and statutes from the mouth of God while he was with him in the mount. If the people of God had obeyed the principles of the ten commandments, there would have been no need of the specific directions given to Moses, which he wrote in a book, relative to their duty to God and to one another."

The *definite directions which the Lord gave to Moses* in regard to the duty of his people to one another, and to the stranger, *are the principles of the ten commandments simplified* and given in definite manner, *that they need not err.*

"The Lord said of the children of Israel, 'Because they had not executed my judgments but had despised my statutes, and had polluted my Sabbaths, and their eyes were after their fathers idols. Wherefore I gave them also statutes that were not good, and judgments whereby they should not live.' Because of continual disobedience, the Lord annexed penalties to the transgression of his law, which were not good for the transgressor, or whereby he should not live in his rebellion.

"By transgressing the law which God had given in such majesty, and amid glory which was unapproachable, the people showed open contempt of the great Lawgiver, and death was the penalty."—*Spirit of Prophecy,* Vol. 1, pages 261-265. See also *Patriarchs and Prophets,* chap. 32, pars. 1-4.

It is true that the sacrificial system was also given, added, because of transgressions. This is true as to the sacrifices originally, with Adam and Abraham: it is also true of the Levitical system given to Israel in the wilderness. This is also stated in a passage quoted in previous studies, as follows:—

"A system was then [after the fall] established requiring the sacrificing of beasts, to keep before fallen man that which the serpent made Eve disbelieve, that the penalty of disobedience is death. The transgression of God's law made it necessary for Christ to die a sacrifice, and thus make a way possible for man to escape the penalty, and yet the honor of God's law be preserved."—*Spirit of Prophecy,* Vol. 1, page 261.

"The sacrificial system, committed to Adam, was also perverted by his descendants. Superstition, idolatry, cruelty, and licentiousness corrupted the simple and significant service that God had appointed. Through long intercourse with idolaters, the people of Israel had mingled many heathen customs with their worship; therefore the Lord gave them at Sinai definite instruction concerning the sacrificial service. After the completion of the tabernacle, he communicated with Moses from the cloud of glory above the mercy seat, and gave full directions concerning the system of offerings, and forms of worship to be maintained in the sanctuary. The ceremonial law was thus given to Moses, and by him written in a book. But the law of ten commandments spoken from Sinai had been written by God himself of the tables of stone, and was sacredly preserved in the ark."—*Patriarchs and Prophets,* pages 364, 365.

Thus, of either the moral law or the ceremonial law it is true that it was given, added, because of transgressions. The question then is, *which* one is the law pre-eminently referred to in this clause in Gal. 3:19? And from the specifications already noticed, as to this law having been "ordained. . . in the hand of a mediator," and the direct association of this text with the speaking of the law of God in Heb. 12:20 and Deut. 5:22, it certainly must be the truth that the law which in this passage is pre-eminently intended, is *the law of God,* the ten commandments, in *written form* on tables of stone and in the Bible.

Galatians 3:19

March 6, 1900

"Wherefore then serveth the law? It was added because of transgressions. . . *and it was ordained by angels in the hand of a mediator.*"

This statement in Gal. 3:19 is identical in substance with that by Stephen in his last words to the Sanhedrin, as they were about to stone him to death, when he said, "Which of the prophets have not your fathers persecuted? and they have slain them which showed before of the coming of the Just One, of whom ye have been now the betrayers and murderers; who have *received the law by the disposition of angels,* and have not kept it." Acts 7:52, 53.

This expression by Stephen, that the law was received, "by the disposition of angels," and the expression in Gal. 3:19, that the law "Was ordained by angels," are identical; for Stephen's word translated "disposition," and Paul's word translated "ordained," are the same Greek word precisely, with simply a variation in tense. Stephen's word is *diatage* and Paul's word is *diat-asso*.

Now, what law could it be which, whatever else might be included, was pre-eminently the law referred to by Stephen when, in connection with the law that they had not kept, he charged them with being murderers? What law is it which pre-eminently is not kept by a murderer?—It is the law of God—the ten commandments, one of which says, "Thou shalt not kill." And when the same identical word is used in Gal. 3:19, in the same identical connection, then what law alone can be referred to as pre-eminently the law there referred to, whatever other laws may be included? To have any other than the same law in both places, would be simply to do positive violence to the plain scripture in its whole connection. And since there can be no possible question as to what law is pre-eminently the one referred to by Stephen, there can likewise be no question as to what law is pre-eminently referred to in Gal. 3:19, when the same identical word is used as was used by Stephen, and in the same connection and in the same sense precisely.

What, then, is the thought expressed in the words "the disposition of angels," "ordained by angels"? The root of the two words used by Stephen and Paul is *tasso,* which signifies "to arrange, ordain, establish;" "to set in order, and draw up an army" on parade. or "in battle order." Thus, the specific statement in the two passages is that at the giving of the law referred to in the two places, the angels were drawn up in a grand array, as a king disposes his army, or a general his troops; and that, in the presence of this grand array of the angels of God, the law in question was given by the hand of a mediator.

As was presented in a former study: Since there is but *"one mediator between God and men, the Man Christ Jesus,"* Christ is unquestionably the Mediator in whose hand this law was ordained. And the scene is touched in Deut. 33:2; "The Lord came from Sinai, and rose up from Seir unto them; he shined forth from mount Paran, and he came with ten thousands of saints: from his right hand went a fiery law for them." From his right hand went forth this "fiery law" in the *writing* upon the tables of stone, and also in the *work* of making the tables of stone upon which the law was written by the hand of fire. For "the *tables* were the *work of God,* and the *writing* was the *writing of God,* graven upon the tables." Ex. 32:16.

And when those original tables had been broken by Moses, although Moses hewed out a second two tables like unto the first, he was required to take up these tables into the mount; and there, Moses says, *the Lord* again *"wrote* on the tables, according to the first writing, the ten commandments, which the Lord spake unto you in the mount out of the midst of the fire in the day of the assembly: and *the Lord gave them unto me*. And I turned myself and came down from the mount, and put the tables in the ark which I had made; and there they be, as the Lord commanded me." Deut. 10:4, 5.

Thus the law of the ten commandments, in the completest sense, was given by *the hand* of the "one mediator between God and men, the Man Christ Jesus;" and *no other law* was given. Other law was given by word, or by inspiration, to Moses, which *he wrote* with *his hand;* but no other law than that on the tables of stone was given in or by the *hand* of the Mediator. From his *"hand"* went forth that "fiery law;" and from that *hand* went forth *no other law.* And when from that *"right hand"* went forth that "fiery law," then thousands of saints were present. These ten thousands of saints (or "holy ones," R.V.) were the grand and glorious array of angels ordained, disposed, set in order, by the heavenly King, to behold and to do honor to this wonderful transaction of that most wonderful occasion.

Even Christian people have never yet truly discerned the majesty and glory of the giving of the law at Sinai; and that majesty and glory are only the true measure of the importance of that event. "There were thunders and lightnings, and a thick cloud upon the mount, and the voice of the trumpet exceeding loud:" "mount Sinai was altogether on a smoke, because the Lord descended upon it in fire: and the smoke thereof ascended as the smoke of a furnace, and the whole mount quaked greatly:" "the voice of the trumpet sounded long, and waxed louder and louder:" the voice of thy thunder was in the heaven: the lightnings lightened the world: the earth trembled and shook." Ps. 77:18. And from the midst of that glorious and terrible scene, when "the mountain burned with fire unto the midst of heaven, with darkness, clouds, and thick darkness" (Deut. 4:11), "the Lord spake. . . out of the midst of the fire, of the cloud, and of the thick darkness, with a great voice," the ten commandments (Deut. 5:22), "and he added no more." And "all the people that was in the camp trembled," and "entreated that the word should not be spoken [added] to them any more." And then, with his *hand* of fire, "he wrote them in two tables of stone, and delivered them unto" Moses.

"The chariots of God are twenty thousand, even thousands of angels: the Lord is among them, *as in Sinai,* in the holy place." Ps. 68:17. "The angels, ten thousand times ten thousand, and thousands of thousands, surrounded *the people of God* as they were assembled around the mountain, and *were all above them;* thus making a great living tabernacle, from which every evil angel was excluded, that not one word that was to come from the voice of Jesus should be altered in any mind, nor one suggestion of doubt or evil to a soul be made."

Thus when the law was delivered at Sinai, the glorious Lord and all the people were surrounded with the heavenly host of angels, disposed, ordained, arranged in orderly array. Four-faced and four winged cherubim, six-winged seraphim, and bright angels in glittering golden chariots—all these by the thousands upon thousands accompanied the Majesty of heaven, the Mediator, as in love there went forth from his hand to sinful men his great fiery law of love. Deut. 33:3. Then at the giving of the law of God, the ten commandments, at Sinai, there certainly has been no more majestic scene since the creation of the world. And that is the only law ever given by the hand of the Mediator.

How can there be any question or doubt that this is the law of Gal. 3:19 that was added because of transgressions, and that was ordained by angels in the hand of a mediator?

Galatians 3:19

March 13, 1900

"Wherefore then serveth the law? It was added because of transgressions, till the seed should come to whom the Promise was made; and it was ordained by angels in the hand of a mediator."

By each Particular clause of this verse, considered by itself alone, we have found that the law of God—the ten commandments in written form, as given at Sinai, and as in the Bible—is the law that is pre-eminently meant, and is the only one that meets all the requirements of all the specifications so far considered. What now of this one—" till the seed should come to whom the promise was made"?

There are two laws referred to in Galatians. That is settled. They were both added; and they were both added because of transgressions. But which is *pre-eminently* the law referred to *in that place,* and its connection? That is the question here.

There are also two *comings of the seed,* which is *Christ;* and it is proper and fair to ask, *Which is the coming* referred to here? Why should any one settle and firmly fix *as the coming of this Passage* a coming that requires that a law shall also be settled and fixed *as the law of the passage, which will not meet the requirements* of the Passage in its connection? That is what has been done; and it has been the great defect in the usual consideration of this passage of Scripture.

Those who are the enemies of the law of God in *any* form, and who would be glad to have it abolished in *every* form, but who do not know that that law could not by any possibility be abolished, have always wrung this verse in to do service in that terribly mistaken cause. These eagerly seize upon and settle it that the coming of the Seed here referred to is *the first coming of Christ.* They never look beyond the single clause: it is not to their interest to do so; because the only use they have for this scripture is that they may support their determination that the law of God is abolished. Thus the enemies of the law of God.

On the other hand, the *friends* of the law of God know that it is true that there was a law abolished at the first coming of Christ. And since here is a law that was added "till the seed should come," these friends of the law of God allow, and even settle upon, the claim of the enemies of the law of God, that *the first coming of Christ* is the coming that is here meant: THEN, and CONSEQUENTLY *the law that was abolished* is decided to be the law here referred to. But it must be confessed that this is a weak way of getting at the thing. It bears on its face more the aspect of the begging of the question than of a real study and discovery of the truth as it is in the Word, *for the truth's sake.* As a matter of fact, there is nothing in the passage, nor any where in this whole connection, that suggests the abolition of any law. The *subject* is, Wherefore serveth the law? What is the purpose, the object, the aim, of the law?

But there are two comings of the Seed. There is another, *the second coming*

Galatians 3:19

of Christ as well as there was the first. Is it impossible that this *second coming* of the Seed should be the coming referred to in this passage? There are other similar expressions in the Scripture.

For instance, Eze. 21:27. Speaking of the removing of the diadem and crown of the king of Judah, it says: "I will overturn, overturn, overturn, it; and it shall be no more, until HE COME *whose right it is;* and I will give it to him." What coming is this? The answer to this question can be given only by a consideration of the facts in the case, He came, but instead of receiving that crown, he received a crown of thorns; instead of being seated upon that throne, he was nailed to the cross. So we know that that was not the coming referred to in the text, but that it is his second coming "seated upon *the throne* of his father David, and having on his head many crowns. *Then it is* that the kingdom of this world becomes the kingdom of our Lord, and of his Christ; and he shall reign forever and ever." Rev. 11:15, R.V. And this *is* the *coming* of him whose right it is, that is referred to in the text, and then it will be given him.

Again, it is written that the seed of the woman should bruise the serpent's head. That Seed CAME, and did *not* bruise the serpent's head, but himself was bruised instead. Isa. 53:5. And after he *had come,* and had thus been bruised, even to death; had risen again from the dead; and had ascended to heaven,— even thirty years after these things—it was written: "The God of peace *shall bruise* Satan under your feet shortly." Rom. 16:20.

In Daniel 2 it is written: "In the days of these kings shall the God of heaven set up a kingdom which shall never be destroyed; and the kingdom shall not be left to other people, but it shall break in pieces and consume all these kingdoms, and it shall stand forever." Dan. 2:44. We all know that it is generally held by the ministers of the day that this was done at the first coming of Christ: that there the stone was cut out without hands, and is to roll on, and on, and on, until it fills the whole earth. But *WE* know that when he was here, he said, "My kingdom is not of this world," and "not from hence." John 18:36. And so we know that this scripture is fulfilled at his *second* coming.

Now, why should it be thought impossible that Gal. 3:19 should refer to his second coming? Look at the situation as it is in the text, with its context: "Till the seed should come to whom the promise was made."

What promise?—The promise of *the Inheritance,* unquestionably: as it is written: "For if *the Inheritance* be of *the law,* it is no more of *promise:* but God gave it to Abraham *by promise.* Wherefore then serveth *the law?* It was added because of transgressions, till the *seed* should come to whom the *promise* was made." Thus it is fixed by the Word itself that *the promise* referred to is the promise of the *inheritance*. And whatever *law* it is that is here referred to, it is given, added, till *He comes* to whom *the promise of the Inheritance* was made.

Now, at his *first coming* did he receive any of the inheritance?—No; no more than did Abraham, to whom with him, the promise was made. He "had not where to lay his head." And of him it was equally true, as with Abraham, that he received "none inheritance in it, no, not so much as to set his foot on."

Notice, too, *particularly,* that the clause says, "Till the seed should come to whom,"—not *concerning* whom, but *TO whom*—"the promise was made." That is, the promise referred to was made *to HIM,* personally; and not simply to *somebody, concerning* him. But it is fixed by the text that *the promise* is the promise of *the Inheritance.* This *promise* was made to Abraham and *to his seed,* which is Christ; and this was done when the promise was made to *Abraham.* But, further, it was *also done TO the seed himself* in person, which is Christ. Read it In the second psalm: "The Lord hath said unto me, Thou art my Son; this day have I begotten thee. Ask of me, and I shall give thee the heathen for *thine inheritance* and the *uttermost parts of the earth for thy possession."* Verses 7, 8. Here is the promise *of the inheritance* made direct *to the seed,* which is Christ.

Now, when is this promise fulfilled? And when something should be done, made, or instituted, "till *the seed should come TO* whom" that promise was made, then *which coming* would be the true and the only logical one that could be considered?—Plainly, the coming that would be *at the receiving of the inheritance* REFERRED TO IN THE PROMISE; and *with which alone* the promise is concerned.

Therefore, considering what the promise is plainly in the scriptures declared to be,—the *promise of the Inheritance,*—and considering that *this promise* relates and pertains particularly, and *above all,* to his *second coming,* it is evident that the *second coming of Christ,* rather than his first, is the one referred to in the clause "till the seed should come to whom the promise was made."

And since by every other clause of the verse, we have found that the law of God, as given on tables of stone at Sinai, and in the Bible, is the one preeminently referred to, and the only one that will meet all the specifications of all the clauses; and since the coming referred to in this clause is the coming in connection with the inheritance and the receiving of it, this settles it beyond all possibility of controversy that the law of God, *the ten commandments,* as given on the tables of stone and in the Bible, must remain in *full force and obligation*

UNTIL THE SECOND COMING OF CHRIST *and the end of the world.* And we all know that it will not be abolished *then.*

It is always true that those scriptures that Satan fixes upon and uses most tenaciously to prove the abolition of the law of God are the very ones which, when truly grasped, are seen to most conclusively and most beautifully show its everlasting integrity and obligation.

Look at the subject further. The *inheritance* is the thing referred to in *the promise.* But with what is the inheritance connected?—Plainly, and only, with *God's covenant with Abraham*—the everlasting covenant. Notice in the context that *"the covenant* [that is the covenant with Abraham, the everlasting covenant) that was confirmed before of God in Christ, *the law,* which was four hundred and thirty years after, can not disannul, that it should make *the promise* [the promise of the inheritance of that covenant] *of none effect."* Gal. 3:17.

As we have seen In a former study, the inheritance is the great thing in the covenant with Abraham, the everlasting covenant. Indeed, *the covenant with Abraham* was made by God *in pledge* to Abraham that he should *inherit* that which God had *promised.* For *after* God *had promised* it to him, Abraham said, "Whereby shall I know that I shall *inherit* It?" And, in answer, God made with him, and entered into with him, that blood covenant, in which he pledged his life that the promise of the inheritance should never fail. Gen. 15:8, 18.

And as we also found in the former studies, all that ever come in *after that covenant was made,* was, in blessing men, *to enable them to attain to the fullness of that covenant,* and *to the inheritance* of which that everlasting covenant is the pledge. And this was exactly the object of the giving of the law of God on tables of stone on Mount Sinai, and in the Bible. For if men had kept that covenant, "they would have kept God's law *in mind,* and there would have been no necessity for it to be proclaimed from Sinai or engraved upon the tables of stone." The object of that law, thus written and given to men, bringing transgressions to a head, making sins abound, was and is that men might find the grace of Christ much more abounding,—that through him they might attain to the fullness of that everlasting covenant with Abraham, and so to *the inheritance* of which that covenant was and is the pledge.

And to allow the coming of the seed to whom the promise of the inheritance was made, to be *the second coming* of Christ, and not his first,— this gives opportunity for the law of God, in its written form, to fulfill its grand object, which is the bringing of men, through faith in Christ, to the fullness of that everlasting covenant. The fullness of that everlasting covenant is the righteousness of God—the keeping of "the commandments, and the faith of Jesus." And men must be brought to the fullness of that everlasting covenant in order that they may receive the inheritance, of which that everlasting covenant is the pledge

That this view is the correct one, and is the truth of the matter, is emphasized by *the fact* that the everlasting covenant is *not* met in its fullness, in believers, *until the second coming of Christ;* that is, till the seed really comes to whom the promise of the inheritance was made.

One provision of that everlasting covenant is. "I will put my law in their inward parts, and write it in their hearts." And that provision will not be accomplished in its fullness until, by the Third Angel's Message, men are brought to the actual keeping of "the commandments of God, and the faith of Jesus:" so that the Lord, looking down from heaven upon them, can say, in perfect truth: "Here are they that keep the commandments of God, and the faith of Jesus."

Another provision of that covenant is: "And they shall not teach every man his neighbor, and every man his brother, saying, Know the Lord; for all shall know me, from the least to the greatest." Heb. 8:11. Although we are now living in the times of the new covenant as really as was Abraham, yet neither the world nor we have attained to that point where it is not necessary any more for any man to teach his neighbor or his brother, saying, Know the Lord. And this part of the everlasting covenant will not be met in its fullness until, through the blessing and power of God in the Third Angel's Message, the mystery of God shall have been finished. Col. 1:26, 27; Rev. 19:7.

It is not necessary here to take up all the clauses of the new covenant one by one. These are enough to illustrate the truth that the everlasting covenant, the new covenant, the covenant with Abraham, which is the pledge of *the inheritance* that is promised to the Seed, *is not met* in its fullness in those who accent it, till the *second coming of Christ.*

And if this be not plain enough by the scriptures presented, or is not convincing enough, then read the following sentences from the testimony of Jesus, which is the Spirit of Prophesy:—

"It was at midnight that God chose to deliver his people. As the wicked were mocking around them, suddenly the sun appeared; shining in his strength, and the moon stood still. The wicked looked upon the scene with amazement, while the saints beheld with solemn joy the tokens of their deliverance. Signs and wonders followed in quick succession. Everything seemed turned out of its natural course. The streams ceased to flow. Dark, heavy clouds came up and clashed against each other. But there was one clear place of settled glory, whence came the voice of God like many waters, shaking the heavens and the earth. There was a mighty earthquake. The graves were opened, and those who had died in faith under the Third Angel's Message, keeping the Sabbath, came forth from their dusty beds, glorified, to *hear the covenant of peace* that God was to make with those who had kept his law.

"The sky opened and shut, and was in commotion. The mountains shook like a reed in the wind, and cast out ragged rocks all around. The sea boiled like a pot, and cast out stones upon the land. And as *God spoke* the day and the hour of JESUS' COMING, and *delivered the* EVERLASTING COVENANT *to his people,* he spoke one sentence, and then paused, while the words were rolling through the earth. The Israel of God stood with their eyes fixed upward, listening to the words as they came from the mouth of Jehovah, and rolled through the earth like peals of loudest thunder. . . The wicked could not look upon them [the saints] for the glory. And when the *never-ending blessing* was pronounced on those who had honored God in keeping his Sabbath holy, there was a mighty shout of victory over the beast and over his image."—*Early Writings* pp. 145, 146.

The following quotation also, though concerning in substance what is in the foregoing quotation, contains statements that make it worth printing in this connection:—"With shouts of triumph, jeering, and imprecation, throngs of evil men are about to rush upon their prey, when lo, a dense blackness, deeper than the darkness of the night, falls upon the earth. Then *a rainbow,* shining with the glory from the throne of God, spans the heavens, and seems to encircle each praying company. The angry multitudes are suddenly arrested. Their mocking cries die away. The objects of their murderous rage are forgotten. With fearful forebodings they gaze upon the *symbol of God's covenant,* and long to be shielded from its overpowering brightness.

In the midst of the angry heavens is one clear space of indescribable glory, whence comes the voice of God like the sound of many waters, saying. "It is done." That voice shakes the heavens and the earth. There is a mighty earthquake, "such as was not since men were upon the earth, so mighty an earthquake and so great." Graves are opened, and "many of them that sleep in the dust of the earth" "awake, some to everlasting life, and some to shame and everlasting contempt." All who have died in the faith of the Third Angel's Message come forth from the tomb, glorified, to hear *God's covenant of peace* with those who have kept his law.

"The voice of God is heard from heaven, declaring *the day* and *hour* of

Jesus' coming and delivering *the everlasting covenant* to his people.

"Soon there appears in the east a small black cloud, about half the size of a man's hand. It is the cloud which surrounds the Saviour, and which seems in the distance to be shrouded in darkness. The people of God know this to be the sign of the Son of Man. In solemn silence they gaze upon it as it draws nearer the earth, becoming lighter and more glorious until it is a *great white cloud,* its base a glory like consuming fire, and above it, the *rainbow* of the COVENANT." *Great Controversy* pages 635, 641.

And when the saints of God have thus attained to the fullness of the everlasting covenant, the covenant with Abraham, when the object of the giving of the law from Sinai, and in the Bible, has thus been accomplished, the law will *not* then be abolished, but will be *kept in mind,* in heart, in soul, just as it was by Adam, Enoch, Noah, and Abraham, when as yet there was "no necessity for it to be proclaimed from Sinai, or written on the tables of stone." Instead of being then abolished, it will be observed and lived more fully and more perfectly that ever before by men.

And this is "Wherefore serveth the law?" And *this* is why it is that "it was added because of transgressions, *till* the seed should come to whom the promise [of the inheritance] was made, and it was ordained by [the disposition, the grand array of] angels in the hand of a mediator."

We are thoroughly convinced that more genuine study, and far more profitable study can be put upon Galatians 3:19, and the rest of the chapter, and the whole book, by Seventh-day Adventists, than has ever yet been put upon it by us or anybody else.

Galatians 3:21, 22

March 20, 1900

"Is the law then against the promises of God? God forbid; for if there had been a law given which could have given life, verily righteousness should have been by the law. But the scripture hath concluded all under sin, that the promise by faith of Jesus Christ might be given to them that believe."

The law could not possibly be against the promises of God. For when God had given a promise, why should he, and how could he, set up anything against the promise? Why should he desire to weaken or to frustrate his own promise? Therefore his "God forbid" is set against any such suggestion. Instead of the law being against the promises, it is, as we have again and again seen, an aid to men in attaining unto the promises.

The divine reason here given as to why the law is not against the promises is that "if there had been a law given which could have given life," then "verily righteousness should have been by the law." And if righteousness had been by the law, there would have been no need of any promises. Indeed there would then have been no place for any promises. For "to him that *worketh* [obtains righteousness by the *law*] is the reward not reckoned of grace, but of *debt.*" Rom. 4:4.

If righteousness could be obtained by working, it would be possessed in the very act of the work performed. And when *possessed,* there could not possibly be any room for any *promise* of it.

And if righteousness could be obtained by working, then the *reward* of righteousness would be *earned,* and so would be a debt *due;* and any withholding of it from him who had earned it, and to whom it was so due, would be injustice. Thus again, if righteousness were by the law, there would be no room for any promise; for even to *promise* to a person that which he had already earned, and which was already due, would be a withholding of the thing earned and due, and so would be injustice.

Therefore upon every consideration, if righteousness could be obtained by the law, then the law *would be* against the promises of God. And for any one to expect righteousness by the law, he in that very thing does set the law against the promises of God. But against all thought of obtaining righteousness by the law the Lord sets his "God forbid" that the law should be against the promises.

Another reason given why righteousness can not be by the law is that *the law can not give life*—"if there had been a *law given* which could have *given life,"* THEN "VERILY *righteousness* should have been by *the law."* Thus it is certified by the word of God that *righteousness* and *life* come from precisely *the same source,* and in precisely the same way; and that is, as the free gift of God by his creative power as the Author and Prince of life.

But there is no law that can possibly give life to men; because all men have lost their lives by transgression of the highest law in the universe—the law of God. And since all men have transgressed that highest law in the universe, and so have lost their lives, no law subordinate to that can possibly give them life, and even that highest law itself can not give them life; because, having transgressed it, and so forfeited their lives, they, being sinners and under sentence of death, can not possibly observe it, but can only continue to transgress it. So that for men there is no life in any law.

Now it is true that the law was "ordained to life," but because of transgression it was "found to be unto death." Rom. 7:10. It is true that it is written: "The man that doeth them shall live in them;" but there is none that doeth them. "There is none righteous, no, not one." "They are all gone out of the way, they are together become unprofitable." Rom. 3:10, 12.

But, bless the Lord, "what the law could not do, in that it was weak through the flesh,"—weak through the sinfulness of the flesh—"God sending his own Son in the likeness of sinful flesh" did. "What the law could not do,"—it could not do even that to which it was ordained, it could not give life,—"God sending his own Son" *did.* In the likeness of sinful flesh he "for sin, condemned sin in the flesh; that the righteousness of the law might be fulfilled in us, who walk not after the flesh, but after the Spirit." Rom. 8:34. "For the wages of sin is *death:* but the gift of God is *eternal life* through Jesus Christ our Lord." Rom. 6:23.

Therefore "the Scripture hath concluded *all under sin,* that the promise by faith of Jesus Christ might be given to them that believe." And the only way in which anybody can be concluded "under sin" is by *the law of God*—the law by which alone "is the knowledge of sin." And since the Scripture hath thus concluded all under sin, *that*—so that, in order that—the promise by faith of Jesus Christ might be given to them that believe, it is perfectly plain that instead of the law being against the promises of God, it is the God-given means of men's attaining to the perfect surety of the promises of God by faith of Jesus Christ.

Therefore that law can no more be done away than the promises of God can be done away, and no more than the faith of Jesus Christ can be done away. And any one who would in argument or in thought do away that law, does in argument or in thought do away the promises of God and the faith of Jesus Christ, and so destroys the way of God's salvation to men. But that can not in truth be destroyed—except in the individual experience of men. And to destroy the way of God's salvation in individual experience, is to work eternal destruction to the soul. Therefore the claim that the law of God—the ten commandments—is done away is the most stupendous and destructive error that could possibly be entertained by anybody anywhere.

Galatians 3:23

March 27, 1900

"But before faith came, we were kept under the law, shut up unto the faith which should afterwards be revealed."

This verse repeats, in different words, the particular thought of the two verses immediately preceding. Verse 21 declares that the law is not against the promises of God, and shows that it is a helper unto the fullness of the promises that are in Christ. Verse 22 declares that "the scripture hath concluded all under sin" and this for a purpose. And what is the purpose?— "That [in order that] the promise by faith of Jesus Christ might be given to them that believe."

Now, "By the law is the knowledge of sin;" and it is the law of God, the ten commandments, by which is the knowledge of sin. Then since "the scripture hath concluded all under *sin,"* and "by *the law* is the knowledge of sin," the scripture hath concluded all under *the law.* And it has concluded them all under the law *so that "the promise by faith of Jesus Christ* might be given to them that believe."

Then, that law by which "is the knowledge of sin"—by *that law* it is that "the scripture hath concluded all under sin." And since it is by that law that all are concluded under sin, in order that the promise by faith of Jesus Christ might by given to them that believe, therefore, as stated in the previous verse, the law is not against the promises of God, but is an aid to all men in their attaining to the promise by faith of Jesus Christ.

Now the same thought is carried forward in the verse at present under consideration; namely, "Before faith came, we were kept *under the law."* Under what law?— Plainly under the law by which alone "the scripture hath concluded all *under sin.* Even as it is said in another place: "Now we know that what things soever the law saith, it is said to them who are *under the law,* that every mouth may be stopped, and *all the world* may become *guilty* before God. This is the condition of every soul upon earth before faith comes to him. But when faith does come to him, when he awakes to the exercise of faith, *then* "the righteousness of God *without the law* is manifested,. . . even the righteousness of God which is by faith of Jesus Christ unto all and upon all them that believe." Rom. 3:19-22. Thus it is true, and thus it is, that all are concluded under sin and kept under the law until faith in Jesus Christ delivers them.

However, there is another expression in the verse that is particularly to be noticed: that is, that we were "shut up." We were "under the law," "shut up." We were *"kept* under the law, *shut up."* It was *before faith came"* that "we were kept *under the law, shut up."* And "before faith came, we were kept under the law, shut up *unto the faith* which should afterwards be revealed."

How was it that we were shut up?—*"under the law,* shut up." But to be under the law is to be "guilty before God." Rom. 3:19. To be "under the law" is to be under the dominion of sin. Rom. 6:14. And since we were "under the law, shut up," it was the law that shut us up. And what law is this?—it is the same law as that of the previous verse, by which "the scripture hath *concluded* all *under sin."* And the only law by which anybody can possibly be concluded under sin, is that law by which "is the *knowledge* of sin," which is the law of God, the law of ten commandments.

The Greek word thus translated, "shut up" is the same word that, in the previous verse, is translated "concluded;" and also that in Rom. 11:32 is translated in *the text* "concluded," and in *the margin* "shut up." So that the expressions translated alike in the two verses, would be: verse 22, "The scripture hath *shut up* all *under sin,* that the promise by faith of Jesus Christ might be given to them that believe;" and verse 22, "We were kept *under the law, shut up* unto the faith which should afterwards be revealed."

This makes it certain that the law by which, in verse 22, "we were shut up under sin" is the same law by which, in verse 23, "we were kept under the law, shut up." And by these twin expressions it is plain that to be "under the law" is to be "under sin," for to be "shut up under sin" is to be "kept under the law, shut up;" to be "shut up under the law" is to be "shut up under sin." And the only law by which anybody can be shut up under sin, is that law by which alone is the knowledge of sin; and that law is the law of God, the law of ten commandments.

Therefore, since all are shut up under sin, in order that the promise of faith of Jesus Christ might be given to them that believe; and since the law of ten commandments is the only one by which anybody can be shut up under sin, it is certain that law is not against the promises of God, but is the only certain means of attaining to the true faith, and so to the fullness of the promises in Christ.

Galatians 3:21-23

April 3, 1900

"Is the law then against the promises of God? God forbid:

for if there had been a law given which could have given life, verily righteousness should have been by the law. And the scripture hath concluded [shut up," Greek] all under sin, that the promise by faith of Jesus Christ might be given to them that believe. But before faith came, we were kept under the law, shut up unto the faith which should afterwards be revealed."

All were "shut up under sin." And all were "under the law, shut up." And the only possible way in which anybody can be under sin is by that law by which is "the knowledge of sin" (Rom. 3:20; 7:7); by that law which is "the strength of sin" (1 Cor. 15:56); that law of which "sin" itself is "the transgression." 1 John 3:4. That law is the law which says, "Thou shalt not covet." Rom. 7:7-13. And that is the law of God, the ten commandments. This is so certain that there can be no question about it.

And it is equally certain that the *ceremonial law of sacrifices and offerings* never was intended to, and never could, shut up anybody under the law. On the contrary, that was for the time then present *the way out* from under the law. Notice the following example in illustration, from that ceremonial law:—"If the whole congregation of Israel *sin,...* and they have done somewhat against any of the *commandments of the Lord* concerning things which *should not be done,* and are *guilty;* when the *sin* which they have sinned against it, is known, *then* the congregation shall *offer a young bullock* FOR THE SIN, and bring him before the tabernacle of the congregation. And the elders of the congregation shall lay their hands upon the head of the bullock *before the Lord:* and the bullock shall be *killed before the Lord.* And the *priest* that is anointed shall bring of the *bullock's blood* to the tabernacle of the congregation;... and the priest shall make atonement for them, and *it shall be* FORGIVEN THEM." Lev. 4:18-20.

Now please look that all over, and consider it step by step:
    a. The people sinned. How?
    b. They had done "somewhat against the commandments of the Lord." What commandments of the Lord?
    c. "The commandments of the Lord *concerning things which* SHOULD NOT BE DONE." What are the commandments of the Lord concerning things which should not be done?

Studies in the Book of Galatians

    d. Plainly enough these: "Thou *shalt* have no other gods before me." "Thou *shalt not* make unto thee any graven image." "Thou *shalt not* take the name of the Lord thy God in vain." "The seventh day is the Sabbath of the Lord thy God; in it thou *shalt not* do any work." "Thou *shalt not* kill." "Thou *shalt not* commit adultery." "Thou *shalt not* steal." "Thou *shalt not* bear false witness." "Thou *shalt not* covet."

    e. And when they had *sinned* by doing somewhat against any of these commandments, this *law, of the Lord,* they were "GUILTY." And when the *sin* came to their knowledge, that *guilt* was the *more impressed*—"sin by the commandment became *exceedingly* sinful." And so long as they remained in that attitude and in that place only, they were held under that guilt, "shut up under sin;" so long as they remained there only, they remained the more guilty, and "were *kept* under the law, shut up." But they need not remain there "shut up under sin" and "kept under the law, shut up," held "guilty." They need not remain there, because—

    f. *THERE WAS A WAY OUT.* That way out, the *only* way out, was the way *of the sacrifice* and *the blood* of THE OFFERING; and the *ministration of the priest* who made "AN ATONEMENT."

    g. For when they had offered the bullock, and the priest with the blood had made atonement, the sin was *"forgiven them."*

    h. And when the sin was forgiven them, *they were free.* They were no longer guilty, no longer "shut up under sin," no longer "under the law, shut up." They were *out* and *free;* because they were *at one* with God, because of the at-one-ment made.

    That whole course of the sacrifice and offering was *the way of FAITH.* It was the way of *promise.* And that way was for, and was available for, *only* those who were "guilty" of "sin," and so were "shut up under sin." That sacrifice and blood was the expression of faith in the sacrifice and blood of Jesus Christ. And that ministration of the priest, and the atonement made, was the example and shadow of the ministration of Christ, the great High Priest, and the atonement that he makes.

    That whole course of sacrifice and offering was the way of the *faith of Jesus Christ.* That way of the faith of Jesus Christ was the *way out* for those who were "guilty" of "sin," and so were "shut up under sin. They were guilty of sin, and so "shut up under sin," only because they had done somewhat against any of the commandments of the Lord concerning things which *should not be done.* And those commandments were the ten commandments. Therefore it is by the Scripture indisputable that by the law of the ten commandments, which *showed them guilty,* they were "concluded [shut up] all under sin, *that* [in order that, so that] the promise by faith of Jesus Christ might be given to them that believe."

Now, did the sacrifice and offering bring them to faith? Or did faith bring them to the sacrifice and offering?—The only answer that there can be is that by all conceivable evidence faith brought them *to the sacrifice.* Can this possibly be doubted when it is written: "By *faith* Abel *offered* unto God a. . . *sacrifice* by which he obtained witness that he was righteous"? Heb. 11:4. It was *faith* that brought *to the offering of the sacrifice* Abel and all the others who were ever accepted of God.

But what *brought them* to the *FAITH* that *brought the sacrifice?*—The knowledge of their sin—the conviction that they were "guilty."

And what gave them the knowledge of their sin? What caused the conviction of their guilt?—Their having "done somewhat against any of the commandments of the Lord concerning *things which should not be done."*

Thus "before faith came" *they, as all others of mankind,* "were kept under the law, shut up *unto* the *faith* which should afterwards be revealed." They were "shut up unto *the faith,"* the faith expressed in the sacrifice and offering, because there was no other way out from their guilt of sin. And there was no other way out, because "there is none other name under heaven given among men, whereby we must be saved." Acts 4:12.

Galatians 3:24,25

April 17, 1900

"Wherefore the law was our schoolmaster to bring us unto Christ, that we might be justified by faith. But after that faith is come, we are no longer under a schoolmaster."

These two verses are the conclusion of the argument in verses 21-23. Accordingly they are introduced by "Wherefore." "Where-fore" signifies "for which cause or reason; in consequence of which; consequently." It is easy to see that these two verses are the consequence of the preceding ones.

Notice verse 23: the law is not against the promises of God; but, instead, is an aid in attaining unto the promises. And we know that all the promises of God are in Christ. Then, since the law is an aid in attaining unto the promises; and all the promises are in Christ, evidently the law is an aid in men's attaining unto Christ.

Next, notice verse 22: "The scripture hath concluded [shut up] all under sin, that the promise by faith of Jesus Christ might be given to them that believe." Plainly, then, the law is a means of bringing men to Christ and to the promises by faith in him.

Next, notice verse 23: "Before faith came, we were kept under the law, shut up unto the faith which should afterwards be revealed." As we were "shut up unto the faith," and "were kept under the law, shut up,"—it was the law that shut us up, and it shut us up unto the faith,—plainly the law brought men to faith. But faith is always Christ, and Christ is always faith, for he is "the author and finisher of faith." And since the law brought men to faith and Christ is the substance of all faith, in the nature of things the law brought men to Christ. And so, verse 24 states the fact, as the consequence of all this: "The law was our schoolmaster to bring us unto Christ, that we might be justified by faith."

But the great question with most persons is, What law is that? It is a fair enough question, because, since whatever law it is, it brings men to Christ: and if men take the wrong law, it will not bring them to Christ.

But it can easily be known what law it is. Read again the text: *"The law was our schoolmaster to bring us unto Christ, that we might be justified by faith. But after that faith is come, we are no longer under a schoolmaster"*—we are no longer under *the law*. Now, what is it to be under the law?—It is to be under the dominion of sin; for it is written: "Sin shall not have dominion over you: for ye are not under the law." Rom. 6:14. Then, whoever is under the law, is under the dominion of sin, and this because "sin is the transgression of the law." And what law is it?—It is the moral law—the law which says: "Thou shalt not covet;" for it is written: "I had not known sin, but by the law: for I had not known lust, except the law had said, Thou shalt not covet." Rom. 7:7. And this is the very thought that is before us in Gal. 3:23, 25, and in the verses preceding, of which verses 24 and 25 are only the conclusion.

Verse 22 says: "The scripture hath concluded [shut up] all under sin, that the promise by faith of Jesus Christ might be given to them that believe;" and verse 23 says: "We were kept under the law, shut up unto the faith which should afterwards be revealed." There can be no manner of question that these expressions "under sin" and "under the law" are identical in meaning, and therefore it is plain that to be "under the law" is to be "under sin." And being "under sin," being "shut up under sin," and thus "kept under the law, shut up unto the faith," it is certain that it is the law *by which is the knowledge of sin,*—the law which says, "Thou shalt not covet."—which is the schoolmaster to bring us unto Christ, that we might be justified by faith. And this is the more evident by the fact that after faith is come, after we are justified by faith, we are no longer under the law; we are no longer under the dominion of sin; we are no longer shut up; because we have attained unto the very thing which is the object of the law, which is Christ. For "Christ is the end [the object, the aim, the purpose] of the law for righteousness to everyone that believeth." Rom. 10:4.

Notice again: for what purpose is it that men are brought to Christ?—"That we might be justified by faith." This is the same as the preceding verses: "We were kept under the law, shut up *unto the faith.*" "The scripture hath concluded all under sin, *that the promise by faith of Jesus Christ* might be given to them that believe." Plainly, therefore, whatever law it is, it is a law that brings men to faith.

Now, it is not true, and it never was true, that the ceremonial law of sacrifices and offerings ever brought anybody to faith. It was faith that brought them to that law. "By faith Abel offered unto God... sacrifice." Did the *sacrifice,* or *the offering of it,* bring Abel to faith?—No. *Faith* brought Abel to the *sacrifice.* That sacrifice was a lamb, and, in Abel's faith, it was Christ. And by the faith of Christ, in which he offered that sacrifice, "he obtained witness that he was righteous." Thus he attained to righteousness by faith; to justification by faith. Thus faith brought him to that ceremonial *law* of sacrifices and offerings.

But what brought him to the *faith* that *brought him* to *the law* of sacrifices and offerings?—The *knowledge of sin* brought him to *the faith.* And what brought him to the knowledge of sin?—The moral law, to be sure—the law that says: "Thou shalt not covet"—the law by which alone is the knowledge of sin.

Cain brought an offering: but it was not brought in faith, and therefore was not accepted; and consequently sin still lay at his door. Gen. 4:7. Cain had no faith in Christ, and therefore his offering was of no avail. And even though an offering were made of a lamb, if there was no *faith in Christ* in him who offered it, it would not avail. The faith must be there before he brings his offering at all, or else it is of no avail.

Thus, by every consideration, it is certain that, instead of the ceremonial law of sacrifices and offerings bringing men to the faith, it was faith that always brought men to the sacrifices and offerings. And it must be faith that would do that, or else, the sacrifice and the offering was nothing.

Galatians 3:24-26

April 24, 1900

The law that is here under consideration brings men to Christ, that they may *"be justified by faith."* Justification by faith is the object in view. But from the example of Abel, and from the ceremonial law of Leviticus, which we have already presented in these studies, it has been demonstrated that the ceremonial law of sacrifices and offerings was itself the way of justification by faith; so that it is impossible for a law which in itself is justification by faith, to bring men *to* justification by faith.

On the other hand, what is the necessity for justification?—All have sinned; all have transgressed the law; all are shut up under sin, and so kept under the law. And they never can be justified by *the law.* The only possible escape is by *faith of Jesus Christ.* Their only hope of justification is in justification by *faith.* Consequently, this law is the law by which is the knowledge of sin; the law *"under"* which every man is *"kept"* until he is justified by faith. This law it is that is the schoolmaster to bring men unto Christ in order that they may be justified by faith.

One other word just here. The ceremonial law of sacrifices and offerings is done away. There is no question of that anywhere. Now if it were the ceremonial law of sacrifices and offerings that brought men to Christ, that they might be justified by faith—since that is done away, how can men be brought to Christ? And how can they find justification by faith? If that were the law here referred to, then, of all things, that law never should have been, and it never could have been, in righteousness, done away, and ever since it was done away, men have needed to be brought to Christ, and to be justified by faith, this, in itself, is the most conclusive proof that the ceremonial law of sacrifices and offerings is not at all, and could not possibly be, the law here referred to.

For these reasons that law could be only a law that abides forever—and that law is the MORAL law—the law by which is the knowledge of sin, by which all the world is declared and held guilty before God, until they are justified by faith. For "what things soever the law saith, it saith to them who are *under the law;* that every mouth may be stopped; and all the world may become guilty before God. Therefore by the deeds of the law there shall no flesh be justified in his sight, for by the law is the knowledge of sin.

"But now the righteousness of God *without the law* is manifested, being witnessed by the law and the prophets; *even the righteousness of God* which is *by faith of Jesus Christ* unto all and upon all them that believe; for there is no difference: for all have sinned, and come short of the glory of God.

"Being justified freely by his grace through the redemption that is in Christ Jesus: whom God hath set forth to be a propitiation through faith in his blood, to declare his righteousness for the remission of sins that are past, through the forbearance of God; to declare I say, at this time his righteousness; that he might be just, and the justifier of him which believeth in Jesus. Where is boasting then? It is excluded. By what law? Of works? Nay: but by the law of faith.

"Therefore we conclude that a man is justified by faith without the deeds of the law." Rom. 3:19-28. All this is of the moral law. But it was *with* the very deeds of the ceremonial law of sacrifices and offerings that men were justified by faith. Indeed, a man could not be justified by faith *without the deeds* of the ceremonial law of sacrifices and offerings: because the deeds of the ceremonial law of sacrifices and offerings were the very expression of faith itself. By faith Abel offered unto God a. . . sacrifice." What was the faith worth that brought no sacrifice?—Nothing. That was Cain's faith. The law, then, that brought men to Christ that they might be *justified by faith,* is a law, and must be a law, *without the deeds* of which men are justified by faith. And this is true and can be true *only* of the moral law.

One of the principle sources of misunderstanding of this text, lies in the taking of the word "schoolmaster" in the sense of our everyday word "school-*teacher,"* and knowing that the ten commandments do not of themselves teach, instruct, or tell men about Christ and his work of salvation, while the ceremonial law of sacrifices and offerings does,—because in *figure* it *was* Christ—it is concluded that this law which was the schoolmaster, *must* be, and can be, only the ceremonial law of sacrifices and offerings.

But the word translated schoolmaster does not signify a school-*teacher.* It signifies a school*master,* in the sense of a *master* as a *disciplinarian:* not a school-*teacher,* in the sense of an instructor. It is true that the schoolmaster, the disciplinarian, *might be,* and sometimes was, also a school-*teacher,* an instructor, but that was only an incident. The original and primary thought of the word is that of *master,* as a disciplinarian, a watcher, a corrector. Accordingly, the German of Luther translated it *"Zuct-meisterr*—master of the house of correction." The Greek word corresponds to the Latin and Anglicized word "tutor." But even as connected with the idea of tutor, the thought of *teacher* only incidentally attaches; because the original and primary meaning of "tutor" is simply *"a guardian;* a watcher; a protector."

A guardian may be indeed a teacher also, if he have the ability and faculty to be a teacher also, but that is not the original and primary thought in the word, it is only an incident.

The Greek word translated schoolmaster is *paidagogos* and signifies "a boy-*ward;*" "a child-conductor;" or "child-guide;" *"the slave who went with a boy from home to school and back again,* a kind of a tutor." "Fabius is jeeringly called the *paidagogos* of Hannibal, because he always followed him about:—generally a leader, *demokratias, turannidos."* The thought that he was primarily a person apart from the *teacher* of the boy is emphasized in the word *"paidagogcion*—the room in a schoolhouse *on which the paldagogue waited for their boy."* The Century Dictionary says: "Among the Greeks and Romans the *pedagogue* was *originally* a slave who attended the younger children of his master, and conducted them to school, to the theater, etc., combining, *in many cases* instruction with guardianship." If the thought intended to be conveyed in this verse were that of a school-*teacher,* the word would have to be not *paidagogos,* but *didaskalos.*

The law then here meant is not a law which in itself teaches of Christ; but that which *conducts* men as children *to Christ* that *by him* they may be taught. The law is not in itself the teacher, but that which watches, guards, corrects, and *conducts men* as untrained and unruly children *to Christ* as to *the school* where *by him* they shall be *taught.* And the only law that can possibly fit the thought not only of the single word *paidagogos,* but also the whole context of which verses 24 and 25 are only the conclusion and consequence, is the moral law—the ten commandments. For "the scripture has *shut up* all under sin;" "we were kept under the law shut up UNTO THE FAITH." *"Wherefore"*— consequently—"the law was our *paidagogos*—watcher, warden, guardian, corrector, and conduct-or—unto *Christ,* that [so that, in order that] we might be justified by faith. But after that faith is come we are no longer under *the law*—no longer "kept under the law," "shut up under sin." "For ye are all the children of God by faith in Christ Jesus."

Two correspondents think that this is new doctrine, especially for and in the REVIEW AND HERALD; but whatever and with whomsoever this may be new doctrine, there is one thing certain, and that is that for and in the REVIEW AND HERALD it is *not in any sense new.* Consider: The first number of the REVIEW AND HERALD ever issued, was Vol. I, No. 1, in November, 1850— forty-nine and a half hears ago. No. 5 of Vol. I was issued in January, 1851. In that No. 5 was the first notice of the third chapter of Galatians that was ever made in the REVIEW AND HERALD. It is in an article by J. N. Andrews, on

Galatians 3:24-26

"The Perpetuity of the Law of God." From that article we quote, just as there printed, enough to make perfectly plain to all *now,* the position that was held in and by the REVIEW *then:*—

"Our faith may be expressed in a single sentence: God's LAW COVERS ALL TIME, *and under all dispensations it stands out before men as the rule of their lives, and the sum of their duty to God.* The fall of man left "the work of the law" written in his heart though faintly indeed; then at Mt. Sinai it was written in tables of stone by the finger of God; then, under the new covenant, it is written in the hearts of God's people, even as it was before the fall. We appeal to men of candor and reason. Are not these things so?

"Galatians 3. The great doctrine of justification by faith having been lost sight of by the Galatian church, the apostle argues the point with them; and with great clearness shows that it is our only hope of salvation. Hence, the different covenants which God made with his people are here examined and contrasted. The covenant made with Abraham, which was based on the righteousness of faith, is first introduced. This covenant secured to himself, and to his seed, the inheritance of the earth. Rom. 4:13... The question now arises. Why does the apostle say that the law could not disannul the promise made to Abraham? Is there anything in the law which is against the promise of God?—No, verily. See verse 21. For the law of God, which embodies his requirements, and man's duty, can not be contrary to his own promise.

Why then is it said that if the inheritance be of the law, it is no more of promise? We answer that God made perfect obedience to his law the condition on which he took Israel, the literal seed of Abraham, to be his people. Jer. 11:3, 4; Ex. 19:5-8; 20. This covenant made the works of the law the condition on which they should receive the inheritance, instead of the righteousness of faith which was the condition of the promise made to Abraham. But it is plain that if the deeds of the law be made the ground of justification, then is justification by faith made void. And as it is evident that fallen, guilty man can not be justified by a law which already condemns him, he could then have no hope of salvation... Why, then, it may be asked, did God give to Israel a covenant which recognized perfect obedience as its only condition? We reply, He did it that he might exclude all appearance of heirship from the natural seed except such as should walk in the faith of their father Abraham. Hear the apostle: "For if there had been a law given which could have given life, verily righteousness should have been by the law. *But the Scriptures hath concluded all under sin that the promise by faith of Jesus Christ* MIGHT BE GIVEN TO THEM THAT BELIEVE." Such are the only heirs."

That article on "The Perpetuity of the Law of God" was concluded in No. 6 of Vol. I, and in this Elder Andrews took up the very verses that stand at the head of this present Study in Galatians, as follows:—

"Gal. 3:23-26. . . How is the law a schoolmaster to bring us to Christ? Answer: The law shows our guilt and just condemnation, and that we are lost without a Saviour. Read Paul's account of this school in Rom. 7:7-25. "By the law is the knowledge of sin." Rom. 3:20. "I had not known sin, but by the law." Rom.7:7. Then the instruction of the law is absolutely necessary, that we may know ourselves to be sinners in the sight of God. We find ourselves sinners by past offences, and unable to render present obedience. The just penalty of the law hangs over our heads; we find ourselves lost, and fly to Jesus Christ for refuge." The same thoughts were published again in Vol. II, No. 4, Sept. 16, 1851; and in Vol. III, No. 7, Aug. 5, 1852; so that it plainly stands as the original doctrine of the REVIEW AND HERALD as to the law of God in Galatians 3. And that it was sound doctrine then, and is sound doctrine now, it is certain from the fact that in the REVIEW AND HERALD of April 5, 1898, in the first page article, under the title of "The Perfect Law," the Spirit of Prophecy speaks as follows:—

"The law of God, as presented in the Scriptures, is broad in its requirements. Every principle is holy, just, and good. The law lays men under obligation to God; it reaches to the thought and feelings; and it will produce conviction of sin in every one who is sensible of having transgressed its requirements.

"In his teachings, Christ showed how far-reaching are the principles of the law spoken from Sinai. He made a living application of that law whose principles remain forever the great standard of righteousness.

"Paul's testimony of the law is: "What shall we say then? Is the law sin [the sin is in the man, not in the law]? God forbid. Nay, I had not known sin, but by the law: for I had not known lust, except the law had said, Thou shalt not covet. . . Wherefore the law is holy, the commandment holy, and just, and good.""

"There is no safety nor repose nor justification in transgression of the law. Man can not hope to stand innocent before God, and at peace with him through the merits of Christ, while he continues to sin. He must cease to transgress, and become loyal and true. As the sinner looks into the great moral looking-glass, he sees his defects of character. He sees himself just as he is, spotted, defiled, and condemned. But he knows that the law can not in any way remove the guilt, or pardon the transgressor. He must go farther than this. *The law is but the schoolmaster to bring him to Christ.* He must look to his sin-bearing

Saviour. And as Christ is revealed to him upon the cross of Calvary, dying beneath the weight of the sins of the whole world, the Holy Spirit shows him the attitude of God to all who repent of their transgressions. 'For God so loved the world, that he gave his only begotten Son, that whosoever believeth in him should not perish, but have everlasting life.'"

And all this is—*not* the *law* in Galatians, but—the *gospel* in Galatians—justification, righteousness, by faith,—the Third Angel's Message.

Galatians 3:27-29

May 1, 1900

For as many of you as have been baptized into Christ have put on Christ." The Greek word here translated "put on" expresses the thought of putting on of clothes: "to be clothed in: have on to wear." It well expresses the thought of baptism, as expressed elsewhere: of being buried, lost sight of: baptism being a burial in the water, so that the person baptized is overwhelmed, lost sight of, and shut away from the sight of the world.

Baptism *in water* is but the *form* in which is expressed the *fact* that the individual is buried, overwhelmed, clothed, and lost sight of, *in Christ;* so that instead of the old man being seen in the world and by the world, it is only *Christ* that is seen in the *baptized individual.*

The thought of this verse is expressed in another place: "As ye have therefore received Christ Jesus the Lord, so *walk ye in him."* As you have *put on* Christ, and so are *clothed* in Christ, so wear him as your clothing, that you yourself may be hidden, and only Christ appear.

This is the truth expressed in baptism. Oh, that this truth were indeed always expressed in baptism. How many realize that baptism in the water is not itself the true baptism; but is only the outward expression of that which is the true baptism? For though a person be baptized, buried, overwhelmed, and lost sight of in *the water*—if that be *all,* then it is but nothing. For baptism consists not in the putting away of the filth of the flesh, but the answer of a good conscience toward God. 1 Peter 3:21. And a good conscience is found only in "the blood of Christ, who through the eternal Spirit offered himself without spot to God." Heb. 9:14. When each soul, to be baptized in the water has already been, *by faith,* overwhelmed, clothed, and lost sight of, *in Christ,* and the baptism *in the water* is the expression of *his faith* which has *clothed him* indeed *in Christ,* then baptism will not only bear to Christians its true meaning, but will also bear to the world its true meaning.

"There is neither Jew nor Greek, there is neither bond nor free, there is neither male nor female, for ye are all one in Christ Jesus." Among those who are Christians, there are neither racial, tribal, national, nor any other distinctions, for all are one in Christ Jesus. And, whoever among those professing to be Christians, there are seen any distinctions of any kind, by that very fact it is *therein* declared that among them Christ is not truly apprehended. Accordingly, the Revised Version brings out this very thought, that among those who have been baptized into Christ, and so have put on Christ, "there *can be* neither Jew nor Greek, there *can be* neither bond nor free, there *can be* no male and female," for all are *one* in *only Christ.*

The thought is that, when the man has died, and has been buried—baptized—into Christ, overwhelmed, lost sight of, in Christ, he is forever taken away from himself, and is not himself anymore If he was an American before, he is not an American now: he is a Christian. If he was a Scythian before, he is not a Scythian now: he is a Christian. If he was an African before, he is not an African now: he is a Christian. If he was a slave before, he is not a slave now: he is a Christian. So that among those who are truly Christ's, who have put on Christ, and who are wearing Christ, all manner of racial, tribal, national, or whatsoever distinction, is utterly gone. There is no respect of persons with God, nor with those who are the children of God: it is only *character* that counts and *that* the character of Christ—the righteousness of God which is by faith of Jesus Christ.

And *thus,* "if ye be Christ's then are ye Abraham's seed, and heirs according to the promise. For the promise is only to Abraham, and *to his seed,* which is Christ. Accordingly, that promise, that inheritance, could not possibly fall to any person but to Christ. For, "he saith not, And to *seeds,* as of many; but *as of one.* And to thy *seed,* which is Christ." Then, whosoever shall not be found with Christ, so that *Christ* is the individual who is seen, can never be heir to the inheritance nor receive the promise. And wherever among professed Christians there are divisions or dissensions, the promise of the inheritance is forfeited. Because the promise is not unto *"seeds* as of *many,* but as of *one.* And to thy *seed,* which is Christ;" and *Christ* is *not divided.* He is *one,* and only those who are *one* IN HIM, can possibly receive the inheritance.

Chapter Four

Galatians 4:1-7

May 8, 1900

"Now I say, that the heir, as long as he is a child, differeth nothing from a servant, though he be lord of all; but is under tutors and governors until the time appointed of the father. Even so we, when we were children, were in bondage under the elements of the world: but when the fullness of the time was come, God sent forth his Son, made of a woman, made under the law, to redeem them that were under the law, that we might receive the adoption of sons. And because ye are sons, God hath sent forth the Spirit of his Son into your hearts crying, Abba, Father. Wherefore thou art no more a servant, but a son; and if a son, then an heir of God through Christ."

"God sent forth his Son," *"made under the law,* to redeem them that were under the *law."* As we have seen abundantly, to be under the law is to be under the dominion of sin. And such are all men of themselves, because "all have sinned, and come short of the glory of God," and "what things soever the law saith, it saith to them who are under the law: that every mouth may be stopped and all the world may become guilty before God."

Now, it is these people who are under sin: who are under the curse: who are condemned to death, because "the wages of sin is death;"—it was *them* whom God sent his son to redeem. And in order to redeem them, it behoved him to be made *in all things* "like unto his brethren, that he might be a merciful and faithful high priest in things pertaining to God, to make reconciliation for the sins of the people." Heb. 2:17. Therefore, that he might meet men just where men are and be a complete Deliverer, he himself came to men where they are, and was made like to men where they are. Therefore, he was even made to be *sin.* 2 Cor. 5:21.

He took the place of the transgressor: he became flesh, just as is the transgressor: he was made to be sin, just as the transgressor is sin: he bore the sins of men, "for the Lord hath laid on him the iniquity of us all." He took the condemnation, because the sins of the transgressor were imputed to him. And, as to the transgressor himself, the consciousness of sin is accompanied with the consciousness of guilt and condemnation; so when these sins were imputed to him who knew no sin, it was the sin indeed, with its accompanying sense of guilt and condemnation. He bore the curse, for sin brings the curse; and he bore the curse even unto death, because sin brings the curse even unto death.

Thus, "Christ hath redeemed us from the curse of the law, being made a curse for us." Thus he redeems them that are under the law. All the penalty, all the curse, all the wrath, all the condemnation, that the law can work upon the transgressor met upon him. And, in the divine sacrifice which he thus made, there was rendered all that the law can ever demand of the transgressor. So that everything that can possibly stand between the transgressor and God is swept away in the sacrifice of Christ.

In this, God has reconciled the world unto himself so completely that he can not impute their trespasses unto them (2 Cor. 5:19); and thus is extended freedom—absolute freedom—to every soul in the wide world. And every soul can have it, to the full and to all eternity, merely by accepting it. And, in accepting this redemption from under the law, every soul receives "the adoption of sons;" for, "as man as received him, to them gave he power ["the right, or privilege" margin] to become the children of God by faith in Christ Jesus." Gal. 3:26.

And then, being sons of God, and *"because* ye *are* sons, God hath sent forth the Spirit of his Son into your hearts, crying, Abba, Father. Wherefore thou art no more a servant, but a son; and if a son then an heir of God through Christ."

Before this deliverance, we "were in bondage under the elements of the world." The only elements of the world that there are, are the elements of sin; for "all that is in the world, the lust of the flesh, and the lust of the eyes, and the pride of life, is not of the Father, but is of the world." 1 John 2:16. But, when delivered into the glorious liberty of the sons of God, we "have not received the spirit of *bondage again* to fear;" but "have received the Spirit of adoption, whereby we cry, Abba, Father. The Spirit itself" bearing "witness with our spirit, that we are the children of God; and if children, then heirs; heirs of God, and joint heirs with Christ.: Rom. 8:15-17.

"Joint heirs with Christ." That is, all that he had falls also to each one of the other sons. The inheritance is not divided up in equal shares among all the sons, as if they were equal heirs. No; *all* the inheritance belongs to *each one* of the sons, because they are *joint heirs.* This because God has no favorites among his sons; but *all* that belongs to any one, belongs equally to every other one. Accordingly, all that falls to Christ the Son and heir falls also to each and every other son and heir. And this wonderful truth Jesus wants the world to know; for, in his great prayer for us all, he prayed, "That the world may know that thou has sent me and has *loved them,* as thou *has loved me."* John 17:23.

And, this wonderful fact: that God has no favorite nor preference among his sons, but that all are equal, and, therefore, that each redeemed soul is, in his estimation, equal to Jesus, and takes his stand on a plane, and in the reward, equal in all things to Christ: it is this wonderful fact that caused John, in beholding it, to exclaim: "Behold, what manner of love the Father has bestowed upon us, that we should be called the sons of God. . .

"Beloved, now are we the sons of God, and it doth not *yet appear* what we *shall be:* but we know that when he shall appear, we shall be like him; for we shall se him as he is." 1 John 3:1, 2.

Galatians 4:8-11

May 15, 1900

"Howbeit then, when ye knew not God, ye did service unto ["were in bondage to," R.V. and Greek] them which by nature are no gods. But now, after that ye have known God, or rather are known of God, how turn ye again to the weak and beggarly elements, whereunto ye desire again to be in bondage? Ye observe days, and months, and times, and years. I am afraid of you, lest I have bestowed upon you labor in vain."

The Galatians, having been Gentiles, knew not God, and, accordingly, were in bondage to them which by nature were no gods at all. To them the gospel had been preached. They had believed the gospel, and so were delivered from bondage, and had received the adoption of sons of God, and were, therefore, no more bondmen, but sons; and, being sons, were heirs of God, through Christ. But the Pharisees which believed, knowing nothing of true faith and freedom which Christ gives, had come among the Galatians, with their perverted gospel, which was not the gospel at all, had confused them, and turned them from faith to works; from the Spirit to the flesh, as the means of justification, and the hope of salvation. Gal. 3:1-3

This is certain from the very words of the text, in the inquiry; "But now, after ye have known God, or rather are known of God, how turn ye *again* to the weak and beggarly elements, whereunto ye desire *again* to be in bondage?" The apostle had just stated that before they knew God, they were in bondage unto them which by nature are no gods, and now, having been turned from God, they turned *AGAIN* to those things, and AGAIN to that bondage. And, as seen in the former lesson, these elements whereunto they were formerly in bondage, and to which they were now *AGAIN* in bondage, were "the elements of the world," and the only elements of the world are "the lust of the flesh, and the lust of the eyes, and the pride of life," the works of the flesh—in a word—are only sin.

Among these things in which they had formerly done service unto them which by nature are no gods, were the observances of certain days, and months, and times, and years, to the very things of the heathen which the Lord, even in ancient times had condemned, as it is written: "When thou art come into the land which the Lord thy God giveth thee, thou shalt not learn to do after the abominations of those nations. There shall not be found among you any one that maketh his son or his daughter to pass through the fire, or that useth divination, or an *observer of times,* or an enchanter, or a witch, or a charmer, or a consulter with familiar spirits, or a wizard, or a necromancer. For all that do these things are a abomination unto the Lord, and because of these abominations the Lord thy God doth drive them out from before thee. Thou shalt be perfect; [upright, or sincere" margin] with the Lord thy God. For these nations, which thou shalt possess, hearkened unto *observers of times,* and unto diviners; but as for thee, the Lord thy God hath not suffered thee to do so." Deut. 18:9-14.

In the Galatian backsliding some of these things had entered; for the text says: "Ye observe days, and months, and times, and years." Well enough, therefore, might Paul write, "I am afraid of you, lest I have bestowed upon you labor in vain."

The one great lesson in this particular phase of the experience of the Galatians, is that there is no power but that which is in the righteousness of God which is by faith of Jesus Christ, that can save man from the evil that is naturally in him: there is no half-way ground between the way of the Spirit and the way of the flesh. Every man is either in the freedom of the Spirit and of the righteousness of God, or else in the bondage of the flesh and of sin.

Galatians 4:12-20

May 22, 1900

"Brethren, I beseech you, be as I am; for I am as ye are: ye have not injured me at all. Ye know how through infirmity of the flesh I preached the gospel unto you at the first. And my temptation which was in my flesh ye despised

Galatians 4:12-20

not, nor rejected; but received me as an angel of God, even as Christ Jesus. Where is then the blessedness ye spake of? For I bear you record, that, if it had been possible, ye would have plucked out your own eyes, and have given them to me. Am I therefore become your enemy, because I tell you the truth? They zealously affect you, but not well; yea, they would exclude you, that ye might affect them. But it is good to be zealously affected always in a good thing, and not only when I am present with you. My little children, of whom I travail in birth again until Christ be formed in you, I desire to be present with you, and to change my voice; for I stand in doubt of you."

Where is then the blessedness ye spake of?"—not the blessedness ye *SPEAK* of; but past tense: "ye *spake* of." It was a blessedness which they had had, and had lost; and so it was no more a blessedness which ye *speak* of, but only which "ye *spake* of."

This was the blessing of Abraham—the blessedness of justification by faith; for they had received the true gospel; they had believed in Christ, and thus they knew that Christ had redeemed them from the curse of the law, that the blessing of Abraham might come on them through Jesus Christ, and that they might receive the promise of the Spirit through faith. All this they had experienced. But, by the delusions of the false gospel of "the Pharisees which believed," they had been "bewitched" and driven back from the purity of faith unto justification by works.

This is plain from Paul's appeal, in the first verses of the third chapter: "0 foolish Galatians, who hath bewitched you, that ye should not obey the truth, before whose eyes Jesus Christ hath been evidently set forth, crucified among you? This only would I learn of you, Received ye the Spirit by *the works of the law* or by the hearing *of faith?*". . . "He therefore that ministereth to you the Spirit, and worketh miracles among you, doeth he it by the *works of the law,* or by the hearing of faith?"

But "to him that *worketh* is the reward not reckoned of grace, but of debt. But to him that *worketh not* but *believeth* on him that *justifieth the ungodly,* his *faith* is counted for *righteousness.* Even as David also describeth the *blessedness* of the man, unto whom God imputeth righteousness without works, saying, Blessed are they whose iniquities are forgiven, and whose sins are covered. Blessed is the man to whom the Lord will not impute sin." Rom. 4:5-8.

This "blessedness" is the blessedness which the Galatians had known when they were Christians; but from which they had been drawn away. And now, it was only a memory: only a blessedness which they had spoken of, but which they could not, as a present thing, speak of. This, because faith, and all that is of faith, is only a living, present thing. Faith is the breath of the spiritual life; and when faith is gone, that spiritual life is gone. It must be constantly present, in constant, active motion, to avail for any soul.

This "the Pharisees which believed" did not know; for they had not true faith: they knew not what it is to live by faith. The thought that justification by faith consisted in forgiveness and justification of the sins that are past; but that, being once thus justified, they must *live* by *works*. They thought that justification is *obtained* by *faith*, but is *kept* by *works*. And into this delusion and loss of faith they had persuaded the Galatian Christians, but with the dreadful result of the loss of the blessedness of righteousness by faith, and their relapse into the darkness of heathenism—into the bondage of sin and the works of the flesh.

And that experience is illustrative of the everlasting truth,—and it is written for the instruction of all the people as to that everlasting truth,—that righteousness by faith, true justification by faith, is righteousness and justification by divine, ever-living, *present* faith, "and that not of yourselves: it is the gift of God."

While the Galatians enjoyed this blessedness, its fruit appeared in the love which they showed to Paul. This love was the very self-sacrificing love of Christ—the abundant love of God shed abroad indeed in the heart, by the Spirit which they had received. Seeing the apostle in need of eyes, they would gladly have plucked out their own and given them to him, if such a thing could have been done.

But now, what a change! From that height of blessedness they are driven back into such a condition that he is obliged to appeal to them: "Am I therefore become your enemy, because I tell you the truth?"

And this is yet the mark of the Galatian, wherever he may be—the mark of the man professing Christianity, but who is not justified by faith, who has not the righteousness of God which is by faith of Jesus Christ. Whoever tells him the truth, in that becomes his enemy, and is so counted by him. This, because he does "not obey the truth:" he is not in the way of truth; he does not know the truth. Therefore, truth can not be to him the sole standard and the supreme test: only *himself* in his own personal preferences and ambitions, and his own self-righteousness, can be the standard. And whoever tells him the truth, especially if it be unpleasant, is counted as making a personal attack on him, and is therefore counted only an enemy.

But the man who is the Christian, who is, indeed and in truth, justified by faith of Jesus Christ; who lives by the faith of Jesus Christ; who is righteous only by the faith of Christ, and the righteousness of God, which is by faith—such a one will always count as his friend, or his brother, the one who tells him the truth. However far it may show him himself to be wrong, however directly he himself may be involved, yet he will thankfully receive the truth, whatever it may be, however it may come, and by whomsoever it may be told to him. This, because the truth is his whole and his only salvation. It is the truth which makes him free. The truth is the only Way he has in which to walk. The love of the truth is his only incentive, the Spirit of truth, his only guide.

But, as we have seen, this blessed condition—this condition of "blessedness"—the Christians of Galatia had lost, and so had again become only Galatians, because they had lost true faith, had been turned from faith to works as the way of life and salvation. And this loss of true faith was the loss of the Christ within; for he dwells in the heart by faith. Eph. 3:17. And because of their forlorn condition, which they did not realize, Paul longed for them as a mother for her children; and, in the depth of his longing, expressed their deep need: "My little children, of whom I travail in birth again until *Christ be formed in you."* The Christ within is what they had lost. To the experience of Christ within they must be restored, or they were lost. And this is simply the gospel, which, in itself, is "Christ in you the hope of glory."

The Two Covenants Galatians 4:21-31

May 29, 1900

"Tell me, ye that desire to be under the law, do ye not hear the law? For it is written, that Abraham had two sons, the one by a bondmaid, the other by a free woman. But he who was of the bondwoman was born after the flesh; but he of the freewoman was by promise. Which things are an allegory, for these are the two covenants; the one from the mount Sinai, which gendereth to bondage, which is Agar. For this Agar is mount Sinai in Arabia, and answereth to Jerusalem which now is, and is in bondage with her children. But Jerusalem which is above is free, which is the mother of us all. For it is written, Rejoice, thou barren that barest not; break forth and cry, thou that travailest not: for the desolate hath many more children than she which hath an husband. Now we, brethren, as Isaac was, are the children of promise. But as then he that was born after the flesh persecuted him that was born after the Spirit, even so it is now. Nevertheless what saith the scripture? Cast out the bondwoman and her son: for the son of the bondwoman shall not be heir with the son of the freewoman. So then, brethren, we are not children of the bondwoman, but of the free."

"These are the two covenants." These *what* are the two covenants?—These two women; because since the covenant from mount Sinai is represented by Hagar, the other covenant is represented by Sarah. The Revised Version of verse 24 reads: "For these *women* are two covenants."

These two women were the mothers of the two sons of Abraham. One son was by a bondwoman: the other was by a freewoman. Hagar was the bondwoman: Sarah was the freewoman. The two sons of these two women represent the children of the two covenants.

"These are the two covenants." It is then settled that the subject of the Two Covenants began in the family of Abraham.

"These are the two covenants." Whoever, therefore, would study the Two Covenants, must study *these.*

"These are the two covenants." Any study therefore, of the Two Covenants, that is not a study of *these,* is not truly a study of the Two Covenants.

"These are the two covenants." With *these* the subject of the Two Covenants begins, and whoever would study the Two Covenants must begin where the subject begins. Therefore this is where we shall begin the study of the Two Covenants.

And that we may all begin it together to the best advantage, we ask that all will read between now and this time next week Genesis 15, 16, 17, and 21:1-21—at least seven times.

Galatians 4:21-24

June 5, 1900

"Tell me, ye that desire to be under the law, do ye not hear the law? For it is written, that Abraham had two sons, the one by a bondmaid, the other by a freewoman. But he who was of the bondwoman was born after the flesh; but he of the freewoman was by promise. Which things are an allegory: for these are the two covenants; the one from the mount Sinai, which gendereth to bondage, which is Agar."

Galatians 4:21-24

Thus the two covenants were in the family of Abraham. For "these women are two covenants." Verse 24, R.V.

But how did the two covenants get into the family of Abraham, and one of these even the covenant from Mount Sinai? "For these are the two covenants; the *one from the mount Sinai,* which gendereth to bondage, *which is Agar."*

Since Hagar is one of the two covenants,—the one from Sinai, and the one which genders to bondage,—*the story of Hagar in the family of Abraham is the story of the covenant from Sinai.*

But God had made a covenant with Abraham himself, before ever Hagar was heard of. And this covenant was confirmed in Christ, before ever any mention was made of Hagar.

This covenant was the covenant of God's promise to Abraham and to his seed—not *"seeds,* as of many: but as of *one,* and to thy seed, which is Christ." This was the covenant of God's righteousness,—the righteousness of God which is by faith,—for when God had made promise to Abraham, Abraham "believed in the Lord; and he counted it to him for righteousness."

This promise was to Abraham, that in him should "all families of the earth be blessed,—that to his seed would he give the land of promise, which is the world to come; and that his seed should be as the stars of heaven.

This seed, to whom the promise was made, being Christ, this covenant was made in Christ; and, when Abraham believed God, and it was counted to him for righteousness, this covenant was confirmed in Christ. This is, therefore, the everlasting covenant, which answers to Jerusalem which is above; for, in that covenant, because of that promise, Abraham "looked for a city which hath foundations, whose builder and maker is God."

All this came to Abraham when as yet he had no child; and the promise was to be accomplished in his seed. Several years had passed after the first mention by the Lord of Abraham's seed when as yet he had no child. Abraham was already old when the thought of his seed was first suggested, and was growing older without seeing any seed. Accordingly, he said: "Lord God, what wilt thou give me, seeing I go childless, and the steward of my house is this Eliezor of Damascus? And Abram said, Behold, to me thee hast given no seed: and, 10, one born in my house is mine heir.

"And behold, the word of the Lord came unto him saying, This shall not be thine heir, but he that shalt come forth out of thine own bowels shall be thine heir. And he brought him forth abroad and said, Look now toward heaven, and tell the stars, if thou be able to number them: and he said unto him, So shalt thy seed be. And he believed in the Lord, and he counted it to him for righteousness. And he said unto him, I am the Lord that brought thee out of Ur of the Chaldees, to give thee this land to inherit it." Gen. 15:2-7.

And when Abram asked: "Lord God, whereby shall I know that I shall inherit it?" the Lord "said unto him, Take me an heifer of three years old, and a she goat of three years old, and a ram of three years old, and a turtledove, and a young pigeon. And he took unto him all these, and divided them in the midst, and laid each piece one against another: but the birds divided he not."

Then it was that the Lord, by passing between those pieces, "made a covenant with Abraham," a blood covenant, in which he pledged himself to the fulfillment of every promise that had yet been made to Abraham.

Here, then, was God's own heavenly, everlasting covenant, made and confirmed with Abraham, with God's own life pledged that everything promised should be accomplished, so that nothing promised could any more fail than that the Lord should cease to exist.

But still the time passed, and no child was seen; for "Sarai Abram's wife bare him no children." But Sarai "had an handmaid, an Egyptian whose name was Hagar. And Sarai said unto Abram, Behold now, the Lord hath restrained me from bearing: I pray thee, go in unto my maid; it may be that I may obtain children by her." Gen. 16:1,2. Thus Hagar comes upon the scene, and is brought into the story.

But how was it that Hagar was brought into the story at all? Was it by trusting the promise of God?—No. It was altogether because of distrust. Was it by faith?—No. It was altogether because of unbelief. This is confirmed by the fact that when this part of the program had all been carried through, it all had to be repudiated, and the promised seed had still to be expected by *Sarah herself,* and "through *faith* also *Sarah herself* received strength to conceive seed, and was delivered of a child when she was past age, *because she judged him faithful who had promised."* Heb. 11:11.

This being so *at the last,* why was it, then, *AT THE FIRST,* that "Sarai Abram's wife bare him no children"?—It was simply because of her *unbelief,* and her *not judging* "him faithful who had promised."

Then it was that, in this distrust of God, this unbelief, *Sarai invented the scheme which brought in Hagar.* And this scheme, springing from distrust of God, and unbelief in him, was altogether a scheme of the natural mind—an invention of the flesh—*to fulfill the promise of God.*

The important consideration in this scheme of Sarai's, is that it was to *fulfill the promise of God.* The thought was not merely that the Lord had not fulfilled his promise; but that he had *refused* to fulfill it. For Sarai said plainly,

"Behold now, the Lord hath *restrained* me from bearing." This straightly charged unfaithfulness on the part of the Lord. And since it was held that the Lord had failed to fulfill his promise, it was naturally concluded that they were to fulfill it themselves, by an invention altogether of their own, springing from distrust and unbelief in God.

And even Abram swerved from his trust in God, from his faith in the Lord's promise. Abram fell in with this scheme of distrust and unbelief, this invention of the flesh. "Abram hearkened to the voice of Sarai."

"And Sarai, Abram's wife, took Hagar her maid the Egyptian, after Abram had dwelt ten years in the land of Canaan, and gave her to her husband Abram to be his wife. And he went in unto Hagar, and she conceived." "And Hagar bare Abram a son." Gen. 16:3, 4, 15.

"But he who was of the bondwoman was born *after* THE FLESH." How could he be born of anything else? The whole scheme by which he was ever born at all, was altogether of the natural mind, in distrust and unbelief of God,—an invention of the flesh.

"Which things are an allegory: for *these are the two covenants;* the one from the mount Sinai. which gendereth to bondage, which is Agar. For this Agar is Mount Sinai in Arabia."

The covenant, therefore, for which Hagar stands,—the covenant from Mount Sinai,—is a covenant in which people, in distrust of God and unbelief of his promise, knowing only the natural man and the birth of the flesh, seek by their own inventions, and their own efforts, to attain to the righteousness of God, and to the inheritance which attaches to that righteousness.

But the righteousness of God, with the accompanying inheritance in all its fullness, is a free gift.

Galatians 4:21-25

June 12, 1900

"Tell me, ye that desire to be under the law, do ye not hear the law? For it is written, that Abraham had two sons, the one by a bondmaid, the other by a free woman. But he who was of the bondwoman was born after the flesh; but he of the free woman was by promise. Which things are an allegory: for these are the two covenants; the one from the Mount Sinai, which gendereth to bondage, which is Agar. For this Agar is Mount Sinai in Arabia."

Hagar represents the covenant from Sinai. Hagar was a bondwoman, and an Egyptian. Her Son, therefore, was a bondson. He was a bondson, by whatsoever means he might have been born: because his mother was a bondwoman.

As we have seen, the means by which Hagar's son was born was altogether out of distrust of God and of unbelief in his promise—was only a scheme of the flesh; and, therefore, "he who was of the bondwoman was born after the flesh." But, "The minding of the flesh, the carnal mind, is enmity against God: for it is not subject to the law of God, neither indeed can be. So then they that are in the flesh can not please God." Rom. 8:7, 8, margin.

Accordingly, the covenant for which Hagar stands—the covenant from Mount Sinai—is a covenant in which people, knowing only the natural man and the birth of the flesh, seek, by their own inventions and their own efforts, to attain to the righteousness of God, and to the inheritance which attaches to that righteousness. This, because, as we have also seen, Sarai and Abram had the fullness of the promise of God, and of his righteousness, in *God's covenant* confirmed *in Christ,* before ever the scheme concerning Hagar was invented. And this scheme was invented, and could be invented, only by forsaking that promise and covenant. And to forsake that promise and covenant was to trust only in the flesh.

Did, then, the people at Sinai have any promise of God, or any covenant, in which they could trust, *before they entered into the covenant of Sinai?*— *They had.* They had *the Abrahamic covenant,* exactly as had Abram and Sarai before they entered into the scheme which brought in Hagar.

Not simply did they have this covenant with Abraham, as a far-distant thing, bedimmed by the lapse of time between Abraham and them: but they had it *repeated to them,* directly by the Lord, and *made with them,* as with Abraham; and all this *before they ever left Egypt* at all. Read, "And God spake unto Moses, and said unto him, I am the Lord: and I appeared unto Abraham, unto Isaac, and unto Jacob, by the name of God Almighty, but by my name *JEHOVAH* was I not known to them. And I have also *established my covenant with them,* TO GIVE THEM THE LAND OF CANAAN, the land of their pilgrimage, wherein they were strangers. And I have also heard the groaning of the children of Israel, whom the Egyptians keep in bondage; and *I have REMEMBERED MY COVENANT.*

"Wherefore say unto the children of Israel, *I am the Lord,* and I will bring you out from under the burdens of the Egyptians, and I will rid you out of their bondage, and I will redeem you with a stretched out arm, and with great

Galatians 4:21-25

judgments: and *I WILL TAKE YOU TO ME FOR A PEOPLE,* and *I WILL BE TO YOU A GOD,* which bringeth you out from under the burdens of the Egyptian, and *I will bring you in unto the land,* concerning the which *I DID SWEAR* ("lift up my hand," margin) *to give it to Abraham, to Isaac, and to Jacob;* and *I WILL GIVE IT TO YOU FOR AN HERITAGE; I am the Lord."* Ex. 6:2-8.

Here was given to the children of Israel, in Egypt, all that was ever given to Abraham, to Isaac, and to Jacob. The same covenant precisely that was "made with Abraham, and his oath unto Isaac," and which was "confirmed" unto Jacob, *was made with Israel,* WHILE THEY WERE YET IN EGYPT, when God came down to deliver them from Egypt.

How, then, could it come about that Israel must enter into a covenant at Sinai?—Just as the scheme concerning Hagar had come about. How could another covenant be brought in at all?—Just as Hagar was brought in— altogether because of distrust of God's covenant; altogether because of unbelief of the promise of God confirmed by his oath. For if they had trusted the promises of God which he had made to them in Egypt, they would have had all that Abraham or any other person ever could have, they would have had the righteousness of God, his everlasting salvation, and the inheritance promised to Abraham: and *this* ALL IN CHRIST; for this is how Abraham had it.

True, they had sung the song of triumphant faith at the Red Sea, after crossing; and *if they had continued in this faith,* they would have *continued in God's everlasting covenant* which he *gave them in Egypt:* and there *never would have been any covenant at Sinai.*

But they *did not continue in that faith;* for immediately afterward, when in their journey they came to Marah, they murmured against the Lord. And when the Lord had delivered them from their fears of that place, and they came into the Wilderness of Sin, "the whole congregation of the children of Israel murmured" again. "And the children of Israel said unto them (Moses and Aaron), Would to God we had died by the hand of the Lord in the land of Egypt, when we sat by the fleshpots, and when we did eat bread to the full: for ye have brought us forth into this wilderness, to kill this whole assembly with hunger." Ex. 17:3. And when the Lord had delivered them from their fears that time, and they had left the Wilderness of Sin, and had come to Rephidim, again they murmured, and said: "Wherefore is this that thou hast brought us up out of Egypt, to kill us and our children and our cattle with thirst? And Moses cried unto the Lord, saying, What shall I do unto this people?"

All this shows confirmed distrust of God, and unbelief of him, on the part of Israel. And this distrust and unbelief *hid from them the blessings and the power given to them in the covenant with Abraham. which God had given to them when they were in Egypt.*

They could not *trust God* for the *inheritance* to which they were coming, not for *the righteousness* which alone would entitle them to that inheritance. This they thought that they themselves could earn. And, that they might see how far short of earning it they would come, the Lord gave to them the widest possible opportunity to try. Accordingly, he said: "Ye have seen what I did unto the Egyptians, and how I bore you on eagles' wings, and brought you unto myself. Now therefore, if *ye will obey my voice INDEED, and keep my covenant, THEN* ye shall be a peculiar treasure unto me above all people; for *all the earth is mine;* and ye shall be unto me a kingdom of priests, and an holy nation. (*"So shall ye be my people, and I will be your God."* Jer. 11:4.) These are the words which thou shalt speak unto the children of Israel.

"And Moses came and called for the elders of the people, and laid before their faces all these words which the Lord commanded him. And *all the people answered together,* and said, *all that the Lord hath spoken we will do.* And Moses returned the words of the people unto the Lord." Ex. 19:4-6.

They had not yet heard his voice; but, when they did hear it, the ten commandments were spoken. And so they had agreed to obey the ten commandments indeed. And, even after they had heard his voice in such majesty that they feared and "removed and stood afar off," they declared, *"All that the Lord hath said will we do,* and he *obedient."* Ex. 24:7.

But they corresponded to the child of Hagar the bondwoman, who "was *born after the flesh."* They knew only the birth of the flesh; and so had only the mind of the flesh, which "is enmity against God: for it is not subject to the law of God, neither indeed can be;" and they could no more obey that law "indeed" than Ishmael, the child of the flesh in the family of Abraham, could fulfill the promise to Abraham. In that condition they could no more keep God's covenant than the scheme of Sarai in bringing in Hagar was the keeping of that covenant.

How, then, could such a covenant ever be brought in? Why did they enter into such a covenant?—"They had no true conception of the holiness of God, of the exceeding sinfulness of their own hearts, *their utter inability,* IN THEMSELVES, *to render obedience to God's law,* and their need of a Saviour. All this they must be taught. . . The people *did not realize* THE SINFULNESS OF THEIR OWN HEARTS, and *that without Christ it was impossible for them to keep God's law; AND THEY READILY ENTERED*

INTO COVENANT WITH GOD. Feeling that they were *able to establish THEIR OWN RIGHTEOUSNESS, they declared,* 'All that the Lord hath said will we do, and be obedient.'"—*Patriarchs and Prophets,* pages 371, 372.

They were already in the bondage of sin and self-righteousness; and *in that bondage,* with minds "not subject to the law of God," and which indeed could not be, they *promised* to obey the law of God *"indeed."* But in the condition in which they were, it was inevitable that they would *break their promise:* they simply could not keep their promise. It was not in them to do it. Thus, in *that covenant,* they were *breakers of the law,* and BREAKERS OF THEIR PROMISE *not to break the law.*

And this is all that they *could be,* in that covenant, or by virtue of anything in that covenant. Accordingly that *covenant, AS HAGAR, gendered,* and *could* gender, *only to bondage.* And this, all simply because of *their distrust of God* and *their unbelief of his promise* as revealed *in the covenant with Abraham,* which covenant *was given to them directly,* before they ever started from Egypt at all.

"These are the two covenants; the one from Mount Sinai, which gendereth to bondage, which is Agar. For this Agar is Mount Sinai in Arabia, and answereth to Jerusalem which now is, and is in bondage with her children. *But Jerusalem which is above IS FREE, which is the mother of us all.* . . NOW WE, brethren, *as Isaac was, are the children of promise."*

Galatians 4:21-25

June 19, 1900

"Tell me, ye that desire to be under the law, do ye not hear the law? For it is written, that Abraham had two sons, the one by a bondmaid, the other by a free woman. But he who was of the bondwoman was born after the flesh; but he of the free woman was by promise. Which things are an allegory: for these are the two covenants."

Ishmael was the son of Abraham, born after the flesh. And what was his disposition? Before he was born the Lord described it: "He will be a wild ass man." The Revised Version translates it: "He shall be as a wild ass among men." "His hand will be against every man, and every man's hand against him."

Remember that this child of Hagar, this son that was born after the flesh, this "wild ass among men," was the fruit of the invention of Sarai's, which sprang from her distrust of God and unbelief of his promise to give a son. Accordingly, bear in mind that this son was intended by Sarai to fulfill the promise of God. It was really intended, and even expected by Sarai, and even by Abraham, that this child of the flesh, this wild man, should be accepted by the Lord as the son whom he intended in his promise; and that the promises to Abraham should be fulfilled in him. This is certain, by the fact that, afterward, when the Lord told Abraham that he would give him a son by Sarai, Abraham answered; "O that Ishmael might live before thee!"

Now remember that Hagar, the mother of this "wild ass man," represents the covenant from Sinai; and her son, who was born after the flesh,—this wild man,—represents the children of that covenant from Sinai. And just as, in the invention which brought forth Ishmael, it was intended that he should fulfill the promise of God, and that the Lord's covenant with Abraham should be fulfilled through him, so these children of the covenant at Sinai, like Ishmael, born after the flesh, expected that they could fulfill the promise of God, and that the Lord's covenant with Abraham should be accomplished in its fullness through them; that is, through the flesh.

But Abraham kept the commandments of God. The righteousness of God is an essential part of the covenant with Abraham; for, without it, no one can attain unto the inheritance given to Abraham in the covenant. But how would Ishmael, born after the flesh, keep the commandments of God, when the minding of the flesh is only enmity against God, and is not subject to the law of God, and neither indeed can be? How could that wild ass man keep the commandments of God, with his hand against every man, when one of the two principles of the whole law of God is, "Thou shalt love thy neighbor as thyself"?

And this child of Hagar the bondwoman corresponds to the children of that covenant at Sinai, which gendereth to bondage. As Ishmael, they know only the birth of the flesh, and only "the minding of the flesh," which is enmity against God, and is not subject to the law of God, neither indeed can be, they covenanted to keep the law of God *"indeed"!*

But Ishmael was not the son intended by the Lord: he could not fulfill the promise of God, nor could the promise of God be fulfilled in him. So far as God's promise was concerned, and God's covenant with Abraham, Ishmael's birth was no more than as if he had never been born at all.

Accordingly, when Abraham said to the Lord: "O that Ishmael might live before thee!" "God said, Nay, but Sarah thy wife shall bear thee a son; and thou shalt call his name Isaac: and *I will establish my covenant with him* for

Galatians 4:21-25

an *everlasting covenant* for *his seed* after *him.* And as for Ishmael, I have heard thee: behold, I have blessed him, and will make him fruitful, and will multiply him exceedingly; twelve princes shall he beget, and I will make him a great nation. *But my covenant will I establish with Isaac,* which Sarah shall bear unto thee at this set time in the next year." Gen. 18:19-21, R.V.

At this time Sarai had become a believer in God's promise, and trusted God alone, and the Lord had changed her name to Sarah. And so, "through *faith* Sarah *herself* received strength to conceive seed;" and according to the promise Isaac was born.

Now what was Isaac's disposition?—It is illustrated in his conduct at the time that Abraham and he supposed that he was to be offered as a sacrifice. He submitted, as a lamb, to be offered. It is further illustrated in the record in Genesis 26: After Abraham had died, and Isaac was the heir of the covenant, he dwelt for a time in the land where the Philistines were. "Now all the wells which his father's servants had digged in the days of Abraham his father, the Philistines had stopped them, and filled them with earth. And Abimelech said unto Isaac, Go from us; for thou art much mightier than we. And Isaac departed thence, and encamped in the valley of Gerar, and dwelt there.

"And Isaac digged again the wells of water, which they had digged in the days of Abraham his father, for the Philistines had stopped them after the death of Abraham: and he called their names after the names by which his father had called them. And Isaac's servants digged in the valley, and found there a well of springing water." Gen. 26:15-19, R.V.

These wells were doubly Isaac's. Abraham had digged them, and they therefore belonged to Abraham. And when Isaac became heir of Abraham, these wells became his by inheritance. And now he had digged them again, which was the same as if he had digged them new. Thus they were doubly his. Yet by even more than this they were his, because the Philistines, when the wells were open, had filled them with earth, showing in the strongest possible way that they did not wish them at all.

Yet the Philistines come now to Isaac, and say of the wells which he had opened, and which, by such full right, were his: "The water is ours." Verse 20. Isaac let them have it. But what would Ishmael have done? And what would *you* do? Which of the "two sons" of Abraham are you? "These are the two covenants." Of which covenant are you?

Isaac "digged another well," and the Philistines "strove for that also." But Isaac, instead of striving with them for this, which was by such large right altogether his own, "removed from thence, and digged another well."

131

But what would Ishmael have done? And what would *you* do? Which of the "two sons" of Abraham are you? "These are the two covenants." Of which covenant are you?

When Isaac had digged this last well, for it the Philistines "strove not: and he called the name of it Rehoboth: and he said, *For now the Lord* hath *made room for us,* and we shall be fruitful in the land." Verse 22.

But how was it that the Lord made room for him?—Simply by Isaac's refusal to strive with the Philistines, by his yielding to them all that they claimed, even when it was his by every possible right. But could *the Lord* have ever "made room" for Ishmael and those Philistines? Does the Lord "make room" for *you* and the envious opposers? Which of the "two sons" of Abraham are you? "These are the two covenants." Of which covenant are you?

"And he went up from thence to Beer-sheba. And the Lord *appeared unto him the same night,* and said, I am the God of Abraham thy father; fear not, *for I am with thee,* and will bless thee, and multiply thy seed for my servant Abraham's sake. And he builded an altar there, and called upon the name of the Lord, and pitched his tent there; and there Isaac's servants digged a well."

"Then Abimelec went to him from Gerar, and Ahuzzath one of his friends, and Phicol the chief captain of his army. And Isaac said unto them, Wherefore come ye to me, seeing ye hate me, and have sent me away from you? And they said, *We saw certainly* that *the Lord was with thee. . . Thou art now the blessed of the Lord."* Verses 28-29. But it was only by Isaac's continual yielding before them that they ever had any opportunity to see that the Lord was with him, and that he was the blessed of the Lord. But what would Ishmael have done? And what would you do? What *do you do?* Which of the "two sons" of Abraham are you? *"These* are the two covenants." Of which covenant are you?

And so "it is written that Abraham had two sons, the one by a bondmaid, the other by a free woman. But he who was of the bondwoman was born after the flesh; but he of the free woman was by promise. *Which things are an allegory;* for *these are the* TWO COVENANTS: the one from the Mount Sinai, which gendereth to bondage, which is Agar. For this Agar is Mount Sinai, and answereth to Jerusalem which now is, and is in bondage with her children. But Jerusalem which is above is free, which is the mother of us all." "Now WE, brethren, *as Isaac was,* are the children of promise." Are you?

The Epistle To The Galatians

June 26, 1900

Sabbath, July 7, begins in all Sabbath-schools the study of the book of Galatians. The following article, contributed by Brother L. A. Reed, will be so helpful to all, as preliminary, that we lay over for this week the *regular* "Study in Galatians: the Two Covenants," to give place to this article.

[*Compiler's note: I believe that what Brother Reed had to say will also be helpful to us as we continue on with A. T. Jones in his studies in Galatians, so I have chose to include it here*]

A great deal of interest just now centers in the book of Galatians. It is to be the subject of study for six months now in our Sabbath schools everywhere.

We know that the epistles of Paul were addressed respectively to certain companies or individuals at given times in the early history of the Christian church. They were written to correct certain errors that had sprung up at that time. And as is always true, these errors took on certain *forms* due to the education and customs of the times.

Thus the disciples of Christ in Galatia were told by some that it was not enough to receive the gospel, which is the "law of the Spirit of life in Christ Jesus," or the "power of God unto salvation," but that they must also perform certain ceremonies. There had been a time when these ceremonies were intended for performance; but that day was now past. But the fact that these rites were no longer in force did not affect *the principle* which Paul outlines. Even in the days when these ceremonies were in force, the *mere performance* of them could not, and was not intended to, make the doers thereof righteous. And what Paul attempts to show is that *at no time* could righteousness so come. And if these rites, when in force, would not make the doers thereof righteous, how much more shall they not when abrogated?

These ceremonies we all now acknowledge are of no binding force. There is therefore no danger now that any man will declare obedience to *them* necessary. And if men are now liable to make a mistake similar to that of the Galatians, it is manifest that this latter-day mistake must take on a *form* different from that made back there. In other words, the law of circumcision, animal sacrifices, etc., is now a dead letter, and ceremonialism of *that form* is no longer threatening any man's welfare. And if God, in the message to the Galatians, is referring *only* to the ceremonial law, and ceremonialism of the *particular form,* then—I say it without qualification—all that message of God has become dead, and is of no value only as a record of the mistakes of those of old.

But ceremonialism of *that particular form* is not the only ceremonialism mentioned in Galatians. There is a ceremonialism which any man in any age of this world may drop into. And as God's word is directed to every man and any man, in every age and any age, *that* ceremonialism is the *mistake* which *now you and I* are warned against. And as the things which concern you and me are of more importance to you and me than that which more truly concerns others in some other age, it follows that this *other ceremonialism* which we may drop into in *these* days is of greater interest to us, and should be the burden of our thought and study, rather than that which almost wholly concerned others in another age of the world now long gone by.

But what is ceremonialism?—It is to *think* that a man is justified by the works of the law; and not to *know* "that a man is *not* justified by the works of the law, but by *the faith of Jesus Christ.*" Gal. 2:16,21; 3:5-14, 18-27. Almost every verse in the third chapter is but a declaration, variously made, of this one principle,—not by the works of the law, but by the faith of Christ.

There was a law called the ceremonial law; it was the law of circumcision, sacrifices, etc. It was given for a good and sufficient purpose; but it was never given with any idea that by observance of it righteousness could be won. And he who lost sight of its true import, and attempted to use it as a means of earning righteousness, dropped into mere ceremonialism, into performing a dry round of ceremony. He began to live a Christless life; he fell from grace, fell under the curse.

There is another law—called the law of ten commandments. It was not given from Sinai with the idea that by observance of its precepts any man could win righteousness. He who thus lost sight of its true import, and attempted to use it as a means of earning righteousness, also dropped into mere ceremonialism. He began thereby the performance of a dry round of ceremony, of outward forms. His life at once became Christless, because he chose a way of salvation other than Christ. But Christ is *"the* Way;" and there is no other name under heaven given among men whereby we must be saved. Such a man falls from grace, falls under the curse.

There was yet a manifestation of the law, other than the form given in the commandments; namely, the law of love. But he who takes even *that* manifestation of the law, that outward expression of the law,—love to God and love to man,—and attempts *by his own efforts* to live it out; that is, to earn righteousness by its works,—that man, like the others, drops into

The Epistle To The Galatians

ceremonialism; possibly of another form, but nevertheless ceremonialism. He loses the *true import* of the law of love, falls from grace, and lives a Christless life.

There was still another manifestation of the law, a clearer presentation of its claims, in the "law of the Spirit of life *in Christ Jesus.*" But the man who reads of the working of that law *in Christ,* and then by a *copying* of those *acts* of Christ attempts to earn righteousness, to *make himself* like Christ,—the man does not know the true import of the Christ life. He, too, has dropped into ceremonialism, dry routine, *dead* works, yea, Christlessness.

Furthermore, *ceremonialism* in *any* of its *forms* must have to do with the "ten commandment law of God." This is true of that form of ceremonialism which takes its root in a *misapprehension* of the ceremonial law. He who so misread God's purpose relative to the ceremonial law, must misread his purpose relative to the moral law. The constitution of the mind itself would produce this. And the fact that the ceremonial law of sacrifices and offerings was but a form of the gospel for the time then present, and therefore was a preaching of the moral law, would also bring it about. And the ceremonialism of the Jews not only in the things of the law of sacrifices, but in the things of the moral law, testifies that the two forms of ceremonialism go hand in hand. He who made the one mistake made the other.

When God indicted the book of Galatians, he did not strike at a few particular *forms* of error, but at the *great principle* which was at the bottom of that error. The error might take on many forms; a form at one time giving way to another form at a later time. A word directed merely at one form, must go out of date when that particular form vanished; but a word directed at the *principle* underlying the various forms, and aimed to destroy the principle that gave rise to them,—that word, I repeat, must forever be needed, so long as human hearts and minds are liable to misapply the principle, and thus create these various forms.

What, then is *now* the message of the book of Galatians?—It is, as we have said, to show that righteousness is a gift of God; that it comes by promise; and that it is by faith in Christ; and that it is not by the works of the law; "for by the works of the law shall no flesh be justified." Gal. 2:16.

And what is the ceremonialism which in the book of Galatians *you and I* are warned against? Is it not that ceremonialism which now is the only ceremonialism possible for us to drop into—that ceremonialism which is an outward conformity, or attempted outward conformity, to the ten commandment law, and especially to the fourth commandment of that law?—Yes, such are the works of the law which *you and I* are apt to trust to; and so the message of the Galatian epistle *now* is relative to the ten commandments, and even the fourth of the ten, or any one of the ten, or all of the ten. It can mean nothing else *to us now;* and whatever more it may have included, only lends force to this other *one warning* not to trust in attempts to outwardly keep that law.

If you will, in the light of these things, open your Bible with a prayerful heart, and read, not having in your mind those who lived two thousand years ago, but having only your own case in mind, and your own soul in the judgment balance,—I say, if you will so read, having in mind only your mistakes and liabilities to mistakes, and your own responsibility to God, I will trust your conclusions as to what law God's Spirit reads to you out of Gal. 3:19, or any other part of the epistle.

Galatians 4:21-31

July 3, 1900

"Tell me, ye that desire to be under the law, do ye not hear the law? For it is written, that Abraham had two sons, the one by a bondmaid, the other by a free woman. But he who was of the bondwoman was born after the flesh; but he of the free woman was by promise. Which things are an allegory: for these are the two covenants; the one from the Mount Sinai, which gendereth to bondage, which is Agar. For this Agar is Mount Sinai in Arabia, and answereth to Jerusalem which now is, and is in bondage with her children. But Jerusalem which is above is free, which is the mother of us all. For it is written, Rejoice, thou barren that bearest not; break forth and cry, thou that travailest not: for the desolate hath many more children than she which hath an husband. Now we, brethren, as Isaac was, are the children of promise. But as then he that was born after the flesh persecuted him that was born after the Spirit, even so it is now. Nevertheless what saith the scripture? *Cast out the bondwoman and her son:* for the son of the bondwoman shall not be heir with the son of the free woman. So then, brethren, we are not children of the bondwoman, but of the free."

The scheme invented by Sarai, and agreed to by Abram, which brought forth Ishmael, the son of the bondwoman, who was born after the flesh, proved unsatisfactory to the whole company, from the first step taken toward carrying it out.

"Sarai Abram's wife took Hagar her maid the Egyptian, after Abram had

Galatians 4:21-31

dwelt ten years in the land of Canaan, and gave here to her husband Abram to be his wife, And he went in unto Hagar, and she conceived: and when she saw that she conceived, *her mistress was despised in her eyes."* Gen. 16:3, 4. And although, as the record says, Sarai was the first to propose this plan, and that *"Sarai. . . took Hagar* her maid the Egyptian,. . . and *gave her* to her husband Abram to be his wife," yet, as soon as she found herself despised by Hagar, and this *because of the success of Sarai's* own plan, she turned in reproach upon Abram, and said: "My wrong be upon thee: I have given my maid into thy bosom; and when she saw that she had conceived I was despised in her eyes." Verse 5.

"But Abram said unto Sarai, Behold, thy maid is in thy hand; do to her as it pleaseth thee." And Sarai dealt so "hardly with her" that Hagar ran away. And though the Lord told Hagar, "Return to thy mistress, and submit thyself under her hands," it is evident that all was not peaceful and pleasant afterward.

Further, as we have seen, when, after Ishmael was born, Abram said to the Lord, "0 that Ishmael might live before thee!" he was not heard; but Ishmael was plainly set aside, and Abram was told that Sarai his wife should bear him a son indeed, and that he should call his name Isaac; "and I will establish my covenant with him for an everlasting covenant, and with his seed after him." Gen. 17:18, 19.

"Sarah conceived, and bare Abraham a son in his old age, at the set time of which God had spoken to him." "And the child grew, and was weaned; and Abraham made a great feast the same day that Isaac was weaned. And Sarah saw the son of Hagar the Egyptian, which she had borne unto Abraham, mocking. Wherefore she said unto Abraham, Cast out this bondwoman and her son: for the son of this bondwoman shall not be heir with my son, even with Isaac. *And the thing was very grievous in Abraham's sight* because of his son. And God said unto Abraham, *Let this not be grievous in thy sight because of the lad* and *because of thy bondwoman;* in all that Sarah hath said unto thee, hearken unto her voice; for in Isaac shall thy seed be called." Gen. 21:2, 8-12.

But not yet was the record clear. Abraham had swerved from the clear promise of God. and had put dependence in the flesh; and not only must the bondwoman and her son be cast out, but every item of that whole scheme which had brought in the bondwoman and her son must be utterly renounced and abandoned. Accordingly, the Lord said to Abraham: "Take now thy son, thine only son Isaac, whom thou lovest, and get thee into the land of Moriah; and offer him there for a brunt offering upon one of the mountains which I will tell thee of." Gen. 22:2.

Isaac was the child of promise. There was no other promise of a child, there could be no other such promise; and there could be no other child without another promise. And now for Abraham to offer Isaac for a burnt offering was, so far as could be seen, to take away all that had been promised. But when Abraham had looked thus far, he looked yet further, even back to the original promise of God, and trusted and expected that when he should offer Isaac, God would certainly fulfill his promise by raising him from the dead—by bringing him back from the ashes when he should have been burned in sacrifice.

This call of the Lord, therefore, to Abraham to offer Isaac for a burnt offering, brought Abraham back to the *night of the original promise,* when God had said to him: "Look now toward heaven, and tell the stars, if thou be able to number them: and he said unto him. So shall thy seed be. And he believed in the Lord; and he counted it to him for righteousness." Gen. 15:5, 6.

Thus Abraham was brought to depend upon and trust in the naked promise of God alone, for all that the promise contained. And if Abraham had stood there from the first and refused Sarai's suggestion with regard to Hagar, there would have been no such family trouble as came between Sarai and Hagar; Ishmael never would have been born; and Abraham would *never have been called to offer Isaac* Had he from the first "staggered not at the promise of God through unbelief" (Rom. 4:20), but been strong in faith, giving glory to God, fully persuaded that what he had promised he was able also to perform, righteousness might have been imputed to him throughout.

"These are the two covenants; the one from the Mount Sinai, which gendereth to bondage, which is Agar." The covenant at Sinai was the fruit of the flesh, of distrust and unbelief in God, just as was the plan that introduced Hagar and brought forth Ishmael. And just as Hagar and Ishmael, the bondwoman and her son, had to be cast out, and the whole scheme that brought them in had to be utterly repudiated, *so the covenant from Mount Sinai had to be cast out,* and all that brought it in had to be utterly repudiated.

As Abraham and Sarah had to cast out Hagar and Ishmael, and repudiate the whole scheme that had brought them in, and themselves come back to the original promise of God, to depend wholly upon that for all that was in it, so must the covenant from Sinai be cast out, and all that brought it in must be utterly repudiated by Israel and everybody else, and God's original covenant with Abraham be depended upon and trusted in, wholly and alone, for all that it promises. And so we read:

In delivering them from Egypt, God sought to reveal to them his power and his mercy, that they might be led to love and trust him. He brought them down to the Red Sea—where, pursued by the Egyptians, escape seemed impossible—that they might realize their utter helplessness, their need of divine aid; and then he wrought deliverance for them. Thus they were filled with love and gratitude to God, and with confidence in his power to help them. He had bound them to himself, as their deliverer from temporal bondage.

But there was still greater truth to be impressed upon their minds. Living in the midst of idolatry and corruption, *they had no true conception of the holiness of God; of the exceeding sinfulness of their own hearts;* their utter inability, *in themselves,* to render obedience to God's law; and *their need of a Saviour. All this they must be taught.*

God brought them to Sinai; he manifested his glory; he gave them his law, with the promise of great blessings *on condition of obedience:* "If ye will obey my voice indeed, and keep my covenant, then. . . ye shall be unto me a kingdom of priests, and an holy nation." Ex. 19:5, 6. The people *did not realize* the sinfulness of their own hearts, *and that without Christ* it was impossible for them to keep God's law; *and they readily entered into covenant* with God. FEELING THAT THEY WERE ABLE TO ESTABLISH THEIR OWN RIGHTEOUSNESS, *they declared,* "All that the Lord hath said will we do, and be obedient." Ex. 24:7.

They had witnessed the proclamation of the law in awful majesty, and had trembled with terror before the mount; and yet only a few weeks passed before *they broke their covenant with God,* and bowed down to worship a graven image. They *could not hope for the favor of God through a covenant which they had broken,* and *NOW, seeing their sinfulness and their need of pardon, they were brought to feel* THEIR NEED OF THE SAVIOUR *REVEALED IN THE ABRAHAMIC COVENANT, and shadowed forth in the sacrificial offerings. NOW* by *faith* and *love* they were bound to God as their *deliverer from the bondage of sin. NOW* they were *prepared to appreciate the blessings of THE NEW COVENANT.—Patriarchs and Prophets,* pages 371, 372.

Galatians 4:21-24

July 10, 1900

"Tell me, ye that desire to be under the law, do ye not hear the law? For it is written, that Abraham had two sons, the one by a bondmaid, the other by a free woman. But he who was of the bondwoman was born after the flesh; but he of the free woman was by promise. Which things are an allegory: for these are the two covenants: the one from the Mount Sinai, which gendereth to bondage, which is Agar."

The covenant from Mount Sinai is the covenant that God made with the children of Israel when he took them by the hand to lead them out of Egypt.

That covenant was *faulty*. "For if that first covenant had been *faultless*, then should no place have been sought for the second." Heb. 8:7.

That covenant was faulty in *the promises:* for the second covenant is "a better covenant" than that, in that it "was established upon better promises." Heb. 8:6.

The fault in that covenant was primarily, in *the people*. "For finding fault *with them,* he saith, Behold the days come, saith the Lord, when I will make a new covenant." Heb. 8:8.

Therefore, since the fault of that covenant was in *its promises,* and the fault was primarily in *the people* themselves, it follows that the promises upon which that covenant was established were primarily the promises of the *people.*

What, then, were these promises?—They are in the covenant which was made with them when they came forth out of Egypt, and here is that covenant:—

"Ye have seen what I did unto the Egyptians, and how I bare you on eagles' wings, and brought you unto myself. *Now therefore,* if ye will obey my voice indeed, and keep my covenant, *then* ye shall be a peculiar treasure unto me above all people: for all the earth is mine: and ye shall be unto me a kingdom of priests, and an holy nation." "And all the people answered together, and said, All that the Lord hath spoken we will do." Ex. 19:4-6, 8.

In this agreement, all the people *promised* to obey the voice of the Lord. They had not yet heard what that voice would speak. But in the twentieth chapter, they heard that voice speaking the words of the *ten commandments,* to which, when the Lord had spoken, "he added no more." And when they had heard this, they solemnly renewed their promise" "All that the Lord hath said will we do and be obedient."

That this is the covenant that the Lord made with them when he took them by the hand to bring them out of Egypt, is made certain by the following words:—"For I spake not unto your fathers, nor commanded them in the day that I brought them out of the land of Egypt, concerning burnt offerings or sacrifices; but this thing commanded I them, saying, *Obey my voice,* AND *I will be your God, and ye shall be my people:* and walk ye in all the ways that I have commanded you, that it may be well unto you." Jer. 7:22, 23.

And this certainly is confirmed in the following words: "Thus saith the

Lord God of Israel: Cursed be the man that obeyeth not the words of this covenant, which I commanded your fathers in the day that I brought them forth out of the land of Egypt, from the iron furnace, saying, *Obey my voice,* and do them, according to all which I command you; *so shall ye be my people and I will be your God."* Jer. 11:3, 4.

Note carefully each of these three statements of the covenant, and see how the promises lie. The first one runs, on the part of the Lord: "If ye will obey my voice indeed, and keep my covenant, *THEN*... ye shall be unto me a kingdom of priests and an holy nation," etc. By this *the Lord's* promises could not come in until they had fulfilled *their promises;* for the covenant begins with an "if." *"IF* ye will" do so and so, *"THEN"* so and so.

This is the arrangement also in the second statement, "Obey my voice *AND* I will be your God, *AND* ye shall be my people." According to this agreement, he was not to be their God, nor they his people, until *they had done what they promised;* until they had *obeyed his voice,* as they had *promised.*

The third statement stands the same: "Obey my voice and do them according to all which I command you: *SO* shall ye be my people, and I will be your God." This makes it perfectly plain, not only that none of *the Lord's part* could come in *until they had done what they had promised;* but that the Lord's part *was to come in* BY THE DOING of what they had promised. "Obey my voice," "and do;" *"SO* [in this way, by this means] shall ye be my people, and I will be your God.

Since, then, in this covenant the Lord's part, what the Lord could do, the Lord's promises, could come in only in the *secondary way* as a consequence of the *people's* doing what they had *promised,* it is perfectly plain that that covenant rested, was established, only upon *the promises* of the *people.*

What, then, were these promises of the people worth? What had they promised? They had promised to obey the voice of the Lord indeed. They had promised to obey his law,—to keep the ten commandments, *indeed.*

But what was their condition when they made these promises?—It corresponded to the condition of Ishmael in the family of Abraham. They corresponded to Ishmael: they had been born only of the flesh, and knew only the birth of the flesh, and so had only the mind of the flesh. But "the minding of the flesh is enmity against God: for it is not subject to the law of God, neither indeed can be." "They that are in the flesh can not please God."

This being their condition, what could be the worth of any promises that they might make to keep the ten commandments *indeed?*—Any or all such promises could be worth simply nothing at all.

Accordingly, in that covenant, the people promised to do something that it was simply impossible for them to do. And since the Lord, with his promises, could not, *in that covenant,* come in until they had fulfilled *their promises:* until *they had done* what they agreed, it is certain that, for any practical purpose which the people discerned, or designed, that covenant was worth nothing at all, because the promises upon which it rested were worth nothing at all.

In the nature of things that covenant could only gender to bondage; because *the people* upon *whose promises* it rested were themselves already subject to the bondage of the flesh, the bondage of sin; and instead of keeping the commandments of God indeed, they would break them. And not only would they break the commandments, which they had promised *not to break,* but they would inevitably *break the promises* that they had made *not to break the commandments.* This simply because they were in a condition in which they were not subject to the law of God and could not be.

And this was demonstrated immediately. For, when Moses had gone up into the mount, to receive a copy of the law, which they had promised to "obey *indeed,"* he had been gone but forty days when they exclaimed: "Up, make us gods, which shall go before us; for as for this Moses, the man that brought us up out of the land of Egypt, we wot not what is become of him." Ex. 32:1. And they made themselves a golden calf—the god of Egypt—and worshipped it, after the manner of Egypt; which shows that, in heart, they were still in Egyptian bondage, and were indeed *as Ishmael,* the son of Hagar *the Egyptian,* "born after the flesh."

And though all this is written for the understanding of all people who should come afterward, and for our admonition "upon whom the ends of the world are come," it is a singular fact that even today there are persons who, knowing only the birth of the flesh, not having been born again, not knowing the birth of the Spirit, yet *will enter into exactly such a covenant;* and will sign to it, to keep all the commandments of God *indeed.* But the trouble with these is just the trouble that was with the people at Sinai, as it is always the trouble with people at Sinai: "They had no true conception of the holiness of God; of the exceeding sinfulness of their own hearts. . . Feeling that *they were able* to establish *their own righteousness,* THEY DECLARED: 'All that the Lord hath said will we do and be obedient.'"

Of course the questions arise here, Why, then, were they allowed of the Lord to enter into such a covenant? Why did the Lord make such a covenant with them? The answer to these questions will be given next week.

Galatians 4:21-31

July 17, 1900

"Tell me, ye that desire to be under the law, do ye not hear the law? For it is written, that Abraham had two sons, the one by a bondmaid, the other by a free woman. But he who was of the bondwoman was born after the flesh; but he of the free woman was by promise. Which things are an allegory: for these are the two covenants; the one from the Mount Sinai, which gendereth to bondage, which is Agar. For this Agar is Mount Sinai in Arabia, and answereth to Jerusalem which now is, and is in bondage with her children. But Jerusalem which is above is free, which is the mother of us all. For it is written, Rejoice, thou barren that bearest not: break forth and cry, thou that travailest not: for the desolate hath many more children than she which hath an husband. Now we, brethren, as Isaac was, are the children of promise. But as then he that was born after the flesh persecuted him that was born after the Spirit, even so it is now. Nevertheless what saith the scripture? Cast out the bondwoman and her son: for the son of the bondwoman shall not be heir with the son of the free woman. So then, brethren, we are not children of the bondwoman, but of the free."

The first covenant was faulty. It was faulty in the promises; because it rested primarily upon the promises of the people wherein the people promised something that it was impossible for them to do.

Why, then, were they allowed of the Lord to enter into such a covenant? Did he not know that the people could not do what they promised?—To be sure, he did.

But *the people* did not know it. "Living [in Egypt] in the midst of idolatry and corruption, they had *no true conception* of the *holiness of God;* of the exceeding *sinfulness of their own hearts;* their *utter inability,* in themselves, to render obedience to God's law; and *their need of a Saviour.* ALL THIS THEY MUST BE TAUGHT. God brought them to Sinai; he manifested his glory; he gave them his law, with the promise of great blessings *on condition* of obedience. . . The people *did not realize* the sinfulness of their own hearts, and *that without Christ* it was *impossible for them* to keep God's law; and they *readily entered into covenant* with God. *Feeling that they were able* to establish *their own* righteousness, *they declared,* 'All that the Lord hath said will we do, and be obedient.'"

Since the people did not know these essential things concerning themselves;—"their utter inability, etc.;—since they would not believe God, so that they could know;—and since "all this they must be taught,"—the only sure means by which they could be caused to learn this which they did not know was to have them try, *and fail;* and so learn by experience that they could not of themselves establish their own righteousness as the righteousness of God. Then they would be willing to accept by faith God's righteousness, which is established by faith.

This is all perfectly plain from the circumstances of the case.

As we have seen in a former study, before they left Egypt the Lord had said: "I will take you to me for a people, and I will be to you a God: and ye shall know that I am the Lord your God." Now is it not perfectly plain that if they had known that was already the Lord their God (Ex. 6:7), would they have needed to promise that they would keep his law "indeed" *so* that they might be his people, and he be their God?—Plainly, no.

If they had believed that the Lord would "give" to them "for an heritage" the inheritance that he had sworn to give to Abraham, to Isaac, and to Jacob (Ex. 6:8), could there ever have been found any place for *a bargain* into which they would enter, and according to which they would, *by works,* earn that inheritance?—Plainly, no.

In other words: If they had known, and had been in, God's covenant *with Abraham,* the everlasting covenant, would they have ever needed to know, or to enter into, this other covenant at Sinai, which in substance was only *their own,* because it rested only on *their* promises?—Plainly, no.

Following back the thought to its original in the parallel, in these verses in Galatians, the parallel question is,—

If Sarai and Abram had believed God's promise, and had held fast only to that, would Ishmael ever have found a place in the family of Abraham? Would two sons ever have been born to Abraham?—Plainly, no.

Plainly, then, there never was any need of Abraham's having more than one son, the son that God had promised. Yet, *"these* are the *two covenants;* the one from the Mount Sinai, which gendereth to bondage, which is Agar."

And just as there was never any need of Abraham's having but one son,—the son that God had promised,—so there was no need for Israel ever to have but the one covenant—the covenant of God with Abraham—the everlasting covenant.

Just as there was no need of those *two* sons, so there was no need of the *two* covenants.

And as, through unbelief and distrust of God, Hagar and Ishmael were brought in on the side; just so, through unbelief and distrust of God, the covenant at Sinai was brought in on the side.

Galatians 4:21-31

And as Hagar and Ishmael never had any recognition at all in the promise that God made to give Abraham a son, just so the covenant at Sinai never had any recognition at all in God's promise of salvation to mankind.

As Hagar and Ishmael had to be cast out, and all that had brought them in had to be utterly repudiated, in order that the son whom God had promised should have the place that belonged to him; just so the covenant at Sinai had to be cast out, and all that brought it in had to be utterly repudiated, on the part of the people, upon whose promises alone that covenant rested, in order that God's original covenant—the covenant with Abraham—the everlasting covenant—should have the place that belongs to it, in the life and salvation of men.

Yet, as the troubles and the failure of Sarai and Abram in the scheme that brought in Hagar and Ishmael, were instrumental in bringing them at last to the point where they did trust implicitly in the promise of God alone; so the trouble and the dismal failure that Israel experience in the first covenant brought them to the point where they appreciated, and implicitly trusted in, *God's original covenant,*—the covenant with Abraham,—his everlasting covenant,—*which he had given them* before they left Egypt at all.

For, as we have seen, Israel broke both the law of God and their covenant not to break it. And when Moses came down from the mount, having in his hands the table of the law that they had covenanted to obey "indeed," and saw what they had done, "he cast the tables out of his hands, and brake them beneath the mount" (Ex. 32:19), "thus signifying that as they had broken their covenant with God, so God had broken his covenant with them."—*Patriarchs and Prophets,* page 320.

They thus found themselves stranded, and utterly helpless, with all their resources utterly exhausted. For "They could not hope for the favor of God through a covenant which they had broken; and now, *seeing their sinfulness* and their need of pardon, they *were brought to feel their need of the Saviour* revealed in *the Abrahamic covenant,* and shadowed forth in the sacrificial offerings. *Now* they were *prepared to appreciate* the blessings of the *new covenant."—Id.,* page 372.

Thus the covenant from Sinai brought them to the covenant with Abraham. The first brought them to the second covenant. The old covenant brought them to the new covenant. And thus the law, which was the basis of that covenant,—*the broken law*—was the schoolmaster to bring them to Christ, that they might be justified by faith.

Please study this study closely and carefully; for, in the next studies, we pass from this to the study of the new covenant.

Galatians 4:21-24, 28

July 24, 1900

"Tell me, ye that desire to be under the law, do ye not hear the law? For it is written that Abraham had two sons, the one by a bondmaid, the other by a free woman. But he who was of the bondwoman was born after the flesh; but he of the free woman was by promise. Which things are an allegory: for these are the two covenants. . . Now we, brethren, as Isaac was, are the children of promise."

As Ishmael was born altogether of the flesh, without any promise of God, but from distrust and unbelief of the promise of God, so was the first covenant—the covenant from Sinai.

And as Isaac was born altogether of the promise of God, solely from dependence upon that promise, so is the new covenant—the everlasting covenant.

The first covenant rested upon the promises of the people, and depended solely upon the efforts of the people. The second covenant consists solely of the promise of God, and depends upon the power and work of God.

The first covenant runs: *If* ye will" do so and so. The new covenant has neither "if" nor any of men's doing, but is altogether the doing of the Lord. Look at them as they stand together:—

THE OLD COVENANT	THE NEW COVENANT
"*If* ye will obey my voice indeed, and keep my covenant, *then* ye shall be a peculiar treasure unto me above all people: for all the earth is mine: and ye shall be unto me a kingdom of priests, and an holy nation." "Obey my voice, *and* I will be your God, and ye shall be my people." "Obey my voice, and do them, according to all which I command you: *SO* shall ye be my people, and I will be your God." Ex. 19:5, 6; Jer. 7:23; 11:4.	"I will put my laws into their mind, and write them in their hearts: and I will be to them a God, and they shall be to me a people, and they shall not teach every man his neighbor, and every man his brother, saying, Know the Lord: for all shall know me, from the least to the greatest. For I will be merciful to their unrighteousness, and their sins and their iniquities will I remember no more." Heb. 1:10-12.

Galatians 4:21-24, 28

Let us read the new covenant, beginning with "If ye will," etc. *"If ye will* put my laws into your minds, and write them in your hearts, then I will be your God, and ye shall be my people." "Put my laws in your minds, and write them in your hearts, *that* I may be your God, and ye may be my people."

If the new covenant read thus, how many persons could ever become the Lord's people? And of how many persons could He ever be the God?—None at all; because no person can write the law of God in his heart; no person can put the law of God into his mind; for "the carnal mind is enmity against God, for it is not subject to the law of God, neither indeed can be." Nothing short of the power of God alone, through the eternal Spirit, can ever put the law of God in anybody's mind, or write it in his heart.

Yet, to do just this, was practically what the people of Israel agreed to do at Sinai, in the old covenant. For they agreed to keep the law of God "indeed," which no person can do without that law being put into his mind, and written in his heart. They agreed to keep the law of God "indeed," so that, in order that, they could be his people, and he be their God. Their agreement, therefore, was plainly in effect that they themselves would put the law of God in their minds, and write it in their hearts; and this when, as yet, they knew only the birth of the flesh; when, as yet, they had only the carnal mind, which "is enmity against God, for it is not subject to the law of God, neither indeed can be."

Thus it was by their own efforts that they were to be righteous; and *by this righteousness* they were to make themselves God's people, and win him to be their God.

Thus that covenant was altogether one of works; of righteousness by works; of winning the favor of God by works; of salvation by works.

It was a covenant in which, because of their works, the reward was to be not reckoned of grace, but of debt.

It was a covenant by which there was no such thing as the forgiveness of sins: it was of bondage, and gendered only to bondage.

And this is why that covenant is brought into this letter of instruction to the Galatians. The Galatians were seeking righteousness by works, by their own efforts. They were seeking to be "made perfect by the flesh." But whatsoever Christian seeks righteousness, or to be perfect, *in that way,* has fallen from grace. He has indeed forsaken grace; because "to him that worketh is the reward not reckoned of grace, but of debt." And "if it be of works, then it is no more grace." Rom. 4:4; 11:6.

This was the position and the condition of "the Pharisees which believed," who had led the Galatians astray. Into a system of righteousness by works, and of seeking to be made perfect by the flesh, the Pharisees that believed had turned everything that God had given them to save them from the bondage of self-righteousness and the works of the flesh; and they would even have perverted to that false system the very gospel of Christ itself.

On the other hand, the new covenant is wholly of grace, and of the work of God by grace.

It is a covenant in which the work is solely the work of God, and righteousness is the righteousness of God.

It is a covenant in which every one who shares it is born of the Spirit, and who thus receives a new mind and a new heart, in which mind the law of God is put, and upon which heart that law is written by the Spirit of the living God.

It is a covenant in which, by the creative power of the promise of God, each one who submits to that promise is *created* a child of God. "For we are his *workmanship,* created in Christ Jesus unto good works, which God hath before ordained that we should walk in them." Eph. 2:10

It is a covenant in which, solely because of the mercy of God, and by his promise, there is obtained forgiveness of sins, full and free: the sins and iniquities to be remembered no more forever.

It is a covenant by which indeed forgiveness must be found for the sins of the people even under the *first covenant.* For "he [Christ] is the mediator of the new testament, that by means of death, for the redemption of the transgressions that were under the first testament, they which are called might receive the promise of the eternal inheritance." Heb. 9:15.

Note, again, that in the new covenant there is no mention of any doing on the part of *the people.* The doing is all of God: *"I* will put my laws into their mind, and write them in their hearts." *"I* will be to them a God." *"I* will be merciful to their unrighteousness, and their sins and their iniquities will I remember no more."

In the new covenant it is God who is the worker; "For it is *God which worketh* in you both to will and to do of his good pleasure." Phil. 2:13. It is "through the blood of the *everlasting covenant,"* that "the God of peace" makes "you perfect in every good work to do his will, *working in you* that which is well pleasing in his sight through Jesus Christ." who is the "surety" of this "better testament." Heb. 13:20, 21; 7:22.

The only way in which the people come into this covenant is passively: they must *submit* themselves unto the righteousness of God. Rom. 10:3. They *"yield" themselves* unto God and *their "members* as instruments of righteousness *unto God."* Rom. 6:13.

Thus, whoever is partaker of this covenant in any way whatever, is partaker of it wholly by *the promise of God;* and *so* becomes, "as Isaac was," a child of promise.

There is no other way to be a partaker of the new covenant than by the promise of God: for there is nothing in the covenant but the naked promises of God. There is no way to be a child of God, but by the promise of God: that promise accepted by faith. Our sins are forgiven, our unrighteousness is pardoned, because God says it, and by the word of that promise we know it. He who accepts and depends only on the promise of God is of the people of God because God has said it. God is his God, because God has said it. The law of God is in his mind, and is written upon his heart, because God has promised that he will put it in his mind and write it on his heart; and he has submitted himself to God to have it done by God. And having so submitted himself to the righteousness of God, he rests securely in the promise of God *in Christ,* who is the mediator and the surety of the new covenant. And "this is the work of God, that ye believe on him whom he hath sent."

The old covenant consisted, and ever consists, of the promises and the works, of the righteousness, of *people* who know only the birth and the mind of the flesh. The new covenant consists forever of the promises and the works of righteousness *of God* in those who know the birth of the Spirit by the promise of God.

Galatians 4:21-31; 5:1

July 31, 1900

"Tell me, ye that desire to be under the law, do ye not hear the law? For it is written, that Abraham had two sons, the one by a bondmaid, the other by a free woman. But he who was of the *bondwoman* was born after the flesh; but he of the free woman was by promise. Which things are an allegory: for these are the two covenants; the one from the Mount Sinai, which gendereth to bondage, which is Agar. For this Agar is Mount Sinai in Arabia, and answereth to Jerusalem which now is, and is in bondage with her children. But Jerusalem which is above is free, which is the mother of us all. For it is written, Rejoice, thou barren that bearest not; for the desolate hath many more children than she which hath an husband. Now, we, brethren, as Isaac was, are the children of promise. But as then he that was born after the flesh persecuted him that was born after the Spirit, even so it is now. Nevertheless what saith the scripture? Cast out the bondwoman and her son: for the son of the bondwoman shall not be heir with the son of the free woman. So then, brethren, we are not children of the bondwoman, but of the free. Stand fast therefore in the liberty wherewith Christ hath made us free, and be not entangled again with the yoke of bondage."

The first covenant depended upon the promises of a people, who knew only the birth of the flesh. These promises were that they would keep the ten commandments "indeed." But, knowing only the birth of the flesh, they were, at the time, transgressors of the law of God, and so were in bondage to sin. And knowing only the birth of the flesh, and having only the mind of the flesh, their promise to obey the law of God "indeed," was worthless, because the minding of the flesh is enmity against God: for it is not subject to the law of God, neither indeed can be."

If they had made no promise at all to obey the law, they would have broken it; because they knew only the birth of the flesh, and "they that are in the flesh can not please God." Therefore, without any promise to keep the law, without the new birth, they would have continued in the bondage of sin. And when they promised to keep the law "indeed," and then broke their promise (which, having only the mind of the flesh, it was inevitable that they would do), this brought them only yet deeper into bondage, because to "vow a vow unto the Lord," and then "slack to pay it," is "sin in thee." Deut, 23:21.

Therefore, that covenant being entered into by those who were already in bondage, and being a covenant which, by its terms, gendered to bondage, it was only a covenant of bondage—a covenant in which their very efforts to deliver themselves from the bondage in which they already were, brought them only deeper into bondage, the bondage of sin, the bondage of their own works and broken promises, which were only sin.

Consequently, all that was seen, or could be seen, in the first covenant was, *and is, the broken law.* And that this should be forever so plain that no one could fail to see it, when Moses came down from the mount and saw their idolatry, he, having the tables of the law of God in his hands, "cast the tables out of his hands, and brake them beneath the mount." Ex. 32:19.

They were at first breakers of the law. They promised nevermore to break the law. They again broke both *the law* and *their promise not to break it.*

And when, therefore, because of this, Moses cast out of his hands the tables of the law of God, and broke them, this was to give to them, and to all people forever, a divine object lesson, that in the first covenant, in all their

Galatians 4:21-31; 5:1

efforts at self-righteousness, and in all their promises not to break the law, no one can ever see anything but THE BROKEN LAW.

But, there was *then and there present* the Abrahamic covenant, the covenant of faith, God's everlasting covenant, to *deliver them* from the bondage and the yoke of bondage that was upon them because of the covenant of works, of unbelief, into which they had entered. "They could not hope for the favor of God through a covenant which they had broken"—through a covenant in which nothing could be seen but the broken law of God. "And now, seeing their sinfulness and their need of pardon, they were brought to feel their need of the Saviour, revealed in the *Abrahamic covenant* and shadowed forth in the sacrificial offerings.

It was *the covenant with Abraham,* Isaac, and Jacob which Moses pleaded to God, *for mercy to the people* worshipping the golden calf at the foot of the mount, while he was yet in the mount, before he had come down the first time. Notice: in Ex. 32:1-6 is given the account of the people's making the golden calf and worshipping it. In verse seven "the Lord said unto Moses, Go, get thee down; for thy people, which thou broughtest out of the land of Egypt, have corrupted themselves: they have turned aside quickly out of the way which I commanded them; they have made them a molten calf, and have worshiped it... Now therefore let me alone, that my wrath may wax hot against them, and that I may consume them." Verses 7, 10.

And Moses besought the Lord his God, and said, Lord, why doth thy wrath wax hot against thy people which thou hast brought forth out of the land of Egypt with great power, and with a mighty hand?. . . Turn from thy fierce wrath, and repent of this evil against thy people. *Remember Abraham, Isaac, and Israel,* thy servants, to whom *thou swearest by thine own self,* and saidst unto them, I will multiply your seed as the stars of heaven, and all this land I have spoken of will I give unto your seed, and they shall inherit it forever. *And the Lord repented* of the evil which he thought to do unto his people." Verses 11-14.

Thus it was the Abrahamic covenant, God's everlasting covenant, that saved the people from the bondage and the curse of their sins, in the first covenant. And so it is ever. Heb. 9:15.

Then Moses came down from the mount, with the tables of the law in his hands, and cast out of his hands the tables of the law, and broke them, thus "signifying that as they had broken their covenant with God, *so* God had broken his covenant with them;" and signifying that in that covenant there was nothing to be seen but the broken law; and that they "could not hope for the favor of God through a covenant which they had broken." And "now, seeing their sinfulness and their need of pardon, they were brought to feel their need of *the Saviour revealed in the Abrahamic covenant,* and shadowed forth *in the sacrificial offerings. Now* by *faith* and *love* they were bound to God as *their deliverer* from *the bondage of sin.* Now they were prepared to appreciate the blessings of the new covenant."—*Patriarchs and Prophets,* p. 373.

Thus the covenant from Sinai brought them to the covenant with Abraham. The first covenant brought them to the second covenant. The old covenant brought them to the new covenant. And thus the law, which was the basis of that covenant,—the broken law,—was the schoolmaster to bring them to Christ, that they might be justified by faith.

Thus "the Lord said unto Moses, Hew thee two tables of stone like unto the first: and I will write upon these table the words that were in the first tables, which thou breakest." Ex. 31:1. And, says Moses, "I made an ark of shittim wood, and hewed two tables of stone like unto the first, and went up into the mount, having the two tables in mine hand. And he wrote on the tables, according to the first writing, the ten commandments, which the Lord spake unto you in the mount out of the midst of the fire in the day of the assembly: and the Lord gave them unto me. And I turned myself and came down from the mount, and *put the tables in the ark* which I had made; and *there they be* as the Lord commanded me." Deut. 10: 3-5.

There was then established among the people the *sanctuary service,* with the *Saviour shadowed forth in the sacrificial* offerings:" and with Christ, "the Mediator of the new covenant," the "one Mediator between God and men," represented in the high priest in his ministration in the sanctuary. To that sanctuary they brought, in penitence and faith, their offering, and confessed their sin. The blood of their offering was taken by the high priest into the sanctuary, atonement was made for them, and the sin was forgiven. And in the great day of atonement the blood of the offering for all the people was sprinkled *upon* the mercy seat, and *before* the mercy seat, which was upon the *top of the ark, over the tables of the law.*

Thus *between* the *sinner* and *the law* there was always the *sacrifice,* representing Christ (and which, in his faith, *was Christ,* the Surety of the "better testament"), by which was brought to the sinner the forgiveness of sins, and the *righteousness of God,* which satisfied all the demands of the law. And thus, through faith in Christ, in this covenant in which Christ is Mediator, and of which he is the Surety, there is seen *only* the *unbroken law.*

Such was, and *is,* the true meaning of the new order of things at Sinai, after the breaking of the table, and after the complete nullification of the first covenant. It was the way of faith, the way of the "righteousness of God which is by faith of Jesus Christ unto all and upon all them that believe."

But, behold, in their unbelief Israel afterward turned all this into a system of works, precisely as was the first covenant. And those sacrifices and offerings, and the ceremonies connected therewith, were given by the Lord to be altogether the expression of faith. But Israel, in their unbelief, missed all this, and made it only a system of works, of ceremonialism. Instead of righteousness coming by faith, and the sacrifices and offerings being but the expression of the faith, they expected righteousness by means of the offering *itself,* and because of *their good work* in *making the offering.*

Thus it was in the time of Christ on earth, and in the time of Paul and the Galatians. Thus it was with "the Pharisees which believed," who had confused the Galatians and driven them back from righteousness by faith to righteousness by works and ceremonialism. And, therefore, Paul could write, and did write, "that Abraham had two sons, the one by a bondmaid, the other by a free woman. But he who was of the bondwoman was born after the flesh; but he of the free woman was by promise. Which things are an allegory: for *these are the two covenants;* the one from the Mount Sinai, which gendereth to bondage, which is Agar. For *this Agar* is Mount Sinai in Arabia, and *answereth to Jerusalem which now is,* and *is in bondage* with *her children."*

Thus the very means that God had given to deliver them from the bondage of the old covenant they, through unbelief, had turned into a system of bondage, which corresponded exactly to that bondage of the old covenant. They had, indeed, perverted the new covenant as then expressed, into the very principle of the old covenant—righteousness by works. That which was the gospel as expressed in the sacrifices, offerings, and ministry *of that time,* they perverted to the bondage of righteousness by works, and ceremonialism, exactly as among the Galatians the "Pharisees which believed" were perverting the gospel as expressed in the sacrifice and ministry of Christ himself.

And just as Hagar and Ishmael were cast out, that God's covenant with Abraham might be fully enjoyed; and just as the covenant at Sinai had to be repudiated and cast out, that the blessings of the Abrahamic covenant, the new covenant, might be enjoyed; so when Christ came, and, by the sacrifice and offering *of himself* and by *his own ministration,* brought in the *fullness of the gospel*—in order that this should be fully enjoyed, there must be repudiated and cast out that system of ceremonies and ceremonialism, that system of righteousness by works, into which Israel had perverted that which in its time was indeed the expression of the true gospel, of righteousness by faith. "Jerusalem which now is. . . is in bondage with her children. . . Nevertheless what saith the scripture? Cast out the bondwoman and her son, for the son of the bondwoman shall not be heir with the son of the free woman." "Jerusalem which is above is free, which is the mother of us all. . . Now, we, brethren, as Isaac was, are the children of promise

And thus was cast out forever the very principle of ceremonialism—the very principle of the bondage of righteousness by works in whatever form it might present itself; and there was established it its place the principle of divine liberty in righteousness by faith. "So then, brethren, we are *not* the children of the bondwoman, but of the free." And because of this there is sounded to all people forever the blessed rallying cry, *"Stand fast therefore in the liberty wherewith Christ hath made us free, and be not entangled again with the yoke of bondage."*

The old covenant, the covenant from Sinai, is summed up in the word *"SELF."* The new covenant, the everlasting covenant, is summed up in the word *"CHRIST."*

The old covenant is self and his righteousness. The new covenant is Christ and the righteousness of God.

The old covenant is self and the bondage of sin and works of law. The new covenant is Christ and the liberty of righteousness which is by faith.

The old covenant—*self*—must be cast out, and utterly repudiated, that the new covenant—*Christ*—may have its proper place and may manifest its saving power, for the son of the bondwoman can *never* be heir *with* the son of the free.

Chapter Five

Galatians 5:2-4

August 14, 1900

"Behold, I Paul say unto you, that if ye be circumcised, Christ shall profit you nothing. For I testify again to every man that is circumcised, that he is a debtor to do the whole law. Christ is become of no effect unto you, whosoever of you are justified by the law; ye are fallen from grace."

Through unbelief and distrust of the promise of God in his covenant with Abraham, the eyes of Sarah and Abraham were hidden from the truth and blessings of the Abrahamic covenant, God's everlasting covenant. Therefore, the real truth and spirit of that covenant they must be taught. Through the disappointing experience of Sarai's scheme in bringing in Hagar and her son Ishmael, Sarah and Abraham were brought to sincerely trust in the promise of God by which they received the child of promise; and by which Abraham was enabled to see the day of Christ, and, in seeing it, to rejoice and be glad. John 8:56.

Through the darkness of Egypt, which was upon their minds and hearts,—the darkness of unbelief and self-righteousness,—Israel *at Sinai* could not discern the truth and blessings of the Abrahamic covenant. "All this *they* must be taught." By their experience in the covenant at Sinai, they were brought to the knowledge of themselves, of "their need of the Saviour revealed in the Abrahamic covenant and shadowed forth in the sacrificial offerings" and "were prepared to appreciate the blessings of the new covenant."

Through the darkness of Egypt, which was upon their minds and hearts,—the darkness of unbelief and self-righteousness,—Israel *before Calvary,* and at Calvary, and "the Pharisees which believed" *after* Calvary, could not discern the Saviour revealed in the Abrahamic covenant and shadowed forth In the sacrificial offerings—the blessings of the new covenant. All this *they* must be taught. And by Stephen, and especially by Paul; and by the church in council at Jerusalem, and especially by Inspiration in the epistle to the Galatians, they were taught that there was not to be put upon the necks of Christians the yoke which neither their fathers nor themselves were able to bear; but that Christians are to stand fast in the freedom of the Abrahamic covenant,—God's everlasting covenant,—"the liberty wherewith Christ hath made us free."

Therefore it is written: "Behold, I Paul say unto you, that if ye be circumcised, Christ shall profit you nothing."

It is the truth that Timothy was circumcised, and it is also the truth that Christ did profit Timothy unto the very fullness of the salvation of God. How, then, can it be true that "if ye be circumcised, Christ shall profit you nothing," and yet Timothy be both circumcised and profited by Christ?

The key to this problem lies in the *purpose* for which circumcision was employed. The Pharisees which believed, who had confused the Galatians, and were making this contention against Paul, "taught the brethren, and said, Except ye be circumcised after the manner of Moses, ye can not *be saved.*" Acts 15:1. With them, then, circumcision was the means of salvation; and *to be saved* was the object in the circumcision. And how entirely salvation was made to depend upon circumcision is shown in the fact that this was said to persons who *were already saved* by the faith of Jesus Christ.

The Galatians had heard the gospel in its purity, preached by Paul. They had believed the gospel; and in that they had believed on the Lord Jesus, and had received him as their Saviour. Thus, they were already saved by faith in Christ; for by that they received the gospel, which is "the power of God unto salvation [working salvation] to every one that believeth." And it was to *these Christians* who were *already saved* by Christ, through the faith of Christ,—to these it was that "the Pharisees which believed" had said, "Except ye be circumcised... ye *can not be saved.*"

This was, therefore, nothing else than to put circumcision above Jesus Christ as the way of salvation. It was to set Christ aside as the Saviour, and to put circumcision in his place as the savior. Therefore it is perfectly plain, in itself, that whosoever was circumcised under that scheme and for that purpose, Christ would profit him nothing; because, in the very process, he set Christ aside for circumcision; he repudiated Christ as the Saviour, and took circumcision as his savior.

And while that controversy was going on, as yet unsettled, Paul would not give countenance for a moment to any suggestion to circumcise Titus, or anybody else. But when the controversy had been settled by the Holy Spirit, and the decree had been published by the Holy Spirit from the council at Jerusalem that people are saved by Christ, without circumcision, and where there was no question of salvation in the circumcision that was performed,—*then* Paul circumcised Timothy, so that a wider door should be open to both Paul and Timothy in the preaching of the gospel without circumcision.

Now, with those "Pharisees which believed" circumcision was the badge, the seal, the very pinnacle of works, of self-righteousness, and of *salvation* by works of self-righteousness. And these works included the law,—all law, moral and ceremonial, which the Lord had given,—and the ceremonies which the Pharisees had heaped upon all that the Lord had given. So that the scheme meant justification, salvation, by "law" and works of law, by ceremonialism, *not* by Christ and the faith of Christ. Therefore exactly as he wrote of circumcision, so now he writes of law: "Christ is become of no effect unto you, whosoever of you are justified by law; ye are fallen from grace." The Greek is *nomos, law,* in general: not *ho nomos, the law,* in particular.

In this controversy the question was not whether it is right or wrong to *keep* the law of God. The question is whether or not men are *justified,* saved, by works of law, whatever law it may be. These people were already saved by Christ, and by faith in him; and now, to those who were saved by Christ, and by faith alone in him, these "Pharisees which believed" insisted that these must be circumcised, and keep the law, *in order to be saved.*

This was putting the law, the keeping of the law, above Christ. It was, in fact, the setting aside of Christ as Saviour, and putting in his place *as the Saviour* their own works of law. And therefore, plainly enough, in the very fact of so doing they were "fallen from grace." For, for any one to turn from Christ, for any purpose whatever,—and, above all, for the purpose of being saved,—is most definitely to fall from grace.

And all this is true forever. Men are never saved by any of their own works in the keeping of any law. They are saved alone by Christ, and the faith of Christ: saved to the uttermost.

Galatians 5:3

August 21, 1900

"For I testify again to every man that is circumcised, that he is a debtor to do the whole law."

"Debtor to do the whole law." It is curious that men, in considering this statement, have made it mark a distinction between two laws, and have made it exclude the law of God from the subject under consideration, by allowing to the word "debtor" only the sense of "obligation."

They know, by the scripture, that it is the whole duty of man to fear God and keep his commandments. They know that there can not be any other Scripture to contradict that. They know that every man is under obligation to keep the whole law of God, whether he is circumcised or uncircumcised. And, allowing that this term implies only obligation,—that if he is circumcised, he is under obligation to do the whole law,—they conclude that this must exclude the law of God: they conclude that it must be some law that no person is under any obligation to do unless he be circumcised; and that therefore the "whole law" here under consideration must be only the whole ceremonial law of sacrifices and offerings.

On the other hand, there are those who hold themselves under no obligation whatever to keep the law of God, who bring in this text to support them in their disobedience and opposition. They will have it that only those who are circumcised are under any obligation to keep the law of God, and that it was only by being circumcised that the obligation comes; and they know that they are not under any obligation to be circumcised. From this they argue that they are under no obligation to keep the ten commandments.

But both of these are wrong; both of them fail to see the thought that is in this verse. And the cause of this failure is in their allowing to the word "debtor" only the sense of "obligation."

It is true that the word signifies "obligation." But, in this place, and in every other place in its connection with men's moral obligations, the word has a meaning so much broader and deeper than that of mere obligation that the sense of mere obligation becomes really secondary.

The word "debtor" in this verse—Gal. 5:3—signifies not only that a person is in debt, and under obligation to pay; but that, beyond this, he is overwhelmingly in debt, with *nothing at all wherewith* to pay. If a man is debtor, and so under obligation, to pay one thousand dollars, and yet has abundance, or even only the ability to pay the one thousand dollars, that is easy enough. But if a man is debtor, and so under obligation, to *pay fourteen millions* of dollars ($14,000,000) and has not a single cent wherewith to pay, and is in prison besides, and has no ability whatever to make a cent wherewith to pay his debt, to *that* man the word "debtor" signifies a great deal more than mere "obligation to pay."

And that is precisely the case here. That is the thought in this verse. That is the meaning embodied here in the word "debtor." This because the word "debtor," when used in connection with morals, implies, and can imply, only sin: that the man is a sinner.

This word "debtor" in Gal. 5:3 is precisely the word that is used in Luke 13:4,—"Those eighteen, upon whom the tower in Siloam fell, and slew them, think ye that they were *sinners* above all men that dwelt in Jerusalem?"—where the word "sinners" is in the text, is "debtors" in the margin.

It is the word used in the Lord's prayer (Matt. 6:12). "Forgive us our *debts*, as we forgive our *debtors;*" and which, in Luke's version of the prayer, plainly expresses the thought of sin, in the words: "Forgive us our *sins;* for we also forgive everyone that is *indebted* to us." Luke 11:4.

It is the same word also that is used by the Saviour in Luke 7:41, 42: "There was a certain creditor which had two *debtors;* the one owed five hundred pence, and the other fifty. And when they had *nothing* [with which] *to pay,* he frankly forgave them both."

It is the same word also that is used in the parable in Matt. 18:23-35. Indeed, from the verse, Luke 13:4, where the word "sinners" is used in the text and "debtors" is in the margin, the *reference* is direct to this parable in Matthew 18. That is the parable in which it is said that when a certain king "had begun to reckon" with his servants, "one was brought unto him, which owed him ten thousand talents,"—about fourteen million four hundred thousand dollars,—and he had *nothing* with which to pay. Then the lord "forgave the *debt.*" But, when the servant found one of his fellow servants who owed him about fifteen dollars, he would not forgive him the debt, but cast him into prison until he should pay the fifteen dollars. Then the king called up his debtor, "and delivered him to the tormentors, till he should pay all that was due unto him. So likewise shall my Heavenly Father do also unto you, if ye from your hearts forgive not every one his brother their *trespasses.*" Matt. 18:23, 35.

That thought of delivering the debtor to the tormentors until he should pay all that was due to his lord, belongs with the word; for "the use of the word involves the idea that the debtor is one that must expiate his guilt." And "sin is called *hamartia,* because it involves expiation and the payment of it as a debt, by punishment and satisfaction."

From these scriptures the attentive reader can begin to see that in the words of Gal.5:3,—"he is debtor to do the whole law,"—there is far more suggested than that he is merely under obligation to accept the claims of the law upon him, and do his best to meet them. All this shows that he is not only under obligation to recognize the binding claims of the law of God, but that he is actually *debtor* to render to that law all the claims that it has upon him. And in this it is further shown that, of himself, he must everlastingly be *debtor,* because he has absolutely nothing wherewith to pay, and of himself has no means of acquiring anything with which to pay.

And this indebtedness lies not only in his obligation to do the law from this time forward; it also lies in obligation to make satisfaction for *all that is past,*— for all the accumulations of the past, up to the present time.

Accordingly, of himself, every man is everlastingly a debtor in all that is implied in this thought in Gal. 5:3, and the kindred texts that we have here cited; because "all have sinned, and come short of the glory of God." And whosoever would be circumcised in order to be saved and thus seek to be saved by works of self-righteousness, thereby takes upon himself the obligation to pay to the law of God his whole debt, from the beginning of his life unto the end of it. And in that, he also takes upon himself the obligation to *expiate all the guilt* attaching to his transgressions, and accumulated thereby.

That is what it is to be "debtor to do the whole law." That is what is stated in the words: "I testify again to every man that is circumcised, that he is a *debtor* to do *the whole law."* He is not only debtor; but, by that transaction, he himself voluntarily assumes of *himself* to discharge all that is involved in his indebtedness.

Now it is true that every man in the world is, of himself, that kind of a debtor. It is also true that any man today who seeks justification by his own works, even in the doing of the ten commandments, or of anything else that the Lord has commanded, does thereby assume, and bind himself to pay, all that is involved in the indebtedness. But he can not pay. There is not with him the first element of any possibility, in himself, to pay any of the debt. He is overwhelmed and lost.

But, thanks be to God, whosoever has the righteousness *of God* which is by *faith of Jesus Christ,* whosoever depends *only* on *the Lord Jesus* and that which *Jesus has done,* though he be of himself debtor just like any other man, yet, *in Christ,* he has wherewith abundantly to pay *all the indebtedness.* Christ has expiated, by punishment and satisfaction, all the guilt of every soul; and by the righteousness of God which he brings, Christ supplies abundance of righteousness to pay all the demands that the law may ever make in the life of him who believes in Jesus.

Thanks be unto God for his unspeakable gift of the unsearchable riches of Christ. Oh, believe it! Oh, receive it! Poor, overwhelmed, lost "debtor," "buy of me gold tried in the fire, that thou mayest be rich;" and white raiment, that thou mayest be clothed." "Yea, come, buy. . . without money and without price."

Galatians 5:5

August 28: 1900

"For we through the Spirit wait for the hope of righteousness by faith."

Galatians 5:5

Notice, it is not that we wait for righteousness by faith. This is the free gift of God, always open to every soul in the world, and does not have to be waited for for a moment. Rather, it waits, in the longsuffering of God, for men to awake to receive it.

The word is, We "wait for *the hope* of righteousness by faith." That is, righteousness by faith is the foundation of a *"hope"* not yet realized, but which is certain to be realized.

What, then, is this hope?—it is the Inheritance, which none can receive except they have eternal life. And none can have eternal life—the *life* of God—who have not eternal righteousness—the righteousness of God.

This hope was referred to by Paul in his answer before King Agrippa: "And now I stand and am judged for *the hope* of the promise made of God unto our fathers: unto which promises our twelve tribes, instantly serving God day and night, *hope* to come. For which hope's sake, King Agrippa, I am accused of the Jews." Acts 26:6, 7. The promise made of God unto the fathers was the promise to Abraham, which embraces the world, even the world to come. As it is written: "By faith he sojourned in the land of promise, as *in a strange country,* dwelling in tabernacles with Isaac and Jacob, the heirs with him of the same promise: for he looked for a city which hath foundations, whose builder and maker Is God." Heb. 11:9, 10.

Paul said that it was for this *"hope's sake"* that he was accused of the Jews, when he made his answer before King Agrippa. But before Paul was brought before Agrippa, he had also stood before Festus the governor; and before that, he had made answer before Felix the governor. And in his word before Felix, he said, I *"have* hope toward God, which they themselves also allow, *that there shall be a resurrection of the dead,* both of the just and unjust." Acts 24:15.

But even before this, Paul had been obliged to stand before the Sanhedrin and answer; and there "he cried out in the council, Men and brethren, I am a Pharisee, the son of a Pharisee: of *the hope* and *resurrection of the dead* I am called in question." Acts 23:6. Of the hope of the dead, and the resurrection of the dead; that is, even the dead have hope, if they be of the righteousness of faith; for it is written: "The wicked is driven away in his wickedness: but the righteous hath hope *in his death."* Prov.14:32. Therefore again it is written: "If in this *life* only we have hope in Christ, we are of all men most miserable." 1 Cor. 15:19. Not only in his *life,* but in his *death,* he who is in Christ has hope: and, being dead, his flesh rests in hope as did that of him in whom all the hope and promises of God are yea and amen.

The resurrection of the dead is an essential part of "the hope" which rests on righteousness by faith—this hope of the promise made of God unto our fathers. Indeed, the resurrection is the essential means of receiving "the hope." For, though God promised to Abraham the land in which he sojourned, yet "he gave him none inheritance in it, no not so much as to set his foot on," though "he promised that he would give it to him for a possession, and to his seed after him, when as yet ye had no child." Acts 7:5.

And even at that time, the Lord taught Abraham that it was through the resurrection of the dead that he was to receive the inheritance. For, in his call to the offering of Isaac, in whom was called the promised "seed," he was brought to the point wherein he accounted "that God was able *to raise him up, even from the dead; from whence also he received* him in a *figure.*" Heb. 11:19.

It was through the seed only that Abraham was to receive the promised inheritance. And thus, in his receiving that seed "from the dead," "in a figure," upon his accounting that God was able to raise him up even from the dead, he was taught the resurrection of the dead.

There is another bright element that enters into this hope which is begotten by righteousness by faith. Without *the coming of the Lord* there can be no resurrection of the dead. For he said to his disciples: "Wither I go, ye can not come." (John 13:33); but, "let not your heart be troubled. . . *I will come again, and receive you unto myself; that where I am, there ye may be also.*" John 14:1-3.

And so all the fathers, "having obtained a good report through faith," "died in faith, not having received the promises," "God having provided some better thing for us, that they without us should not be made perfect." Heb. 11:39, 13, 40.

Therefore, "this we say unto you by the word of the Lord, that we which are alive and remain unto the coming of the Lord shall not prevent them which are asleep. For the Lord himself shall descend from heaven with a shout, with the voice of the archangel, and with the trump of God; and the dead in Christ shall rise first; then we which are alive and remain shall be caught up together with them in the clouds, to meet the Lord in the air: and so shall we ever be with the Lord." 1 Thess. 4:15-17.

Thus the *second coming of the Lord* is the *crowning essential* in "the hope of righteousness which is by faith." We can not have the inheritance without the righteousness of God, we can not receive the inheritance *without the resurrection of the dead.* And having the righteousness of God, and *the hope* of the resurrection of the dead, there can not be the resurrection of the dead without *the coming of the Lord* in power and great glory.

Therefore, they who have the righteousness of God. which is by faith, are ever "looking for that blessed hope, and the glorious appearing of the great God and our Saviour Jesus Christ." Titus 2:13.

And, so, it is the present truth forever that "we, through the Spirit, wait for *the hope* of righteousness by faith."

Galatians 5:6

September 4, 1900

"For in Christ Jesus neither circumcision availeth anything, nor uncircumcision; but faith which worketh by love."

This is the climax of Paul's argument in answer to the "Pharisees which believed," who preached to those who were saved by faith of Jesus Christ, that "except ye be circumcised and keep the law, ye can not be saved."

The force of it is more fully discerned when there is understood just what was claimed for circumcision, and what it represented to those who there preached it. By them it was held that "so great is circumcision, that, but for it, the Holy One, blessed be he, would not have created the world:" that "but for circumcision, heaven and earth could not exist." And "how great is circumcision, since *it is equivalent* to ALL *the commandments of the law."* Thus, in their estimation; he who was circumcised *had, in that,* all the keeping of all the commandments. How this emphasizes the weight of that sentence of Paul's: "I testify again to every man that is circumcised, that he is a debtor to do the whole law." Instead of his having *in circumcision* all the keeping of the commandments, he had *by that* none of it at all; but was still in debt to do *the whole law,* with nothing at all wherewith to pay.

From the value which they gave to circumcision, it is easy to see how the "Pharisees which believed" could insist that persons who *believed in Jesus,* and so *were saved* by the faith of Jesus, must yet be circumcised *in order to be saved.* This was so, and was so easy, simply because to them circumcision was greater than was Jesus; and because to them, in every sense, circumcision stood exactly in the place that Christ *in truth* occupies.

Thus the question involved between Christianity and "the Pharisees which believed," the question which was settled by the Holy Spirit, and which is made plain in Galatians, is: Are men saved by faith of Christ, or by *something else?* Is Christ the true Saviour, or is something else the savior?

Yet, in reality, though that was the question, it did not stand exactly that way. Notice: the people to whom came preaching the "Pharisees which believed," were already *believers in Jesus,* and the "Pharisees which believed" did not say that men should not believe in Jesus. They admitted that it is proper to believe in Jesus. They themselves professed to believe in Jesus. But they insisted that the faith of Jesus is *not enough* to save: salvation must be by the faith of Jesus and *something else.*

Therefore the question in reality stood: Is Christ alone sufficient for salvation? or must salvation be by Christ *and something else?*

Does faith in Christ alone save the soul? or is it by Christ *and circumcision?*

It is by Christ alone? or is it by Christ *and penance?*

Is it by faith of Christ alone? or is it by faith *and works?*

Is it *by faith* which comes from God as the gift of God, and therefore itself works the works of God? or is it by a so-called faith which springs from mere assent of the mind, is thus "of yourselves," and therefore must be supported by the works of the law in self and self-righteousness.

Is it by faith *which* works? or is it by faith *and* works? And to this question, in all the various and subtle ways of insinuating self in place of Christ, the divine answer stands full and complete forever, in the single mighty sentence, *"In Christ Jesus neither circumcision availeth anything, nor uncircumcision; but faith which worketh by love."*

"In Christ Jesus"—that is, *with whomsoever believeth in Jesus*—"neither circumcision availeth anything, nor uncircumcision; but *faith.*"

"In Christ Jesus"—with whomsoever believeth in Jesus—"neither circumcision availeth anything nor uncircumcision,"—neither works availeth anything, nor no works,—"but *faith WHICH* WORKS."

"In Christ Jesus"—with whomsoever believeth in Jesus—"Neither circumcision. . . nor uncircumcision"—neither keeping the commandments availeth anything, nor not keeping the commandments; "but FAITH W*HICH worketh by LOVE*"—FAITH *WHICH keepeth the commandments* of God; for *"this is the* LOVE *of* GOD, *that we keep his commandments."* And he who *has Christ,* and *is in Christ,* has IN CHRIST *all the keeping of all the commandments.*

Even as it is written in another place in Galatians: "In Christ Jesus neither circumcision availeth anything, nor uncircumcision; but *A NEW CREATURE."* Gal. 6:15. And this, simply because "if any man be in Christ he IS a new creature." 2 Cor. 5:17. If he is not a new creature, his profession of being in Christ is only a profession, and is in vain.

And as it is written yet again in another place: "Circumcision is nothing and uncircumcision is nothing; but the keeping of the commandments of God" *is something.* But this *only* when the man "is *a new creature;"* only when the keeping of the commandments is the result of faith, which is of God, and which therefore works the works of God; only when the keeping of the commandments is the *effect,* of which the sole *cause* is *"faith WHICH worketh* BY LOVE"— faith which is of God and worketh by the love of God, which love in itself is expressed and can be expressed *only* in the keeping of the commandments of God, and which therefore *is* the keeping of the commandments of God; all of which is because of *Christ* within,—"Christ IN YOU the hope of glory,"—by whose obedience alone every believer in Jesus is made righteous.

Galatians 5:7-15

September 11, 1900

"Ye did run well; who did hinder you that ye should not obey the truth? This persuasion cometh not of him that calleth you."

Verse 8 here ought to make plain to all who is the one, in chapter 1, verse 6, that called them into the grace of Christ. Some are inclined to hold that Paul refers to himself in that scripture, in the words, "I marvel that ye are so soon removed from him that called you into the grace of Christ unto another gospel." They think that Paul is marveling that the Galatians should be so soon removed from himself, because they think that Paul was the one who called the Galatians into the grace of Christ. But this is a mistake. Paul did not draw men to himself: and this for the simple reason that he did not preach himself. He preached Christ—Christ and him crucified, and Christ crucified in every place where Paul preached. Consequently, men saw Christ instead of Paul— Christ with themselves, just where they were. And Christ, being thus lifted up in person, drew men to himself. And since, even in that, it is forever true that no man can come to Christ except the Father draw him, It is evident that in this work of the grace of Christ it is God who called these people into the grace of Christ. And when men come to them, preaching another gospel, which was not another, but was a perversion of the gospel of Christ, as many as trusted in that false gospel were, by that, removed, not from Paul, but from Christ, who had drawn them to himself; and from God, who had called them into the grace of Christ, which drew them to himself.

And thus verse 8 of the present study—"This persuasion cometh not of him that calleth you"—shows that it could not refer to Paul, because he had not been near to them, so that the persuasion could be an alternative between them and the others. But God was present with them, with his persuasion and his calling, so that whatever persuasion and calling were against that gospel which they had at first heard, could not possibly come from him who had called them, who was God.

"A little leaven leaveneth the whole lump. I have confidence in you through the Lord, that ye will be none otherwise minded: but he that troubleth you shall bear his judgment, whomsoever he be. And I, brethren, if I yet preach circumcision, why do I yet suffer persecution? Then is the offense of the cross ceased. I would they were even cut off which trouble you."

As we saw in last week's study, if he had preached circumcision, it would have been but to put circumcision in the place of Christ; and that, in itself, would have been to reject the grace of Christ, Christ and him crucified; and so the offense of the cross would have ceased, and the persecution with it, in the preaching of circumcision.

"For, brethren, ye have been called unto liberty; only use not the liberty for an occasion to the flesh, but by love serve one another. For all the law is fulfilled in one word, even in this: Thou shalt love thy neighbor as thyself."

Every soul, in being called unto Christ, is called to liberty; and every soul who receives Christ is delivered from bondage, in to the glorious liberty of the sons of God. Jesus Christ came into the world only to set men free, and to plant in their souls the genuine principle of liberty. And this liberty with which Christ made men free is liberty actuated only by love. It is a liberty too honourable to allow itself to be used as an occasion to the flesh, or as a cloak of maliciousness. It is a liberty led by a conscience enlightened by the Spirit of God. It is a liberty in which he who has it, is made free from all men, yet it makes him who receives it so gentle by love that he willingly becomes the servant of all, in order to bring them to the enjoyment that same liberty. This is freedom indeed: this is the freedom which Christ gives to whomsoever believes in him: for "whom the Son makes free is free indeed."

And thus "all the law is fulfilled in one word, even in this: Thou shalt love thy neighbor as thyself." This, because all that law, of which this *"one* word" is but one of the two great principles upon which the whole hangs,—that law is itself "the *law of liberty.*"

This is Christianity: this is the gospel and the liberty of the gospel. "But if ye bite and devour one another,"—if so ye repudiate the gospel and deny the liberty which it brings: if ye be critical, narrow, and intolerant,—"take heed that ye be not consumed one of another." For that is the only consequence that can come of such a course, with utter destruction at the last.

Galatians 5:16-18

September 18, 1900

"This I say then, Walk in the Spirit, and ye shall not fulfill the lust of the flesh. For the flesh lusteth against the Spirit, and the Spirit against the flesh: for these are contrary the one to the other: so that ye can not do the things that ye would. But if ye be led of the Spirit, ye are not under the law."

"If ye be led of the Spirit, ye are not under the law;" because "as many as are led of the Spirit of God, they are the sons of God." As sons of God, these have the mind of the Spirit, the mind of Christ; and so with the mind they "serve the law of God." Accordingly, whosoever is led of the Spirit of God, and thus has the mind of Christ, fulfill the law; because, by that Spirit, there is shed abroad in the heart the love of God, which, in itself, is the fulfilling of the law, in whomsoever has it.

On the other hand, whomsoever is *led of the flesh,* and so has *the mind of the flesh,* does *the works of the flesh,* and so *serves the law of sin.*

And the two ways, the way of the Spirit and the way of the flesh, are *always open before every man.* As certainly as the flesh is there, it "lusteth against the Spirit;" and as certainly as the Spirit is there, it "lusteth against the flesh." Whosoever is led of the flesh can not do the good that he would; he serves the law of sin, and so is under the law. But whosoever is "led of the Spirit is not under the law."

And every man is always free to choose which shall be his way—the way of the Spirit, or the way of the flesh. "If ye live after the flesh, ye shall die; but if ye through the Spirit do mortify the deeds of the body, ye shall live." Rom. 8:13.

Note that, in the text of Galatians now under consideration, and its kindred texts in Romans and also in Colossians, it is stated in words, and constantly held in view, that the flesh, in its true, fleshly, sinful nature, is still present with him who has the Spirit of God; and that this flesh is warring against the Spirit.

That is, when a man is converted, and is thus brought under the power of the spirit of God, he is not so delivered from the flesh that he is actually separated from it, with its tendencies and desires, so that, by the flesh, he is no more tempted, and that with it he has no more contest. No; that same degenerate, sinful flesh is there, with its same tendencies and desires. But the individual is *no longer subject to them.* He is delivered *from subjection to the flesh,* with is tendencies and desires, and is now *subject to the Spirit.* He is now subject to a *power* that *conquers,* and brings under, crucifies, and keeps under, *the flesh,* sinful as it is, with all its affections and lusts. Therefore, it is written that "ye *through the Spirit* do mortify the deeds of the body." "Mortify therefore *your members which are upon the earth;* fornication, uncleanness, inordinate affection, evil concupiscence, and covetousness, which is idolatry." Col. 3:5. Note that all these things are there in the flesh and would live and reign *if the flesh were to rule.* But since the *flesh itself* is brought *into subjection* to the *power of God,* through the Spirit, all these evil things are killed at the root, and thus prevented from appearing in the life.

This contrast between the rule of the flesh and the rule of the Spirit, is clearly shown in Rom. 7:14-24 and in 1 Cor. 9:26, 27. In the seventh of Romans is pictured the man who is under the power of the flesh, "carnal, sold under sin," who longs to do good, and wills to do good, but is subject to a power in the flesh that will not let him do the good that he would. "For the good that I would I do not; but the evil which I would not, that I do." "I find then a law, that, when I would do good, evil is present with me. For I delight in the law of God after the inward man: but I see *another law IN MY MEMBERS, warring against the law of my mind,* and bringing *me* into *captivity to the law of sin* which is *in my members.* 0 wretched man that I am! who shall deliver me from the body of this death?" That describes the man who is subject to the flesh, "to the law of sin" that is in the members. And when he would break away from the power of the flesh, and would do good, that power still brings him into captivity, and holds him under the dominion of the flesh, the law of sin, which is in his members.

But there is *deliverance from that power.* Therefore, when he cries out, "0 wretched man that I am! who shall deliver me from the body of this death?" there is given instantly the answer: "I thank God through Jesus Christ our Lord." There is the way of deliverance; for Christ alone is the Deliverer.

And now this man, though he is thus delivered, *is not delivered from* A CONTEST: he is not put into a condition where he has no fighting to do *with the flesh.* There is a fight still to be carried on; and it is not a make-believe fight; it is not the fighting of a phantom. Here is the man of 1 Cor. 9:26, 27: "So fight I, not as one that beateth the air." "But I keep under *my body,* and *bring it into subjection:* lest that by any means, when I have preached to others, I myself should be a castaway."

Thus, in the battle that the Christian fights, is *his body,* is *the flesh,* with its affections and lusts. The body is to be, by the Christian, kept under, and brought into subjection, by *the new power* of *the Spirit of God,* to which he is now subject, and to which he became subject when delivered from the power of the flesh and the law of sin.

This is made yet more expressive by the fuller rendering of the Greek word translated "keep under," in 1 Cor. 9:27: "I keep under my body." It means literally, "to strike under the eyes, hit and beat the face black and blue." Accordingly, Conybeare and Hawson translate this passage thus: "I fight not as the pugilist who strikes out against the air; but I bruise my body and force it into bondage."

Thus the seventh of Romans shows *the man* subject to the power of *the flesh* and the law of sin that is in the members, but longing for deliverance. The ninth of first Corinthians shows *the flesh* subject to *the man* through the new power of the Spirit of God. In the seventh of Romans, *the flesh is ruling, and the man is under.* In the ninth chapter of Corinthians, *the man is ruling, and the flesh is under.*

And this blessed reversal of things is wrought in conversion. By conversion the man is put in possession of the power of God, so that, by that power, he is made ruler over the flesh, with all its affections and lusts; and, through the Spirit, he crucifies the flesh with the affections and lusts, in his fighting "the good fight of faith."

Men are not saved by being delivered utterly from the flesh; but by *receiving power to conquer* and *rule over* all the evil tendencies and the desires of the flesh. Men do not develop character (in fact, they never could) by being delivered into a realm of no temptation; but, by *receiving power,* in the field of temptation exactly where they are, *to conquer all the temptation.*

If men were to be saved by being delivered utterly from the flesh just as it is, then Jesus need never have come to the world. If men were to be saved by being delivered from all temptation, and set in a realm of no temptation, then Jesus need not have come into the world. But never, by any such deliverance as that, could man have developed character. Therefore, instead of trying to save men by delivering them utterly from the flesh, just where they were, Jesus came to the world, and *put himself* IN THE FLESH, just where men are; and met *that flesh,* JUST AS IT IS, with all its tendencies and desires; and by the divine power which he brought by faith, he "conquered sin *in the flesh,*" and thus brought to all mankind that divine faith which brings the divine power to man to deliver him from the power of the flesh and the law of sin, just where he is, and to give him assured dominion over the flesh, just as it is.

Instead of Jesus' trying to save men in a way in which they would be limp and characterless, by setting them in a realm of no temptation, he came to man, just where man is, *in the midst of all his temptations.* Jesus came in the *very flesh such as man has;* and *in that flesh,* he met all the temptations known to that flesh, and conquered every one of them; and by that conquest brought victory to every soul in the world. Bless his name.

And every soul can have in its fullness that victory, who will receive and keep *"the faith of Jesus."* For "this is the victory that overcometh *the world,* even our faith."

Galatians 5:19-21

September 26, 1900

"Now the works of the flesh are manifest, which are these: adultery, fornication, uncleanness, lasciviousness, idolatry, witchcraft, hatred, variance, emulations, wrath, strife, seditions, heresies, envyings, murders, drunkenness, revelings, and such like: of the which I tell you before, as I have also told you in time past, that they which do such things shall not inherit the kingdom of God."

Fornication, uncleanness, and lasciviousness are but different forms of the practice of adultery; as Jesus said: "Ye have heard that it was said to them of old time, Thou shalt not commit adultery: but I say unto you, that whosoever looketh on a woman to lust after her hath committed adultery with her already in his heart." Matt. 5:27, 28.

Thus, adultery begins in the unclean thought, the lascivious desire. Indeed, truly and strictly speaking, it begins in any thought which, if carried to its ultimate extent, could possibly lead to adultery. This is why it is that the commandments of God are "exceeding broad." Each of the commandments of God forbids the ultimate act, by forbidding the imagination of the thought, which, if followed up, could possibly lead to the ultimate act. And thus the law of God, with its eternal "Thou shalt not," forbids all unrighteousness of men, and asserts the righteousness of God.

Idolatry is the having of other gods before the Lord. And anything that, in the estimation of any one, stands, to him, before the Lord, is an idol; and he who so allows such a thing is an idolater. Perhaps the clearest and most comprehensive statement of what is idolatry, is that by John: "Love not *the world,* neither the things that are in the world. If any man love the world, the love of the Father is not in him. For *all that is in the world,* the lust of the flesh, and the lust of the eyes, and the pride of life, is *not of the Father,* but *is of the world.* And the world passeth away, and the lust thereof: but he that doeth the will of God abideth forever." 1 John 2:15-17. As expressed by James, it is, "Know ye not that the friendship of the world is enmity with God? whosoever therefore will be a friend of the world is the enemy of God." James 4:4.

The world, with its ways, is not of God, but is of Satan; for it is written: "The whole world lieth in the wicked one." 1 John 5:19, R.V. And it is "the god of this world" who blinds "the minds of them which believe not, lest the light of the glorious gospel of Christ, who is the Image of God, should shine unto them." 2 Cor. 4:4. Accordingly, any way of this world that is followed by any one in preference to the way of God—that is idolatry to that person, and he is an idolater.

Witchcraft is, literally, sorcery; and in other translations is mostly rendered sorcery. The original word is *pharmakeia,* which means "the preparing or using of medicine," and is the original of the present English word "pharmacy," the art of compounding medicines and drugs. From the original meaning of "the preparing of medicine," the word was applied to "the using of any kind of drugs, potions, or spell." Hence, it signifies "the use of supernatural knowledge or power gained in any manner, especially through the connivance of evil spirits, magic art, enchantment, witchcraft, spells, or charms."

And how natural a work of the flesh is that tendency to divination! How many persons there are who like to know their fortune; and who, therefore, are always ready to respond to the invitations of a gypsy or a crone. And how ready people naturally are to wish to feel the experience of being mesmerized, or hypnotized! All these things come under the heading of this word *pharmakeia,* witchcraft, or sorcery. They are all works of the flesh. And bear in mind that it is written that "they which do such things shall not inherit the kingdom of God." In the eternal righteousness, the eternal life, and the eternal promises, which God has given in Jesus Christ our Lord, the Christian already knows his fortune, even to the depths of all eternity; and he needs no pharmacy, no drugging, no charms, spells, witchcrafts, or sorcery, at any time, not in any way whatever.

Hatred, being the opposite of love, all the following-named works of the flesh—"variance, emulations, wrath, strife, seditions, heresies, envyings, murders"—are but variations of it, just as we have seen that fornication, uncleanness and lasciviousness are simply various forms of adultery. The commandment which says, "Thou shalt not kill," and which, in that, forbids hatred, is, in itself, murder. For "whosoever hateth his brother is a murderer." As defined in the sermon on the mount, the thought stands: "Ye have heard that it was said to them of old time, Thou shalt not kill; and whosoever shall kill shall be in danger of the judgment: but I say unto you, That whosoever is angry with his brother without a cause shall be in danger of the judgment; and whosoever shall say to his brother, Raca, shall be in danger of the council: but whosoever shall say, Thou fool, shall be in danger of hell fire." Matt. 5:21, 22.

However, it is well to look at each of these words, that we may get as clear a view as possible of the subtlety and deceitfulness of sin in the works of the flesh. This, because few persons realize that they hate a person unless they actually do regard them "with a strong and passionate dislike, or aversion," or "with extreme ill-will." But when there is borne in mind the principle that the law of God in forbidding the ultimate act of evil, forbids the very imagination of the thought which, if carried out, could possibly lead to that ultimate act; and when it is borne in mind that, according to the Lord's own definition, to hate a person, or to speak ill of a person, is to break the commandment that says, "Thou shalt not kill,"—then it can be easily understood that hatred can be indulged without that direct and extreme ill-will and aversion to the presence, or even the thought, of the person hated, which alone is commonly recognized as hatred.

"Variance" suggests "difference," especially "difference that produces disagreement or controversy; dispute; disuasion; discord." The original word signifies "strife, quarrel, debate, wordy wrangling, disputation, contention." The spirit and tendency, therefore, of "variance," is a readiness to differ and to raise questions, and then hold tenaciously to personal views, and run the difference into debating and dissension; then to ill-will, which, in itself, is hatred, which, in itself, in turn, is the breaking of the commandment that says, "Thou shalt not kill."

It is not in vain that, in the Scriptures, debate is catalogued with "envy, murder," "deceit," and "malignity," and is placed definitely between *murder* and *deceit*. Whoever, therefore, would avoid murder must avoid hatred; and whoever would avoid variance must diligently avoid the spirit that raises questions and indulges differences that lead to controversy, debate, and its further train of evils, which continues unbroken unto hatred, which itself is murder. And this thought is worthy of special attention everywhere in the study and recitation of the Sabbath-school lessons.

"Emulations" is the "love of superiority; desire or ambition to equal or excel others;" "the desire and the resulting endeavor to equal or surpass another, or others, in some quality, attainment, or achievement," It is the expression of sheer love of self-superiority, and inability to endure the thought that another should be superior. The original word is, literally, "jealousy;" and in other translations it is so rendered; and the declaration of the word of God, as to jealousy, is that it "is cruel as the grave." Its synonym is "envy:" and envy is "a feeling of uneasiness, mortification, or discontent, excited by the contemplation of another's superiority, prosperity, or success, accompanied with some degree of enmity or malignity, and often, or usually, with a desire or an effort to discomfit or mortify the person envied." Emulation appears first, and aims to attain to a standing of superiority over another. And when that can not be attained, then envy sweeps in with its tide. When emulation has obtained its aim, it is succeeded immediately by exaltation at the defeat of the foe. When emulation in itself is defeated, it is immediately followed by envy, which, being "enmity prompted by covetousness," waits in secret for an opportunity to vent its malignity, which, it itself, is hatred.

It is easy to see how, in association with variance, emulations, and envyings, there should also appear "wrath, strife, seditions [a going apart], heresies [a choosing for one's self]," and, finally "murder," which is but the ultimate of any *one* of the works of the flesh named in this list, beginning with "hatred" and ending with "murders."

Drunkenness and revelings are simply all manner of intemperance, which, in itself, is idolatry, and carries in its train a multitude of the evils already described in the dreadful works of the flesh.

"And such like" of the which I tell you before, as I have also told you in time past, that *they which do such things* SHALL NOT INHERIT THE KINGDOM OF GOD.

Galatians 5:22-26

October 2, 1900

"But the fruit of the Spirit is love, joy, peace, long-suffering, gentleness, goodness, faith, meekness, temperance: against such there is no law. And they that are Christ's have crucified the flesh with the passions and the lusts. If we live in the Spirit, let us also walk in the Spirit. Let us not be desirous of vainglory, provoking one another, envying one another."

We have seen somewhat of the essential evil and deceitfulness of the works of the flesh. But, thank the Lord, there is a better picture.

The Spirit of God, which, in his fullness, is freely given to every believer, lusteth against the flesh, so that in him who is led by the Spirit of God the flesh can not do the things that it would. In such the Spirit of God rules, and causes to appear in the life "the fruit of the Spirit," instead of "the works of the flesh."

And though it be true "that they which do such things" as we described in the list of the works of the flesh, "shall not inherit the kingdom of God," yet in the gift of the Holy Spirit, through the grace of Christ, God has made full provision by which every soul, in spite of all the passions, lusts, desires, and inclinations of the flesh, *can* "inherit the kingdom of God."

In Christ the battle has been fought, on *every point,* and the victory has been made complete. He was made flesh itself—the *same flesh and blood* as those whom he came to redeem. He was made in all points like these; he was "in all points tempted like as we are." If in any "point" he had not *been* "like as we are," then, on *that* point he could not possibly have been tempted *"like as we are."*

He was *"touched"* with the *feeling* of our infirmities," because he "was in *all* points *tempted* like as *we are."* When he was tempted, he felt the desires and the inclinations of the flesh, precisely as we feel them when we are tempted. For "every man is tempted, when he is drawn away of his own lusts [his own desires and inclinations of the flesh] and enticed." James 1:14. All this Jesus could experience without sin; because to be tempted *is not sin.* It is only "when lust hath conceived," when the desire is cherished, when the inclination is sanctioned,—only then it is that "it bringeth forth sin." And Jesus never even in a thought cherished a desire, or sanctioned an inclination, of the flesh. Thus, in such flesh as ours, he was tempted in all points as we are, and yet without a taint of sin.

And thus, by the divine power that he received through faith in God, he, *in our flesh,* utterly quenched every inclination of that flesh, and effectually killed at its root every desire of the flesh; and so "condemned sin *in the flesh."* And in so doing, he brought *complete victory,* and *divine power to maintain it,* to every soul in the world. All this he did "that the righteousness of the law might be fulfilled in us, who walk not after the flesh, but after the Spirit."

This victory, in its fullness, is free to every soul in Christ Jesus. It is received

Galatians 5:22-26

by faith *in Jesus.* It is accomplished and maintained by "the faith *of Jesus,"* which he has wrought out in perfection, and has given to every believer in him. For "this is the victory which overcometh *the world,* even our faith."

He "abolished *in his flesh* the enmity" that separated mankind from God. Eph. 2:15. In order to do this, he took *the flesh,* and *must take* the flesh, *in which that enmity existed.* And he "abolished in his flesh the enmity," "for to make," in order to make *"in himself* of twain," God and the estranged man, "one new man, so making peace."

He "abolished in his flesh the enmity," in order "that he might reconcile both" Jew and Gentile—all mankind who are subject to the enmity—"unto God, in one body by the cross, having slain the enmity *in himself."* Eph. 2:16, margin. "The enmity" was "in *himself,"* by being "in his *flesh."* And there *"in his flesh"* he slew it and abolished it. And he could do this only by its being indeed "in his flesh."

Thus Jesus took upon him the curse, in all its fullness, precisely as that curse is upon mankind. This he did by "being made a curse for us." But "the curse causeless shall not come," and never came. The cause of the curse is sin. He was made a curse for us, because of our sins. And to meet the *curse* as it is *upon* us, he must meet *sin* as it is *in* us. Accordingly, God "hath made him to be sin for us, who knew no sin. And this "that we might be made *the righteousness of God IN HIM."* 2 Cor. 5:21.

And though he thus placed himself entirely at the same great disadvantage as are all mankind—made in all points like us and so, "in all points tempted like as we are,"—yet not a single tendency or inclination of the flesh was ever allowed the slightest recognition, even in thought; but every one of them was effectually killed at the root by the power of God, which, through divine faith, he brought to humanity.

And thus, "as the children are partakers of *flesh and blood,* he *also* HIMSELF *LIKEWISE* took part of *THE SAME;* that through death he might destroy him that had the power of death, that is, the devil; and *deliver them who* through fear of death were all their lifetime *subject to bondage.* For verily he took not on him the nature of angels; but he took on him the seed of Abraham. Wherefore in *all things* it behoved him to be *made like unto his brethren,* that he might be a merciful and faithful high priest in things pertaining to God, to make reconciliation for the sins of the people. For in that he himself hath suffered *being tempted,* he is able to succor them that are tempted." Heb. 2:14-18.

And this victory which Christ wrought out in human flesh, is brought by the Holy Spirit to the rescue of everyone in human flesh who today believes in Jesus. For by the Holy Spirit the very presence of Christ himself comes to the believer; for it is his constant desire to "grant you, according to the riches of his glory, to be strengthened *with might* by *his Spirit* in the inner man; *that Christ my dwell in your hearts by faith;* that ye, being rooted and grounded in love, may be able to comprehend with all saints what is the breadth, and length, and depth, and height; and to know the love of Christ, which passeth knowledge, that ye might be filled with *all the fullness of God."* Eph. 3:16-19.

Thus the deliverance from the guilt of sin and from the power of sin, which holds the believer in triumph over all the desires, the tendencies and inclinations, of his sinful flesh, through the power of the Spirit of God,—this is wrought today by the personal presence of Christ Jesus IN HUMAN FLESH in the believer, *precisely as it was wrought* by the personal presence of Christ in human flesh eighteen hundred and seventy years ago.

Christ is ever the same—"the same yesterday, and today, and forever." The gospel of Christ is ever the same—the same yesterday, and today, and forever. The gospel of Christ today is the same that it was eighteen hundred and seventy years ago. *Then* it was "God manifest in the flesh;" and *today* it is the *same*—"God manifest in the" *same flesh,* the flesh of sinful men, human flesh, just as human nature is.

That gospel is "Christ in you, the hope of glory,"—Christ in you *just as you are,* sins, sinfulness, and all; for he gave himself for our sins, and for our sinfulness. And you, *just as you are,* Christ has bought, and God "hath made accepted" in him. He *has received you* just *as you are* . and the gospel, "Christ in you, the hope of glory," brings you under the reign of the Spirit of God, makes you so subject to the power of Christ and of God that "the fruit of the Spirit" appears in you, instead of "the works of the flesh."

And the fruit of the Spirit is—

LOVE—the love of God which is shed abroad in the heart by the Spirit of God. And instead of hatred or any of its kin ever being allowed, even in thought, no man can possibly do anything to you that can cause you to do anything but love him. For this love, being the love of God, is "the same yesterday, and today, and forever;" and loves not for reward, but for the mere sake of loving; it loves simply because it is love, and *being* only that, it can not *do* any thing else.

JOY—Is "ardent happiness arising from present or expected good." But in this case, the alternative "or" is excluded; for this joy is ardent happiness arising from present *AND* expected good; for the cause of it is eternal. Accordingly, it is everlastingly present, and is everlastingly to be expected. And therefore, it is "exultant satisfaction."

PEACE—perfect peace that rules in the heart—"the peace of God, which passeth all understanding," and which *"keeps* the *heart* and *mind"* of him who has It.

LONGSUFFERING, GENTLENESS, GOODNESS, FAITH—This faith—*pistis*, Greek—is "firm persuasion; the conviction which is based upon *trust*, NOT upon *knowledge* [the faith of "the *heart,"* not of the *head;* the faith of *Christ,* not of the creed,]: a firmly relying confidence cherished by conviction, and bidding defiance to opposing contradictions."

MEEKNESS, TEMPERANCE—Temperance is self-control. Thus, the Spirit of God delivers the man from subjection to his passions, lusts, and habits, and makes him a free man, master of himself.

"Against such there is no law." The law of God is against nothing but sin. In human lives the law of God is against everything that is not the fruit of the Spirit of God. Therefore it is certain that everything in human life that is not the fruit of the Spirit of God, is sin. And this is but stating, in another way, the eternal truth that "whatsoever is *not of faith* is sin.

Therefore "if we live in the Spirit, let us also walk in the Spirit." And because we do live in the Spirit and walk in the Spirit, *"let* us not"—yea, we shall not; yea, we can not—"be desirous of vainglory, provoking one another, envying one another."

Chapter Six

Galatians 6:1

October 16, 1900

"Brethren, if a man be overtaken in a fault, ye which are spiritual, restore such an one in the spirit of meekness; considering thyself, lest thou also be tempted."

Note that when a man is overtaken in a fault, the only thing that the Scripture commands the Christians to do is to "restore such an one." There is no commandment to condemn him, to set him at naught, to ostracize him, to talk about either him or his fault; but only to "restore" him.

This is the only spirit that there is in Christianity; for "God sent not his Son into the world to condemn the world; but that the world through him might be saved." Condemnation is not what anybody needs in this world; for everybody is already condemned over and over, by his own sins and by his own knowledge of his own faults. And, surely, it could be nothing but an essentially vindictive spirit that would crowd more condemnation upon a person who is, already, and many times, doubly condemned. And Christianity is not of such spirit: Christianity is the spirit of love, of the very love of God; and God's love is manifest in his sending of Christ, not to condemn the world, but to save it. Such alone is the spirit of Christianity, everywhere, and forever.

This is shown also in the text, in directing that "ye that are *spiritual* restore such a one." There is no direction to anyone who is not spiritual to make any attempt to restore such a one: and this for the simple reason that any such one could do it. The first consideration, therefore, when the Christian receives the knowledge that one is overtaken in a fault, is that that one is to be *restored*. The next is, Am I spiritual, so that I can hope to restore him? This brings the one who is to attempt the restoring, face to face with himself and God, in an examination of his own standing before God, as to whether he is truly spiritual.

And when this is found to be so, when one has found himself truly spiritual, then, in the spirit of meekness, which is only the spirit of Christ, and which can be only in him who is truly spiritual, seek to restore the one overtaken in the fault: at the same time "considering thyself, lest thou also be tempted;" putting yourself in his place, asking yourself how you would like to be approached, how you would like to be treated, if you were in the fault in which the brother has been overtaken.

Bear in mind also that it is the man who is "overtaken" in the fault who is to be restored—not one whom you imagine to have committed a fault; not one whom you think has done what you think to be a fault. This word gives no countenance whatever to any spirit of fault-finding, or of searching for faults in a brother. It is counsel to be followed and applied only when one is "overtaken in a fault;" when it has become apparent that there is actually a fault. Then, and only then, is the matter to be touched; and then only "ye *which are spiritual, restore* such a one in the spirit of meekness; considering thyself, lest thou also be tempted."

Jesus has also given *specific* directions as to how Christians shall go about to "restore" the one overtaken in a fault. He says: "Go and tell him his fault between thee and him alone." Matt. 18:14. In all the word of God there is no counsel plainer than this of the Lord Jesus; yet what counsel of his is more, and more positively, disregarded by those who profess to be his?

It is the truth well known to all, that the majority of professed Christians do go and tell anybody, and almost everybody, *else than the one* who has committed the fault. But how can they do so and be a Christian? Such a course is natural to the natural man, because it is natural to each man in the world to think every other man his enemy, and, consequently, to have no confidence in him; and then he concludes that it would do no possible good for him to go and tell the man his fault, because it would only make the man still more his enemy.

But it is not so with Christians. The believer in Jesus is sure that all other believers in Jesus are not his enemies, but are his brethren; he counts them as such; he has confidence in them as such. Therefore, he who is really a Christian has confidence in his brother, that his brother will listen to him and will hear him in what he has to say, even though it be to tell him his fault "between thee and him alone."

Therefore, it is lack of confidence in a brother's sincerity in the fear of the Lord, which is the cause that any professed Christian will not go and tell his brother his fault "between thee and him alone." But lack of Christian confidence is only the mark of the lack of brotherly love, which in itself, is a lack of Christianity. So the true analysis of such a course shows that it is simply the lack of Christianity that causes any professed Christian to tell it to anybody else than *the one in fault,* and *not* to "go and tell him his fault between thee and him alone." But go as a Christian, as a brother, and "tell him his fault between thee and him alone; if he shall hear thee, thou hast gained thy brother." To *"gain"* him, to "restore" him, is all the purpose of your going to him at all.

And when one is not a Christian, there is indeed no need for him to go and tell a man his fault, because he is not in a condition to be able to tell it in a way that will do the man any good; for even when one is a Christian, and is spiritual, and "in the spirit of meekness "goes and tells a man his fault, between the two alone, it is possible that even then the man will not hear him. And "if he will not hear thee, then take with thee one or two more, that in the mouth of two or three witnesses every work may be established." Matt. 18:16. Not that you are to go and *tell* one or two more, but you are to *take* one or two more, and go and *tell him,* in their presence as witnesses.

"And if he shall neglect to hear them, tell it unto the church; but if he neglect to hear the church, let him be unto thee as an heathen man and a publican." Verse 17.

He who, against all this attempt to restore him, holds on his own way, rejecting all attempts of his brethren to help him, has demonstrated that he has not the spirit of Christian brotherhood, and has separated himself from the company of the brethren. And then all that the church can do is to recognize the truth of the situation thus developed, and "let him be unto thee as an heathen man and a publican." As it is written in another place; "A man that is an heretic [one who chooses for himself, against the word of God. against all considerations of brotherhood] after the *first* and *second* admonition reject; knowing that he that is such is subverted, and sinneth, being *condemned of himself."* Titus 3:10, 11.

Galatians 6:2

October 23, 1900

"Bear ye one another's burdens, and so fulfill the law of Christ." Thus it is seen that the law of Christ is self-sacrifice to serve others; the spending of self to help others.

And so it is written in another place: "We then that are strong ought to bear the infirmities of the weak, and not to please ourselves."

And again: "Let every one of us please his neighbor for his good to edification."

Galatians 6:2

And this because "even Christ pleased not himself; but, as it is written, The reproaches of them that reproached thee fell on me." Rom. 15:1-3.

Again: this law is expressed thus: "Let nothing be done through strife or vainglory: but in lowliness of mind let each esteem the other better than themselves." Phil. 2:3. When each esteems the other better than himself, it becomes a pleasure to serve the other: it is more of a pleasure to serve the other, by helping him, than it is to serve self.

So in truth each can please himself *more,* in *pleasing his neighbor* for his good, by serving and helping him, than he can in seeking to please himself by serving only himself. This is the true Christian joy, because it was "for the joy that was set before him" that Christ "endured the cross, despising the shame" and the reproach which must be, and which were, endured to deliver us from our shame and reproach.

Therefore, again this law of Christ is expressed in the words: "Look not every man on his own things, but every man also on the things of others." Phil. 2:4.

And that all may know for certain that this is precisely the law of Christ, and that the observance of it is therefore the keeping of all the law of God,—yea, even the keeping of all the law and the prophets,—Jesus himself spoke for all mankind this law of Christ. And here are the words: "All things whatsoever ye would that men should do to you, do ye even so to them; for this is the law and the prophets." Matt. 7:12.

Notice, it is not, "All things whatsoever ye would that men should do to you, do" that to *yourself.* Nor is it to *have them do that to you;* but it is "do *ye even so* to *them.*"

Thus the knowledge of this law of Christ is the easiest of all knowledge to attain, and the observance of this law is the easiest of all observances, to him who really has the heart to do it. To know what the law of Christ is, all that is required is that I shall simply think of what I would have any man do to me. In this transaction, at this particular moment, *what would I choose* that that man should do to me, if I were in his place, and all these circumstances applied to me? And whatsoever that may be, I know that that is the thing that it is right for me to do to him just at that moment, in that particular transaction, and in those circumstances. And since it is always perfectly easy for any man to know what he would that another should do to him in given circumstances, it is thus easy for him to know, at any moment, just what is the law of Christ; just what is the law of God; just what is "the whole duty of man."

And just as easy as it is to *know* it, just so easy it is to *do* it, when I have the heart to do it; when I have Christ before me, instead of myself; and when I have his law in my heart, instead of my own self-seeking. But it is plain that this requires the utter emptying of self, and the appearing of Christ in the life; because none of this is the way of self; and self will never go that way. That is the way of unselfishness; that is the way of the crucifixion of self; the utter death of self, and the living of Christ.

Therefore immediately following the word, "Look not every man on his own things, but every man on the things of others," the sum of all is written: "Let this mind be in you which was also in Christ Jesus; who being in the form of God: thought it not robbery to be equal with God, but emptied himself, and took upon him the form of a servant, and was made in the likeness of men, and being found in fashion as a man, he humbled himself, and became obedient unto death, even the death of the cross." Phil. 2:5-8.

Certainly it is true that without the mind of Christ no man can fulfill the law of Christ. Then wherever there is a lack of fulfilling the law of Christ, a lack of esteeming others better than ourselves, a lack of looking on the things of others, it is evident that the cause of the failure is in not having the mind of Christ. And the remedy is to receive and to retain the mind of Christ.

If this law of Christ were fulfilled daily by individuals, by the managers of our Conferences and our institutions, the loud cry of the Third Angel's Message would shortly fill the earth, the gospel of the kingdom would speedily be preached to all the world, and very soon the end would come. "Bear ye one another's burdens, and so fulfill the law of Christ."

Galatians 6:3

October 30, 1900

"For if a man think himself to be something, when he is nothing, he deceiveth himself."

It is bad enough for a man to be deceived by another; but it is worse to be deceived by himself. But this verse gives the true corrective and preventive of self-deception—and it is found in a man's thinking himself truly what he is; that is, nothing.

But this is not natural. The natural thing is for each one to think himself something; and then continue so to think until he becomes more and more something, and the chiefest of all. That is simply the secret and the spirit of self-exaltation.

But the truth is that of himself man is nothing; and the true way for any man to find this truth is to confess that he is nothing. That is simply the way of self-abnegation.

And then he can become something.

Now the reason of all this is that man is separated from God; and this separation was accomplished by his accepting the suggestion, and following the way, of the one who originally in his self-exaltation, declared: "I will be like the Most High." And the end course, with that one, is that he shall be absolutely nothing. For of him at the end of his course it is written: "Never shalt thou be any more." Eze. 28:19. And when he entered upon that course which inevitably ends only in his being absolutely nothing, then it is certain that at the beginning of it he practically made himself nothing, and that all through his course he was truly nothing.

It is so also with the man who accepted the leadership, and followed in the way, of this one. By this the man made himself nothing. And so it is written: "All nations before him are as nothing: and they are counted to him less than nothing, and vanity." Isa. 40:17. And "they that war against thee shall be as nothing, and as a thing of naught." Isa. 42:12.

Yet the original leader, and, from him, all who are led in this course, really think themselves to be something, when, in very truth, they are nothing.

Now there is a way out of this nothingness into that which is something, and in which each one shall be truly something. And this was in the way of Christ—the way of the cross. Christ is the example: he has led the way; for "he emptied himself, and became obedient unto death, even the death of the cross." Thus he gave himself up to be, and to become, lost and nothing, that he might redeem those who are lost and nothing.

Therefore all are exhorted: "Let this mind be in you, which was also in Christ Jesus: who, being in the form of God, thought it not robbery to be equal with God: but emptied himself," and became nothing. And because he did this, and through his doing it, "God also hath highly exalted him, and given him a name which is above every name: that at the name of Jesus every knee should bow, of things under the heaven, and things in earth, and things under the earth; and that every tongue should confess that Jesus Christ is Lord, to the glory of God the Father." Phil. 2:5, 9-11.

Therefore the first of all things for any man to do to help himself, to set himself in the way of deliverance from nothingness, is to recognize truly that he is nothing. Then, *in Christ* he becomes *something,* and shall be something, even though, in himself, he is ever nothing. As it is written: "In nothing am I behind the very chiefest apostles, though I be *nothing."* 2 Cor. 12:11. This, because we are not "sufficient of ourselves to think *anything* as of ourselves; but our sufficiency is of God." 3:5. "As God hath said, I will dwell in them and they shall be my people." 6:16. This is "the mystery of God;" God manifest in the flesh: "Christ in you, the hope of glory."

And these things are written "that ye might learn in us not to think of men above that which is written, that no one of you be puffed up for one against another. For who maketh thee to differ from another? And what hast thou that thou didst not receive? Now if thou didst receive it, why dost thou glory, as if thou hadst not received it?" 1 Cor. 4:6, 7.

When it is true of every man that he has nothing, absolutely nothing, even to his existence, which he did not receive from God; then, without God, what is he?—Plainly, he is nothing. And that is just the condition of men as they are in the world, naturally, "without God in the world." Eph. 2:12.

Thus, it being strictly true, in the nature of things, that, without God, any creature is nothing; man, being without God, is truly nothing. Then, when, in this condition, man thinks himself something, in that very thing he asserts self-existence—equality with God. And this is true of man in his condition of sin and separation from God; because that was the very thing which was asserted to him and expected by him when sin entered: "Ye shall be like God."

But self-existence is not true of any creature: self-existence is true only of God. All persons and things are from him, and by him; and in him all things "live, and move, and have their being:" each in itself nothing, but in him something, according as his mind, his will, his purpose, is manifest therein.

Thus the self-deception of a man in his thinking himself to be something, when, in absolute truth, he is nothing, is the worst and most destructive of all deceptions, because it is the deception of asserting of himself self-existence,—divinity; "showing himself that he is God,"—the only end of which is to become, indeed, absolutely nothing, in the awful consummation that is declared. "For yet a little while, and the wicked *shall not be:* yea, thou shalt diligently consider his place, and it shall not be." Ps. 37:10.

But only let a man accept, in his heart and life, the truth that he is nothing; let him accept the manifestation of Christ, which alone can ever hold him in the place where he shall know that, in truth, of himself he is nothing; let Christ live in him; let God be manifest in his flesh; let the mind, the will, the purpose, of God thus be manifest in him,—and of him it will be also true that, because of this, "God also hath highly exalted him." For it is written: "To him that overcometh will I grant to sit with me in my throne, even as I also overcame, and am set down with my Father in his throne." Rev. 3:21. Jesus said, "Without me ye can do nothing." This is so because, without him, ye are nothing. For to be without Christ is to be "without God in the world" (Eph. 2:12); and to be without God is to be nothing.

Only the way of Christ, the way of the cross, is the way of life, the way of something. Any other way is only the way of death, the way of nothing.

"Let this mind be in you, which was also in Christ Jesus: who. . . emptied himself."

Galatians 6:4-10

November 6, 1900

"But let every man prove his own work, and then shall he have rejoicing in himself alone, and not in another."

The word "prove" here signifies, as to the thing proved, the test put upon metals by the assayer; and it is well known that such a test is the most thorough that can be employed. It goes even so far as to the testing by fire to such an extent that the fire itself shall be through and through the metal; so that the very metal itself shall be so fairly on fire that everything that is not of the metal itself, is utterly consumed.

As relates to the person who does the proving, the word signifies "to scrutinize," "to keep an eye upon," "to watch narrowly," "to play the spy upon," "to examine intently."

This is what every Christian is particularly called upon to do respecting his own work—respecting the things he does, and which, from mere impulse, he finds himself apt to do.

The same thought is expressed in 2 Cor. 13:5, and is applied to the *whole person himself,* and not only to "his own work:" "Examine yourselves, whether ye be in the faith; *prove* your own selves.

Let each one test his own work, and himself, in all things examine yourselves, whether ye be in the faith; *prove* your own selves."

Let each one test his own work, and himself, in all things in the light of the word of God, illuminated by the Spirit of God, thus holding himself and all his work up to the judgment of God And to all who do so the blessed promise will be found sure: "Then shall he have rejoicing." For of this same thing it is written in another place: "If we would judge ourselves, we should not be judged." 1 Cor. 11:31.

All this is to say that in Christianity, in the faith of Christ, God gives to every man in this world the opportunity safely to pass the judgment. And everyone who will thus enter into God's judgment, who will put himself through the severest tests that the law of God can ever demand, and will thus judge himself in the light of God's countenance, he thus passes the judgment, and has nothing to fear "when God riseth up."

And all such have God's promise that they shall "have rejoicing," and that they have nothing to fear in the great day of judgment itself. This, because they live constantly in the presence of the judgment of God. Their constant prayer is, "Search me, O God, and know my heart; try me, and know my thought: and see if there be any wicked way in me, and lead me in the way everlasting." Ps. 139:23, 24. And they find it all so; and, so, shall surely be led only in the way everlasting.

He shall have "rejoicing in himself alone, and not in another." The parallel thought is in Prov. 14:14: "A good man shall be satisfied from himself." "The sentiment is that he will find in himself a source of pure joy. He will not be dependent on the applause of others for happiness. In an approving conscience; in the evidence of the favor of God; in an honest effort to lead a pure and holy life, he will have happiness. The source of his joys will be within; and he will not be dependent, as the man of ambition, and the man who thinks of himself more highly than he ought, will, on the favors of a capricious multitude, and on the breath of popular applause.

"Here is the true secret of happiness. It consists (1) in not forming an improper estimate of ourselves; in knowing just what we are, and what is due to us; in not thinking ourselves to be something, when we are nothing; (2) in leading such a life that it may be examined *to the core,* that we may know exactly what we are without being distressed or pained; that is, in having a good conscience, and in honest and faithful discharge of our duty to God and man; (3) in not being dependent on fickle applause of the world for our comfort.

"The man who has not internal resources, and who has no approving conscience; who is happy only when others smile, and miserable when they frown is a man who has no security for enjoyment. The man who has a good conscience, and who enjoys the favor of God and the hope of heaven, carries with him a source of perpetual joy. He can not be deprived of it. His purse may be taken, and his house robbed, but the highwayman can not rob him of his comforts. He bears about with him an unfailing source of happiness when abroad, and the same source of happiness abides with him at home; he carries it into society, and it remains with him in solitude; it is his companion when in health, and when surrounded by his friends, and it is no less his companion when his friends leave him, and when he lies upon a bed of death."

"For every man shall bear his own burden."

This is the plain conclusion from all the thought of the preceding verse; and the whole thought on both sides is expressed in Prov. 14:14, complete: "The backslider in heart shall be filled with his own ways: and a good man shall be satisfied from himself." And, again, "I the Lord search the heart, I try the reins (the conscience), even to give every man according to his ways, and according to the fruit of his doings." Jer. 17:10.

Every man is free to choose. To every man the Lord has said, "Choose ye this day whom ye will serve." God has made most abundant provision, even to all the fullness of God, for everyone grandly to succeed who chooses the service of God; and the burden of him who so chooses is only a burden of rejoicing and gladness, forevermore. But he who chooses not the way of the Lord, but his own way, against all the call of the Lord,—he, too, must bear his burden; it is the burden which he has freely chosen to bear, but it is a burden which can not be borne, and only works his undoing.

"Let him that is taught in the word communicate unto him that teacheth in all good things."

This word "communicate" means much more than simply to talk or write to a person: it means "to have things in common," "to be partakers or equal partakers in things." It is the same word and the same meaning as that given in 1 Cor. 10: 16, 17. "The cup of blessing which we bless, is it not the *communion of the blood of Christ? The bread which we break, is it not the *communion of the body of Christ? For we being *many are one bread,* and *one body;* for we are all *partakers* of that *one bread.*" So those who are taught in the word count him that teacheth equal partners with themselves, count all other things common with him, and communicate unto him "in all good things."

And so it is written in another place: "If we have sown unto you spiritual things, is it a great thing if we shall reap your carnal things?" 1 Cor. 9:11. And also in yet another place: "Now I go unto Jerusalem to minister unto the saints. For it hath pleased them of Macedonia and Achaia to make a certain contribution for the poor saints which are at Jerusalem. It hath pleased them verily; and their debtors they are. For if the Gentiles have been made *partakers* of their spiritual things, their duty is also to *minister unto them* in carnal things." Rom. 15: 25-27.

And, upon all this, the exhortation in the four verses, which follow is sufficient, and sufficiently forcible, without any further enlargement or explanation: "Be not deceived; God is not mocked: for whatsoever a man soweth, that shall he also reap. For he that soweth to his flesh shall of the flesh reap corruption; but he that soweth to the Spirit shall of the Spirit reap life everlasting. And let us not be weary in well doing; for in due season we shall reap, if we faint not. As we have therefore opportunity, let us do good unto all men, *especially* unto them who are of the *household of faith.*"

Galatians 6:11-18

November 13, 1900

"Ye see how large a letter I have written unto you with mine own hand."

This is, literally, "with what large letters;" relating to the size of the letters which he was obliged to make because of his defective eyesight.

This itself was an appeal which would tenderly touch the Galatians, and revive in them the memory of the blessedness of their first days in Christianity; for, in the fifteenth verse of the fourth chapter, he says: "Where is then the blessedness ye spake of? For I bear you record, that, if it had been possible, ye would have plucked out your own eyes, and have given them to me." This was their love to him when they enjoyed the blessedness of the true gospel which they had received, and Paul gladly witnessed to it. But there never would have been any need, nor any ground for thought, of plucking out their eyes and giving them to him if there had not been in him a manifest need of eyes.

This defect in his eyes was the result of the consuming glory of Christ that day when the Lord appeared to him as he was on his way to Damascus; for, when the vision was past, he was unable to see; and "they led him by the hand, and brought him into Damascus." And there "he was three days without sight," until Ananias was sent by the Lord to put his hand on him "that he might receive his sight." And when Ananias had so done, "immediately there fell from his eyes as it had been scales." But forever there was thus in his flesh that mark which he calls "my temptation which was in my flesh."

And now, in his last words to the Galatians, when he says, "Ye see with what large letters I have written unto you with mine own hand," it is a delicate and touching way in which he would call their attention to this affliction which they, in their love at the first, would have remedied by plucking out their own eyes and giving them to him. This expression shows to them that he had written this whole letter with his own hand in spite of this affliction, which obliged him to write in exceptionally large letters, in order that he himself might be able to see his writing. This of itself would be a powerful testimony to them of his tender love still for them, and that, whatever he had said, in none of it was there any ill-feeling toward them, but a great fear lest they should be caused to lose the great salvation that had been so freely given to them.

This writing of a whole letter in Paul's own hand was unusual. He usually wrote the body of a letter by an amanuensis. For instance, the actual body of the letter to the Romans was written by Tertius. Rom. 16:22. But always, Paul would sign the letter with his own name, with his own hand, as, for instance, 1 Cor. 16:21: "The salutation of me Paul with mine own hand;" Col. 4:18: "The salutation by the hand of Paul;" and 2 Thess. 3:17: "The salutation of Paul with mine own hand, which is the token in every epistle: so I write." This, indeed, became essential, because 2 Thess. 2:2 shows that there were those who were circulating letters as from Paul, which were fraudulent.

"As many as desire to make a fair show in the flesh, they constrain you to be circumcised; only lest they should suffer persecution for the cross of Christ. For neither they themselves who are circumcised keep the law; but desire to have you circumcised, that they may glory in your flesh."

It must be borne in mind that those who had confused the Galatians and caused all the trouble there were "Pharisees which believed." They were Pharisees at first, and, still holding to their pharisaism, professed to believe in Jesus; and this had made their profession of Christianity merely pharisaism. And pure Christianity at that time, as well as in every other time, could not be made to fit well with pharisaism; because, at that time, it was a very humiliating thing to be known as a Christian outright. The One in whom all Christianity centered had only lately been crucified as a malefactor; had thus died the most disgraceful death, and by the most disgraceful means, known to mankind. In addition to this, there was persecution attached to the outright profession of Christianity, but the Pharisees, still holding to their pride, had not discerned the true glory of the cross of Christ so that they could with confidence, and even with joy, suffer persecution. But in the way of circumcision there was no persecution: that was the way of glory. True, it was worldly glory; it was pharisaic glory; it was self-glory; but that being the only glory which they knew, to them it was the true way of glory. Consequently, so long as they could hold to circumcision, they would escape persecution.

Thus the controversy centered in the question as to the true way of glory—

whether it was by circumcision, or by the cross of Christ. By the *pride* of the Pharisees circumcision was exalted to the pinnacle of the true way of glory. The cross, as already stated, was the most degrading thing in the world. But behold here the illustration of the great truth that "that which is highly esteemed amongst men, is abomination in the sight of God." The Pharisees had made circumcision the greatest of all things, and the perfect highway to glory, while they, and all mankind, looked upon the way of the cross as the most disgraceful thing that could ever come to a man. But that way of the cross, God shows to be indeed the highway of glory. The way which men most despise is the way in which God would most manifest his glory: the way in which men most gloried is indeed the way which is most truly to be despised.

Therefore, it is the true, triumphant exclamation of the Christian everywhere and forever: "God forbid that I should glory, save in the cross of our Lord Jesus Christ, by whom the world is crucified unto me, and I unto the world. For in Christ Jesus neither circumcision availeth anything, nor uncircumcision, but a new creature."

"And as many as walk according to this rule, peace to them, and mercy, and upon the Israel of God." And this is forever true; as many as walk by this rule of the cross of Christ, and of the glorying in the cross of Christ; as many as walk by this rule of being by the cross of Christ crucified unto the world, and the world unto them; as many as walk by this rule that neither circumcision availeth anything, nor uncircumcision, but only a new creature avails in Christ Jesus,—"as many a walk according to *THIS RULE,* peace be on them, and mercy, and upon the Israel of God."

"From henceforth let no man trouble me: for I bear in my body the marks of the Lord Jesus." These marks of the Lord Jesus were those which Paul received in the scourgings, the stonings, and all of the other hardships which left their impress upon him. And another translation gives it: "I the brands of the Lord Jesus in my body bear." These things were the token to all who might see, that he belonged to Christ; these were the marks, the brands, which he bore, signifying Christ's ownership of him. And so it is with the Christian forever.

"Brethren, the grace of our Lord Jesus Christ be with your spirit. Amen."

As to the additional subscription: "Unto the Galatians written from Rome," it is but proper to state that the letter to the Galatians was not written from Rome at all, but from Corinth.

We invite you to view the complete
selection of titles we publish at:

www.TEACHServices.com

or write or email us your praises,
reactions, or thoughts about this
or any other book we publish at:

TEACH Services, Inc.
P U B L I S H I N G

www.TEACHServices.com
P.O. Box 954
Ringgold, GA 30736

info@TEACHServices.com

TEACH Services, Inc., titles may be purchased in bulk for educational, business, fund-raising, or sales promotional use. For information, please e-mail BulkSales@TEACHServices.com.

Finally, if you are interested in seeing
your own book in print, please contact us at

publishing@teachservices.com.

We would be happy to review your manuscript for free.

www.ingramcontent.com/pod-product-compliance
Lightning Source LLC
Chambersburg PA
CBHW070537170426
43200CB00011B/2453